The Mitford Family

Hugh Mitford Raymond

Zymurgy Publishing

Published in the U.K. in 2016 by Zymurgy Publishing,
Newcastle upon Tyne

Printed and bound by CPI Group (UK) Ltd, Croydon, CR0 4YY.

A CIP catalogue record for this book is available from the British Library.

ISBN 978 1903506 44 8

The photograph on the front cover is of Mitford Church, copied from an original taken in 1884 by Lt Colonel John Philip Mitford. Restoration began in 1874 and was completed in 1883.

With fond memory of my wonderful parents and to Yvonne Molinari alias Miss Marple and Dr Laurent Priou alias Dr Froggy with all the love in the world.

La bamba linga shoni
I raise a glass

Hugh

"La bamba linga shoni" is an age old, traditional African saying which means "Don't let the sun set" . In turn, this means when you take the energy from the sun and use it to good benefit, you'll feel the warmth in your heart. Used as a term of deep respect, in greeting or farewell within the old African tribes.

I hope you enjoy reading this book.

France, June 2016

My sincere and heart felt thanks to some and all for a small point taken or a big leap made.

Roger Adams, Philip Adamson and Pamela Brown, Helen Gill Anderson, Simon Baines, Brenda Beagley, Dr Hamlet Berger, Molly Brown, Rosie Burnham, Elisabeth Calmés, John Campbell, Judge & Dulcie Caney, Helen Chambers, Chrissie Courtney, Robert Crickmore, Mark Dezzani, Norma Duffew, James Durrant, Ken Edgar, Pat and Billy Elliot MBE, Martin Ellis, Peter Else, Andrew Gallagher, Wanda Gaynor, Richard & Valerie Gill, Tom Horne & Michael Gaunt of Brumell & Sample, Stephen Mitford Goodson, Peter Gore-Symes, Regina & Michael Healy MBE, Marjorie Henry, Lesley Hepherd, Eddie Heydenrych, Nicola, Anne & Ted Hotchkiss, Vanessa Ilsley, Michael & Shirley James, Aisling Lauder, Jerome Le Goff-Andrews, Mary Lovell, Roger Mariani, Carolyn McKenzie, Bill and Joanna Mitford, Fiona Mitford, Deborah Mitford, Selena Mitford, Yvonne Molinari, Robert Morton, Alison O'Donnell, Theuns Oosthuizen, Barbara & Ted Orzechowski, Danuska Orzechowski, Zyta Orzechowski, Jason Palmer, Sandra Piek, Dr Laurent Priou, Edward Pybus, John & Rosemary Rayner, Angela Cecil Reid, Dr Michael Sagner, Basil & Linda Nissen Samuels, Dr Rosa Sanchez, Benedikt Schmitz, Margaret Seeley, Mike & Meryl Sharp, Anna Smith, Pauline Sonley, John Stanford, Irene Straughan, Trevor & Diane Strydom, Richard Sutton, Charles Taylor, Sonia Vanular, Bruce Weaving, Catherine Welch, Micheal & Gillian Wilkinson, Colin Sydney Wilmot, Mark Witney, Graham, David & Kathy Woodhall and The London Society of Authors and National Union of Journalists.

Contents

1 Introduction 7
2 Where It All Began 13
3 The Feudal Barons Of Mitford 29
4 Kidnapping The Bishop 45
5 Legend Of The Mitford Crest 50
6 Mitford Church And Chapel 52
7 The Squires Of Mitford 62
8 Extraordinary Characters & Notable People
(i) William Mitford 122
(ii) Rev John Mitford 126
(iii) John (Jack) Mitford 129
(iv) Sir Robert Mitford 135
(v) Admiral Robert Mitford 139
(vi) Squire Osbaldeston 143
(vii)Mary Russell Mitford 149
(viii) Edward Mitford FRGS 158
(ix) Algernon Freeman-Mitford 173
(x) Godolphin Mitford 177
(xi) Bertram Mitford FRGS 201
(xii)The Mitford Girls 218
9 Mitford's Estate Act 226
10 Bibliography 236

Two plate sections with illustrations are to be found between pages 96 - 97, and pages 144 - 145.

Chapter 1

Introduction

The Mitford family of Mitford from 1042 to now

It's taken over 960 years and an Act of Parliament to hold one of England's oldest families together. But with no heir it took one man and the stroke of a pen to end a dynasty. From Europe, to the Middle East and Africa, to America, China and Japan, Australia and New Zealand, you'll find the name Mitford.

The family coped with all that was flung at it through the ancient feudal system and medieval wars, through battles and bloodshed, treason, kidnapping, politics and scandal. A family that stood up for freedom as we know it today. The good, bad and the worst of times. Sadly, due to one weak link the Mitford family was unable to adapt, accept change and failed to reinvent itself to continue into the 21st century. A matter of perfect indifference.

The Mitford mainline family was never grand or ostentatious. Unassuming, frugal and eccentric would best describe them. Living life in a modest mansion they waved no flags, other than British flags from flagpoles at Mitford and Hunmanby Hall. The head of the family clan learnt to cope with awkward eccentricities and scandals of other Mitfords, along with the international publicity. One can imagine family conversation along the lines of 'my goodness, how frightful! Not us you know, it's that lot down south that make life so awkward'.

I was born and raised in South Africa; life was a wild and exciting adventure and England was a faraway place. It was only in later years that I came to understand why I was christened with the name Mitford as my parents never fully explained the family story to me. There was always more background and history to what they told me. I knew I was related to someone called Mitford but had no idea who, where and why? And to be honest, who really cared? People would ask, are you related to the Mitford girls – and I would reply, who are they?

It is not only the sisters – to understand the Mitford family it is necessary to understand nearly 1,000 years of family history, politics and intrigue. Mitford heritage includes a massive ancient tumble down castle, manor house, a (modest) Georgian mansion, family chapel and village life on an estate that once covered over 50,000 acres, managed by the family for over 960 years. How would a parent explain all this to a naïve youngster living in a faraway country who had no idea of what life was like – out of Africa?

We lived in South Africa and I had no thoughts whatsoever that I would ever move. I considered South Africa was one of the best countries in the world. My future was in South Africa and I was going to stay and live there, with no plans to emigrate to the rolling green hills of a centuries old sheep farm on the borders of England and Scotland. Many years later the final pieces of the family jigsaw puzzle fell into place. It would never have entered my dreams that I would be part of a centuries old English establishment. But it turned out in reality that I was.

What the family owned for over 960 years was sold as no heir could be found. Obviously, had I known about my family history much earlier, things would perhaps be entirely different today. I was a few years too late. But hold on... there's an Act of Parliament with a term of 900 years that has not been changed, amended or cancelled. More about that later.

Digging into my family roots I discovered an amazing and unique background of family heritage that spawned a worldwide dynasty. The Mitford family has had a say and influence in the history of England and around the world – the Arab countries, British Commonwealth, the Far East and Europe with links to many great people across hundreds of years. From the beginning of England and South Africa, the Mitford family is part of English history.

With my research, my interest grew and it became evident that I needed to create a consolidated and independent family record and reference of this extraordinary, eccentric, charming and crazy family, under one cover. Before I go any further I would like to apologise to all the excellent historians out there! I'm not a historian nor do I wish to upset any historians. This is simply my humble attempt to set the record straight as best I can, from the inside out and not the other way around as it has been up to now. Say the name Mitford and most people think of the Mitford girls! This book sets out to change that – they are a branch of the mainline Mitford family. Undoubtedly their lives make interesting reading, however, it's the original Mitford family and dynasty that provides the most fascinating and amazing story.

This book is by no means a definitive and comprehensive record of the entire Mitford family; the family is too vast. My prime focus goes to the direct mainline and a selection of the most notable Mitfords who have left their mark. The mainline Mitford family represents the ownership and succession to the Barony of Mitford, Mitford Castle, Mitford Manor, Mitford Hall, Mitford Church and Chapel and surrounding farmlands of the Mitford estate since it was granted to the Mitford family by Edward the Confessor in 1042. This is where it all started. The estate has been owned and lived on by 32 generations of the Mitford family for over 960 years, until it was sold in 1993 and then finally, the very last link in 2006. The dynasty sadly ended with the death of the last squire in 2002. Amazingly, the trustees sold the manor tower in 2006 which according to the last Squire, was to remain within the family as a token of the Mitford family presence in Mitford.

There are several other Mitford branches – and related families and individuals in the UK and commonwealth countries who have combined, added or changed their names to include Mitford through marriage, inheritance or choice. However, there is only one bloodline on the direct main line of the Mitford family of Mitford since William the Conqueror in 1066 and Edward the Confessor in 1042.

Dating back in history the line of succession was always 'tail male' which means the first born male inherits. This system kept large estates intact (so they weren't split up between the children) providing greater longevity and succession through future generations. The younger brothers and sisters were left to the challenge of securing suitable marriages to ensure their future. For most without financial means the safest way forward was a career serving the Crown via the church, military, navy or civil service – as you'll note with the Mitford family. A male was preferable, simply because he was expected to fight for his lord and king. It was not a woman's job.

However, there are always exceptions to the rule. For example when a male line died out succession could go via the eldest female with a surviving male line. Name changes happened often and in the case of the Mitford dynasty happened frequently to secure inheritance. On occasion if the name change was not effected within six months the inheritance was lost. Through the years attitudes slowly changed and from 1925 new inheritance laws were passed to keep up to date with trends and circumstances. In essence, if you owned a castle (or the ruins of a castle) or anything…. you could leave it to your favourite dog or cat.

This book is written from information sourced from family archives, books and family records consisting of letters, documents and press clippings and books written by my great uncle, my great-great grandfather and cousins as listed under references at the end of the book. Much of the information used comes from the Mitford Historical Society Archives, started by Peter Else and the village of Mitford. An enormous thank you goes to the excellent scholar and teacher Michael James, a past chairman of the Mitford Historical Society. My emails and telephone calls have been nonstop. A fountain of knowledge and goodwill with all matters Mitford, along with his wife Shirley as Honorary Treasurer.

Many, many thanks to Pat and Billy Elliot MBE, cornerstones of the Mitford village community, with over 50 years on the parish and church councils. They made me feel at home in Mitford. They are warm and wonderful people; generations of their family have lived in Mitford. I have enjoyed afternoon tea, cakes and cream scones in front of a roaring fire on their sheep farm, which is the very essence of English life.

I also dug out an old wooden trunk of letters and envelopes, photographs, documents and newspaper clippings handed down through the generations. The zinc lined, oak trunk was turned into the family archives by my great grandmother, Mary Margaret Mitford, daughter of Squire Edward Ledwich Mitford FRGS.

Back in South Africa, and totally unexpected, my mother received a notice to collect a large and heavy trunk from Durban Docks. I was around 10 years old when I accompanied my mother to collect the trunk. Porters loaded it into my mother's car and we drove back to our home 35 miles away in the country village of Gillitts, Natal, wondering, with great excitement of what was inside! When my father arrived home from work we opened it.

It was a total surprise and quite amazing. Inside was a full length Russian sable fur coat and buried below, a mass of books and papers. Of course, my mother looked wonderful in the exquisite coat; however in South Africa, with no opportunity to wear such a magnificent coat in a temperate climate, she had it altered to best suit the winters of South Africa. Mary Margaret was the younger sister of Bertram Mitford FRGS, the celebrated South African novelist. Due to her robust nature my great grandmother became the Mitford family matriarch. She married money into the Raymond family. Between Edward her father and her brother Bertram, their lives were covered in a total of 48 books spanning 133 years from 1781 to 1914.

Another huge thank you goes to John Campbell in the United States for the archive material from Bertram Mitford's son, Roland Mitford who died in Cannes in 1932. Roland's wife remarried and became Princess Djoumkovsky, her family kindly passed the archive collection on to me.

Inevitably and naturally much of the information in this book has been cross checked from a variety of sources and there are a few instances where I have found what one person says – differs to what others have said. There are always contradictory answers with diverse explanations. We can't escape from a degree of confusion on occasion. One website records over 93,000 Mitford documents! Likewise, there are 100s (perhaps 1,000s) of people who can link their family ancestry and pedigree to the Mitford family. Rule of thumb - it's always best to check in order to avoid inadvertently passing on mistakes.

The very best reference to the early history of my family is contained in the book written by James Fergusson, entitled "Mitford Church - Its History, Restoration and Associations", published in 1884. Inside this book is a hand written letter from my great-great grandfather, Edward Ledwich Mitford FRGS, Squire of Mitford, recommending the facts recorded, dated 7 September 1884. I believe this book was commissioned by the Mitford family, to provide an accurate record of Mitford history and to celebrate the rebuilding and renovation of Mitford Church. The book includes details covering the Mitford family, Mitford Manor, Mitford Hall, Mitford Castle, Mitford Church and village.

Along with various dilemmas encountered, I have always stuck to John Hodgson and his excellent History of Northumberland. Even he was confused with some names and issues, so dear reader; kindly accept my humble apologies in advance for any errors and omissions that you may perhaps find. In our age of modern technology where would we be without Google, Wikipedia and Facebook? They have been wonderful and a very huge and big thank you to Lila Tretikov, Executive Director of the Wikimedia Foundation and Jimmy Wales, founder. These pages will hopefully iron out the inaccuracies, embellishments and innuendoes that I have found covering the Mitford family?

This book takes you on an amazing insight and incredible journey of one of England's oldest families - through 960 years of the history of England and around the world. It sets the record straight. You'll read about many members of the extraordinary, eccentric and yes, crazy Mitford family covering many different places over many years and amazing situations. There are a few clues here and there, perhaps you'll discover of how the Mitford dynasty ended with perfect indifference?

This is a true story.

All photographs within this book are privately owned and in copyright to the author unless otherwise stated. For talks and presentations - supporting this book, there is a dynamic, professionally produced, full colour MS Power Point - computer presentation of 200 slides, covering the Mitford dynasty & village as it was and as it is today, followed by open discussion.

Chapter 2

Where It All Began

A Synopsis of 1000 years

Once the bastion and flag between England and Scotland, nestling in a sheltered hamlet amidst two rivers, surrounded by magnificent rolling countryside, Mitford Castle guards a troubled history. During the castle's early years - the Kings of England and Scotland reduced the castle and village to ruins between 1318 and 1320. That wasn't enough – they also burnt the church with everyone inside.

The ancient Border stronghold of the Mitford family built in accord with William the Conqueror and his conquest of England in 1066, sits on a picturesque hilltop on the banks of the Wansbeck River, near Morpeth, in the county of Northumberland, England.

Like many of the very old castles in England, once destroyed, Mitford Castle was never rebuilt and the old stones went on to build Mitford Manor House, Mitford Hall and numerous other buildings in and around Mitford village. The immense thickness of the walls, standing to this day, is evidence of its vast strength as demonstrated when Alexander II of Scotland in May 1217, besieged Mitford Castle with his whole army… for seven long days before returning home empty handed. It was built on a massive mound of solid rock alongside the Wansbeck River - the engineers of the day very cleverly diverted a part of the river to run around the castle to form a natural moat and a swamp and marsh making it totally impregnable.

It was 951 years later in 1993, the once mighty stronghold of Mitford Castle was conquered. Not by king or foe, but from within – by the stroke of a pen. Who and what influenced the last squire to sell the castle and lands? Born from nothing the Mitford family ended in the most perfect indifference. What drove the family to become a worldwide dynasty? Let's go back to where it all began.

The Mitfords were established in the village of Mitford as early as the time of King Edward the Confessor in 1042 AD. To quote my great-great grandfather Edward Ledwich Mitford, 27th squire of Mitford "Of the precise date when Mitford Castle was built time has no record. During the Conquest it was in possession of the Mitford family". His handwritten notes dated 18th September 1883 explain the origins of the Mitford family.

During the conquest of England in 1066, the Mitford lands were seized by William the Conqueror (1066-1087) then given to Sir Richard Bertram in 1080, one of the Norman invaders from Dignam in Normandy who had travelled over and fought with William. Sybil Mitford, the only daughter and heir of Sir John Mitford was also given in marriage to Sir Richard.

The result of this union was two sons William and Roger, the eldest of whom succeeded to the manor and castle of Mitford and its dependencies, the lands and castle were later made into a barony by Henry I (1100-1135). Sybil also had an uncle - Matthew Mitford and a nephew - Nicholas Mitford from whom the families of Mitford of Mitford, Mitfords of Benhall, Suffolk; William Mitford, of Pittshill, Sussex, and Lord Redesdale - the Exbury branch and the Mitford girls, derive their descent. It is from Matthew that the mainline Mitford family has continuously owned the Mitford estate for 964 years. The Mitford feudal barons died out around the 1300's.

During the generations and years of feudal wars and political squabbles, the castle and its lands passed out of Mitford hands – but were mostly, through goodwill and perseverance recovered by the family. However, the question remains, what does one do with a massive pile of very old stones?

Henry III (1216-1272) restored the Mitford barony to Roger Bertram, and when Lord Brough, in Queen Mary's reign (1553-1558) "Granted to Cuthbert Mitford (1582-1613) and his son Robert, forever all his lands at Mitford, reserving only to himself the site of the castle in 1556 and the royalties, which castle and royalties being in the Crown in the reign of Charles II (1660-1685), were granted by his Majesty to Robert Mitford Esquire" (1612-1674).

The Barony of Mitford originally covered more than 50,000 acres and extended over the whole of the parishes of Mitford 9,595 acres, Meldon 995 acres, Ponteland 10,073 acres, Dinnington 5,538 acres, Felton 12,830 acres, and also included Longframlington 4,962 acres and Brinkburn Chapelry 3,777 acres in the county of Northumberland, and Greatham 3,054 acres, in County Durham, a total of 50,824 acres or 79.4 square miles. The land which is now Newcastle Airport was once part of the Mitford Estate.

The actual parish of Mitford covered 9,595 acres and was divided into 11 townships namely Edlington and Molesden in the west division of Castle Ward on the south side of the Wansbeck – and nine townships in the west division of Morpeth ward, namely Mitford, Newton, Throphill and Nunriding, which lie between the Wansbeck and the Font rivers, and of Spittlehill, Newton Park, Pigdon, Benridge and High and Low Highlaws, with the two Espleys, all on the north side of the Font and Wansbeck rivers.

In 1314, along with his eccentricities, idiosyncrasies and his assumed lover, Piers Gaveston, the troubled Edward II of England was defeated at the Battle of Bannockburn, by Robert the Bruce of Scotland. This major battle was won by the Scottish using highly mobile and opportunistic tactics against the larger, heavily armed and less agile English. The great victory at Bannockburn gave substance to the Scots' claim of independence and to Bruce's leadership of his nation. It did not end the war, which dragged on until 1328, when Edward III signed the Treaty of Northampton, the main clause of which read: "Scotland shall remain to Robert, King of Scots, free and undivided from England, without any subjection, servitude, claim or demand whatsoever."

This freed Scotland from English control and Robert the Bruce continued to pillage and blackmail Northumberland and Yorkshire. He allowed Scottish forces to raid unchecked throughout the north of England. As a result, Mitford Castle was left uninhabited. In 1315 it was placed under the guardianship of Sir John Evers, who in turn, passed on the task to Sir Gilbert Middleton, a King's soldier and past captain of the garrison at Berwick, once an English stronghold and last outpost. This decision and choice proved to be a disaster for both Mitford Castle and England.

A year later Pope John XXII was elected, Edward II considered this an opportune moment to reconcile the damage done in the north and his massive defeat in battle at Bannockburn, sent ambassadors to Rome to persuade the Pope to send papal letters to Britain to arrange a peace between England and Scotland and once and for all bring an end to the border wars. This attempt and carefully laid plan was to be totally scuttled in 1317 by the treasonable deeds of Sir Gilbert Middleton and his brother John covered in more detail on page 45 which sent Edward II into a blind rage.

Covered in later chapters in equal grisly detail, Sir Gilbert Middleton was eventually caught at Mitford Castle and shipped to London, tried, found guilty and condemned to be dragged by horses through the city of London to the gallows, hanged alive, then while still alive to be torn apart and afterwards beheaded. His body was then divided into four parts and sent to Newcastle, York, Bristol and Dover. His head was kept in London. King Edward in his rage also ordered the destruction of Mitford village and castle. Between Edward II, Robert the Bruce and King Alexander III of Scotland, Mitford Castle was finally dismantled and destroyed between 1318 and 1320, so no one else could avail themselves of its protection.

Coincidentally, around 680 years later, another Middleton – features in the Mitford story. Not a specialist in treasonable activities, kidnapping and demolishing castles, but rather…as the legal adviser that ended the Mitford legend. After reading this book and all with facts at your fingertips, you be the judge. Be careful to note the many subtle clues you'll read through the book.

Jumping ahead again…. and just before WW2 an enterprising rabbit catcher received somewhat of a shock when he found four human skeletons beneath a large stone slab just inside the main west walls of the castle. The rabbit catcher was digging for his ferret that had gone to ground when he came across the stone measuring about 6ft by 5ft and about 4 inches thick, believed to be the lid of a Norman grave, dating back to the days of the Conquest.

The castle was excavated to some extent many years ago but no record is known today of the discoveries. Various historians have made appeals but the excavation committee could not proceed due to lack of funds. Further investigation was halted due to the outbreak of war. To this day, it is believed that much lies hidden under the ruins of Mitford Castle. Some ancient coffins, hewn from blocks of stone and the size of small children, were carelessly left lying next to Mitford Church but were removed in 1997 their current location is not known.

Treason & Democracy

The bonds that held and united the massive barony of Mitford together did not continue for long. Two major events sent shockwaves through the families from which it would take generations to recover. Surrounded by the wanton lawlessness and desolation of the northern borders the Barons of Mitford had had enough. There were no other options. They put their necks on the block and gambled all their lands and possessions. Even if their deeds were treasonable, they were in the cause of democracy and good reason.

They drove themselves to it. It was what young spirited knights did in those days. Being brave and courageous, needing to make a statement against the corrupt establishment - they took up arms against the king. It was the only way they had to demonstrate purpose and reason, amidst chaos and ruin, living on the wild and desolate borders of England and Scotland. They crossed the line and gambled away their lives, family and lands.

The first major event was Roger Bertram II joining forces with the English barons to force King John to sign the Magna Carta at Runnymede in 1215. Not a bad idea, but King John managed to get the Magna Carta revoked by the Pope, and in his fury not only destroyed the town of Mitford and burnt Mitford Church with all the villagers inside – he also confiscated the entire Mitford Estate. Roger had to pay a huge fine to reclaim his lands from Philip Ulcotes, to whom King John had given them. Luckily King John died the same year, perhaps divine justice, to be followed by Henry III.

Robin Hood – Broke & Bankrupt

Like father like son. The second major event occurred some years later in 1264, when Roger's son Roger Bertram III, supported Simon Monfort, Earl of Leicester with Roger Godberd (alias Robin Hood), one of Monfort's captains and fought against Henry III, in the 2nd Baron's War of 1263/4. Today, Simon Monfort is known as the father of democracy as he was responsible for being the first person to convoke a parliament for England and was ruler of England for over one year before he was killed in the Battle of Evesham.

Unfortunately, Roger Bertram III was taken prisoner in 1264 and once again….the Mitford Estates were seized by the king and given to the Earl of Pembroke, half brother to Henry III. The Earl of Pembroke was also known as William de Valence 1225-1296, a French nobleman and Knight - he is buried at Westminster Abbey. The remaining parts of the estates which had not been taken in the cause of rebellion, were either sold or mortgaged to raise the sum required for the ransom to release Roger Bertram III from captivity. Sir Roger Bertram III was broke.

Luckily, Roger Godberd survived the battle of Evesham. He continued as a rebel until his capture in 1272, in and around Sherwood Forest. Later to become the character around which the Robin Hood legend is based.

Historians have spent years trying to identify Robin Hood. In historian David Baldwin's book Robin Hood: The English Outlaw Unmasked, Baldwin sets out evidence that Roger Godberd was Robin Hood. According to his research, Roger Godberd lived from the early 1230's to the 1290's and was accused of an array of crimes across the country. It is said that Roger Godberd's career inspired early ballads, leading to the Robin Hood we all know today; for example, Kevin Costner's portraying Robin Hood in the film, Robin Hood: Prince of Thieves (various locations in Northumberland were used in the film).

The Wreck Of The Mitford Barony

The commissioners making inquests contained in the 1275 Hundred Rolls (census of England) have entered numerous accounts against Roger Bertram III for sales of property up to 1275. He sold the village of Glantley in the parish of Felton to Peter Mitford; the village of Swarland to Agnes Cousedine and the village of Overgares to William Mitford.

Roger Bertram III also sold several estates held in return for previous military services to the Crown, which broke his allegiance to the Crown. Great Eland, Merdisfen, Little Eland and Calverdon were sold to the Earl of Pembroke. Mitford Park and Kirkley were sold to Hugh Eure, Babington went to the Umfrevilles, Tropill was given to his illegitimate son Thomas, Newton went to Wyschard de Charun, Meldon and Prestwick to Walter de Cambhow, and so it continued. All these sales were made during the rule of Henry III (1216-1272).

In the time of Edward I (1272-1307) Roger Bertram III gave his granddaughter, Agnes Bertram, Mitford castle, the village of Mitford, Mitford Mill and the village of Mollisdon. Agnes thereafter amazingly sold everything to Eleanor, dowager Queen of England (Born in Aix en Provence 1122-1204 and married to King Henry III & mother of Edward I). Eleanor, in turn, then sold them to Alexander de Balliol (Balliol college at Oxford derives its name from Alexander de Balliol).

The pleadings and inquests made at Newcastle in 1294 provide a greater perspective of the transactions between the Balliols and Bertrams. They record how the wreck of the barony was collected and reorganised by the former family, and the state in which it was given to their successors. It isn't known how Agnes Bertram enjoyed life in Mitford, she died in 1282. Roger Bertram

III was broke and bankrupt or as we say nowadays, financially embarrassed.

Although it's not documented from the time of the Norman conquest - it is surmised that the original estates of John Mitford's brother Matthew, whose daughter Sybil, was presented by William the Conqueror to Richard Bertram, are not mentioned in any statements of the barony, in acquisitions or any documents - is because they were not part of the barony but belonging to the younger brother and his son Nicholas in their private capacity under the Saxon government. When William the Conqueror gave Sir John Mitford's land with his daughter in marriage to Richard Bertram in 1080, he required Bertram to hold those lands by the service of five knight's fees. As previously mentioned, Mitford was only made became a barony during the reign of Henry I.

Farm Management Through 1,000 Years

According to England's feudal laws landed barons were responsible for the successful management and security of their estates and farms. They had to pay taxes to the Crown - it fell upon the feudal barons or lords to provide to the Crown, as and when needed - trained and armed soldiers and knights with horses, armour, accommodation and provisions.

The property of Matthew and Nicholas Mitford was exempt from this feudal obligation and excluded from the Conquest, so was not subject to military tenure. Much later the estate became more consolidated and Robert Mitford (1612-1674) acquired the castle and royalties of Mitford from Charles II (1660-1680). Once again the estate became whole.

In 1663 the squire of Mitford was assessed for the whole township for a rental of £300 a year. Generations later, in 1815, the squire of Mitford was assessed to the property tax upon an annual rental of £10,321. Farming done used the old system of "strip farming" which later changed to open crop management during the agrarian revolution.

In 1928, the Mitford Estate consisted of the following buildings, dwellings, farms and lands.

Dene House, Pigdon House, Pigdon Farm, Spital Hill House, Spital Hill Farm, Mitford Post Office, Newton Park, Newton Mill, Newton Underwood, Newton Underwood Cottage, Newton Red House, Mitford Steads, Maidens Hall, Nunriding Hall, Nunriding Moor, Nunriding House, East & West Throphill, Throphill Cottage, East & Middle Coldside, Molesden Cottage, East & West Molesden, Coalhouses, Lightwater Farm, Smithy & land, Mill Cottage, Covert, Long Framlington, Framlington Quarry, School Gardens, Village Land, River Green, Stable Green, Mitford Mill, Mitford Castle, Mitford Manor, Mitford Parks, Mitford Hall, 2 New Cottages, Font & Wansbeck Rivers & Woodlands.

With this there were 128 inhabited houses, with 134 families and 625 people. Around 500 people or 70% of the village population were employed in farming. Over previous years the population of Mitford averaged 650 residents - today (2010) it has a population of approximately 430 residents.

Mitford School was built by public subscription on land donated by my great-great uncle Lieutenant Col John Philip Mitford, 27th Squire in 1883 and in 1963 was still in use with 45 pupils and two teachers. It eventually closed in 1966. The school house is now a private home. Another great uncle, Robert Mitford, 29th Squire, donated the use of Mitford Park, alongside Mitford Hall as home to the Mitford Cricket Club, still in operation today.

With farming, the main breeds of beef cattle – Shorthorn, Hereford and Angus were typical until just after the Second World War. The breeds that became more fashionable are Charolais, Limousin, Simmental and Belgian Blue. Similarly, dairy cattle – Friesian and Ayrshire etc, have been replaced mostly by Holstein and Canadian Friesian.

Breeds of sheep in upland regions have largely remained the same for several hundreds of years, hardy breeds (such as the Swaledale) being crossed with Longwool sires (such as the Blue Faced Leicester) to produce cross bred ewes. One of the most successful examples is the North of England Mule which through its good mothering abilities, its prolificacy, and ability to produce marketable lambs, became the mainstay of mid level and lowland farming regions.

Before the 1914-1918 war, heavy horses and steam power were the only way to cultivate the land and harvest wheat, root crops and farm animal feed. Transport was by pony and trap. As Mitford was a privately owned estate most of the farms were occupied by tenant farmers. Farm workers who lived on the farms were in tied cottages or, if single, lived in the farmhouse and were known as servant lads and girls. They often did the milking, cleaned the byres and dairy, and looked after the horses.

Most cattle were housed during winter and fed turnips, corn and hay to fatten them up for market. Shepherds were allowed to keep a few sheep of their own to provide an additional income. Bacon, eggs and potatoes were often provided from the farm as part of a worker's wage. Workers were hired on an annual basis from May with the farmer shaking hands and the gift of one shilling. The farmer's wife usually kept hens, made butter and wholesome kitchen produce with the surplus sold at market to help pay household expenses.

The biggest changes in farming were from 1930 onwards when the first tractors began to replace horses. Two horses could plough one acre a day but the tractor could plough 4 to 5 acres, cutting down the time needed to cultivate the land. Travelling threshers became available and farmers began to help each other with the harvesting, with the wives competing to provide the best homemade dinners and teas for anyone who helped.

When war was declared in 1939 many farm workers were called up for active service. The Women's Land Army was formed and many girls who had never done farm work, lived in the country or even set eyes on a cow had to help out. Producing food became a priority. Later, combine harvesters were introduced which radically reduced harvesting time and tractors equipped with hydraulic lifting machinery eliminated time-consuming lifting and carrying. All the back breaking tasks of farm work has been mechanised. Back in the 1920's with 8 men on a 500 acre farm, the farmer today only needs 2 men and machines to do the same work. As a result, crop production has increased dramatically, along with the increased use of artificial fertilizers. When the population of Mitford was higher, agriculture provided employment for many people, there are now only a few people employed in agriculture.

In general, with the increase of cheaper produced and imported foods, some lands have been taken out of production. Many of the smaller family farms are no longer viable and the old traditional farm buildings have become unsuitable for modern farming. Throughout the country many of these buildings have been converted into private housing and business activities.

In 1928 the Mitford Estate grossed an annual, rental income of £6,700 and after deductions this amounted to £5,400. Expenses as follows, covered - Insurance £149, Tithe & Charges £327, Rates & Taxes £2,170, Repairs & Maintenance £1,207, Private & Hall Staff £2,703, Allowances off Rents £377, Improvements £149 and Management & Administration £305. With the total being £7,390 it left a deficit of £1,990 for the then squire, my great uncle, Robert Mitford to find.

There was also a village shop, post office, sawmills, snuff mill, blacksmith and the local village pub The Plough, luckily recently saved from closure by Richard Gill, a centuries established, estate family. The sawmills handled all forms of woodwork from felling, logging, sawing, joinery and produced every form of forestry product from mine pit props, fencing, gates, farm wagons, flagpoles to ships' masts. The sawmills closed in 1979 but much lives on in the Beamish Museum in Durham.

In 1993, after 23 years of disrepair and neglect with no resident landlord, the Mitford Estate of 5,000 acres was sold with five houses and nine let farms generating an income of £48,127 in rents for a reported £2.85 million. The only 4 farms still operating in 2010 were Dene House Farm, Maiden's Hall Farm, Newton Underwood Farm, Mitford Steads Farm and East Coldside Farm. Lightwater, Mill Farm, Newton Park, Newton Mill, Spital Hall and West Coldside are now Mitford Estate private houses.

Mitford - Where Two Rivers Meet

Mitford village is situated between two rivers, the Wansbeck and the Font, two miles from Morpeth. In fact, the origin of the name Mitford is from the old English Myth-ford at the junction of streams or between two fords. Mitford means the lands between two rivers. The scenery along the well-wooded banks of the two rivers is rich, diverse and simply quite beautiful. Much of the soil is rich and fertile and well watered from the two rivers. The village farmed around 4,000 acres and had around 2,000 in grass and meadow lands for pasture with the remainder in woodlands.

At one stage, records show coal mines were worked in Mitford, Nunriding, Newton Park and Coldside, but the coal discovered is apparently of inferior quality and not worth the expense of digging it out. Difficult and dangerous to extract, there is a record of a miner spending eight days in a coal pit with nothing but a little water collected in his shoe in order to survive. When dug out he soon recovered and lived to a ripe old age.

An allied industry to sheep farming, wool manufacturing proved to be unsuccessful and was discontinued. The ancient water-corn-mill at Mitford is now a ruin and the only water mill is at Newton-under-wood, there is a windmill at Edlington. Commercial enterprise by the Mitfords was frowned upon as was the family culture during the nineteenth century. When one looks at the abundant natural resources available it is surprising that no entrepreneurial enterprise was ever undertaken by the Mitford family in order to develop an alternate source of income and revenue other than tenant farming and sheep.

Mitford Church

Mitford Church in pristine condition is one of the most elegant churches in the county of Northumberland. It is quite out of proportion to the size of the village indicating that the village of Mitford was quite large during its prime. Built in 1135 by William Bertram, Baron of Mitford it has survived over 880 years including a troubled history detailed in later pages. At one stage the church had been reduced to a ruin – evidenced by burnt stones and charred wood, proving past plunder and devastation. William also founded Brinkburn Priory which was at one stage, within the Mitford estate. Brinkburn Priory was a medieval monastery built on a bend of the River Coquet nearly 4 miles east of Rothbury, Northumberland. It is a grade 1 listed building in the care of English Heritage. The priory was dissolved in 1536 after Parliament enacted the Dissolution of the Monasteries Act, of monasteries whose income was less than £200 per annum. Roger Bertram's son Roger is buried at Brinkburn where it is possible to see his inscribed tombstone 'Hic Jacet Roger vx Fundator'.

From 1874 to 1877 the church was totally rebuilt from family funds by my great-great uncle Lt Col John Philip Mitford (1809-1895) at a cost of over £14,000 (around £1.4 million today). The church is 130 feet long with an aisle on its south side, the middle wall of which is supported by heavy pillars and plain semi-circular arches. At the top of the bell tower you'll find an exquisite painting of a white dove, painted by my great-great grandfather Edward Ledwich Mitford in 1898. Today, Mitford Church is a most impressive and significant, historical landmark.

From Castle To Manor & Hall In 835 Years

The Mitford family home took on many shapes and sizes through the centuries. A process of making ends meet. Mitford Hall represents the last of the three separate stages of the Mitford family's residence over a period of 835 years. Using the same old family stones, the family built three totally different and independent family homes or "seats". Uniquely, each one overlooks the other. There is no place in England where this is more perfectly combined than at Mitford.

The Border Reivers were families of raiders based on the English-Scottish border. To defend against reivers or raids many dwellings in Northumberland outside towns and villages were fortified and are known as Bastle Houses. Stone built two floor buildings, livestock were kept at ground level and people lived on the second level which was reached by a ladder that could be pulled-up at night when raids took place. George Macdonald Fraser comments on Border Reivers in The Steel Bonnets,

"The Border Reiver is a figure unique in British (perhaps in world) history, a professional cattle-thief who left to posterity a legacy of great poetry... a merciless racketeer and plunderer who also in his country's vanguard in time of war, a murderous pursuer of feud who held little sacred except his pledged word, and who vanished four centuries ago, leaving behind him the word 'blackmail' and a bloodline that has included among others, Presidents Nixon and Johnson, Sir Walter Scott, the Charlton brothers, Rutherford the physicist, Billy Graham, Robert Burns, Deborah Kerr, Thomas Carlyle, T S Elliot and the first man on the moon Neil Armstrong."

With the Union of the Crowns in 1603 peace was restored along the English and Scottish borders. Families no longer needed to live in fortified castles with guards and soldiers. The Scots finally gave up attacking the English and country gentlemen could sleep safely at night. With Mitford Castle destroyed and dismantled by the Scots the Mitford family decided on something a little more comfortable and modern. Mitford Manor House was built in 1637. One of the first non defensible country houses in England.

Built with old stones from Mitford Castle, the 17th century manor house became home to the Mitford family for over 300 years until it was finally destroyed by fire in 1813. The kitchen wing remained intact and was partly repaired and used as a farm house and accommodation for estate staff for many years.

Today all that remains is the central porch-tower with turrets which bears the family crest and the date 1637. The old kitchen wing was sold off and the new owner turned it into an impressive and spacious modern home, built and blending in with the old ruins, all in keeping with the old style. Passed down with the house from an old family collection, there are several pen and ink drawings that show what the manor was like before the fire. There are also two huge, magnificent old trees, a chestnut and a Lebanon cedar tree that add to the graceful, age old elegance and splendour. In this magnificent setting, in mid-June, the annual garden fête was held - a fun day for the entire village with the local band, stalls and raffles, chatter and laughter and British flags flying.

With no family seat Bertram Mitford (see chapter Lords and Squires) commissioned the well known Newcastle architect, John

Dobson, to build a new home for the family in 1810. Finally, in 1828 with stones from the old Manor house, castle, quarry and river, a new Georgian mansion house was built in Mitford Park on the north side of the Wansbeck River, with sweeping views over the manor, church and castle ruins. It was here, except for WW2, when it was occupied by the British army and 400 soldiers, that the Mitford family, bar the last squire, lived, until it was sold in 1993.

From the grand imposing entrance gates with the impressive, sandstone pillared gatehouse, once home to the butlers of Mitford Hall, one drives through a deep, sun speckled and enchanting deer forest to emerge into light and open space and the requisite gravel driveway sweeping up to the imposing entrance of Mitford Hall. Clearly much thought went into the design and approach, with excellent results... referred to as a "modest mansion".

In the library stands a large fire-place, recovered from the old Manor house. It has two statues each side of the fire-place. One is said to represent Adam and the other, Eve. Not perhaps associated with a traditional Victorian family, but apparently fashionable at the time. Outside the dining room used to stand the original butler's table and throughout the house would have been many lovely old family heirlooms, now all auctioned and sold.

As with all grand old homes there was a formidable array of bells, dating from the time the mansion buzzed with butlers, footmen, servant girls and grooms. Years ago, if you had wandered through the rooms you would notice the magnificent walnut furniture and some intricately carved tables from Kashmir and colonial era furniture from South Africa and the British Empire. Sadly, nothing is left.

Today... wander out to the specially built conservatory and you'll find a magnificent camellia tree, said to have been planted by Charles Darwin around 1839. In the spring it's a mass of bright pink and crimson flowers. Quite exquisite - as Charles Darwin and brothers Bertram and Robert Mitford, no doubt intended.

The old ballroom at Mitford Hall once hosted annual fund raising fetes and the Morpeth Hunt Ball, along with many other charitable village events and celebrations. The Hall, grounds and park, are a beautiful event location.

Looking out from Mitford Hall, the past is present. With the magnificent view over the vast, rolling green lawns and river to the old manor house, Mitford Church spire and the ruins of Mitford Castle – it presents a unique and splendid statement to the rise and fall of one of England's oldest and most extraordinary dynasties.

In the next chapters you'll discover what happened to the feudal barons of Mitford and the scoundrel Sir Gilbert Middleton before going on to the succession of the Lords and Squires of Mitford in Northumberland and Hunmanby in Yorkshire and their attempts to hold the estate together for over 960 years.

Chapter 3

The Feudal Barons Of Mitford

The Bertram Barons from 1080 to 1312

Life in a medieval castle was great fun if you didn't mind running around fighting battles and you were a baron. Governed by the pyramid-shaped feudal system, the early kings of England during the 12th century ruled by Divine Right - if you don't do what I say I'll call the Pope…. and some poor fellow would probably be dispatched from England to Rome, on his horse with a plea of help. Which brings to mind the old Monty Python film "Monty Python and the Holy Grail" and the coconuts "clip clop, clippity clop". These well intentioned messengers bringing bad news often got killed, which was why Shakespeare thoughtfully wrote "don't shoot the messenger". The kings… and their appointed nobles and government controlled without much accountability.

In order to enjoy life, kings and queens needed the support and goodwill of their nobles and knights (their ministers) freemen and peasants (civil servants) so they granted lands in return for their loyalty and military services. To maintain power locally they needed a castle to provide protection from enemies, wandering bandits, rustlers and… hooligans. A safe haven in time of need for all the village people as well as the occupants of the castle. To generate money nobles and knights would grant lands to peasants and freemen so everyone owed allegiance to the king and their lord. Everyone was expected to contribute by providing work.

One of the first decisions William the Conqueror made, apart from distributing lands and property to all his followers, to enable construction of numerous fortresses to overawe and repel takeovers, he conducted a national survey which we know as the

Doomsday Book. It registered each and every piece of land and property, its state - be it meadow, pasture, wood, arable land, the owner's name and who rented it and its value. Northumberland was not included in this great public record owing to its state of desolation in the border wilderness of England and Scotland and perhaps more importantly it was under the control of the Prince Bishops in Durham who collected taxes in the area.

As such...all the lands in England were described as "to be held by the king". William I was quite a crafty fellow, he established a system that gave him control. All the vassals of the Crown, lay or clerical, were compelled to have a quota of armed knights, ready and able within 40 days. With this regulation the Crown could raise an army of around 60,000 horsemen as and when needed. The military tenants of the Crown were obliged to attend court at the three great festivals (Christmas, Easter, Pentecost/Whitsuntide) or when summonsed to court. At court earls and barons gathered to discuss the administration of justice and business affairs, hence were called the king's barons and their land baronies. Baronies were held in perpetuity via their legitimate descendants. In case of failure of heirs, felony or treason, the fee was forfeited to the Crown. Fees of inheritance were enjoyed by the nearest heir. When the heir of a fee was a minor he became ward of the lord – when the fee descended to a daughter (as what happened with the Mitford barony), the lord claimed the right to give her in marriage, along with the homage and service of her husband. This system continued until the time of Charles II, when all "tenures of honour, manors and lands were turned into free and common socage" or ownership in the case of Mitford Castle around 1660.

The Normans preserved most of the Anglo-Saxon laws and customs but preferred their own trial by battle as more worthy of freemen and warriors. Trail by battle is to settle a dispute between two individuals, fought in combat – in other words, a judicially sanctioned duel. The Norman Lords or Barons held their lands as they had obtained them – by the sword.

Succession Of The Barony & Mitford Castle 1066 - 1674

1st Baron Sir Richard Bertram & heiress Sybil Mitford
(c. 1045-1086) Son of Lord Dignan in Normandy
& follower of William the Conqueror
2nd Baron Sir William I Bertram (c. 1080-1150) Son of Richard
3rd Baron Sir Roger I Bertram (c. 1130-1177) Son of William
4th Baron Sir William II Bertram (c. 1157-1199) Son of Roger
5th Baron Sir Roger II Bertram (c. 1180-1242) Son of Roger
6th Baron Sir Roger III Bertram (c. 1224-1275) Son of Roger
7th Baron Sir Roger VII Bertram (c. 1275-1311) Son of Roger
8th Baron Agnes Bertram (c. 1267-1311) Daughter of Roger
9th Baron William Fitzwilliam (c. 1312) Son of Agnes

Ownership Of The Barony & Mitford Castle

Via the families of Valence – Balliol – Stutteville – Comyn – Strabolgie – Percy & Burgh
Primarily via the female line

1 William de Valence – 1st Earl of Pembroke (c. 1225-1296)
2 Adomar de Valence – 2nd Earl of Pembrok (c. 1275-1324)
3 John Cumin (or Comyn) (c. 1325)
4 Sir David de Strathbolgie (c. 1307-1335)
5 David de Strathbolgie (c. 1332-1375)
6 Sir Thomas Percy (c. 1364-1388)
7 Sir Henry Percy (c. 1393-1433)
8 Sir Thomas Burgh (c. 1420)
9 Sir Thomas Borough (c. 1431-1496)
10 Sir Edward Borough (c. 1463-1528)
11 Lord Thomas Borough (c. 1480-1549)
12 Sir Thomas Lord Borough (c. 1522-1584)
13 Sir William Burgh (c. 1557-1597)
14 Sir John Burgh
15 Sir Robert Burgh
Returned to the Mitford family of Mitford, Northumberland by royal decree by King Charles II (c 1660-1680)

1st Baron Sir Richard Bertram & Heiress Sybil Mitford (c. 1045-1086)

At the time of the Norman Conquest, the Castle of Mitford in Northumberland, then an Anglo Saxon fort, was held by Sir John Mitford, whose only daughter and heiress, Sybil Mitford, was given in marriage by William the Conqueror to a Norman knight Sir Richard Bertram, son of Guillaume (William) Bertram and Miss de Bostembourg from Dignan (in Brittany, France) Normandy. Sir Richard Bertram and Sybil Mitford produced two sons, William and Roger. The eldest William succeeded to the barony created by Henry I, in the service of five knight's fees. The union of Sir Richard Bertram and Sybil Mitford created the Bertram Barons of Mitford and succession to Mitford Castle.

2nd Baron Sir William I Bertram (c. 1080-1150)

For better or for worse, second baron Sir William joined the family of the neighbouring village of Morpeth. William Bertram married Hawys, daughter of Sir William Merlay, Baron of Morpeth, which was probably a wise decision taken for strategic as well as emotional reasons. Their sons Roger, Guy, William and Richard, founded the Augustinian Priory of Brinkburn, in Northumberland. The deed of foundation was made in the reign of Henry I, who died in 1135, Brinkburn Priory was not actually built until the next generation. Its architectural characteristics are those of the transition period, which corresponds with the time of his son and successor, Roger Bertram I. Medieval monastery Brinkburn Priory never attained the reputation of Newminster Abbey, which was founded in 1138, by brother-in-law Ranulph Merlay of Morpeth. The two brothers-in-law and neighbours appear to have vied and competed with each other in religious promotion. William Bertram laid down the first marker with his priory at Brinkburn. Ranulph Merlay outstripped him in the realization of his design for Newminster Abbey. For a while Brinkburn only existed on parchment while Newminster was built of stone and occupied by a friary of Cistercian monks. To this, William generously assisted his brother-in-law by granting to the monks of Newminster Abbey all the lands between it and Mitford! Alas, Newminster Abbey did not survive generations of conflict and feudal wars. During this time William Bertram's hands were full and resources stretched with building his own castle and church. It is therefore understood that Mitford Castle and church was built during the time of William Bertram I. He died before 1157, for there is evidence that his son Roger was in possession that year. It may therefore be affirmed that by the middle of the twelfth century, or shortly afterwards, the Norman church of Mitford has been built by William Bertram, the second baron. According to Burke's Peerage 1883, William married twice. His second wife was Hawise de Baliol, heiress of Stainton and daughter of Guy de Baliol and Dionysia. Sir William built Mitford Castle into a formidable medieval stronghold.

3rd Baron Sir Roger I Bertram (c. 1130-1177)

It's recorded in 1165 that Roger was beholden to the Crown of Henry II, the first Plantagenet King by the service of five knights fees, as his father and grandfather had previously done under Henry I.

Roger confirmed his father's foundation deeds and grant made to Brinkburn Priory and gave the monks the church of Felton and use of common pasture within Feltonshire as witnessed by Ralph de St Peter, one of the tenants of the barony in 1165. In 1157 to increase village revenue and its prestige, he paid 50 marks to Henry II for rights for a market to be held at Mitford. The market was held on the land between the church and castle see photograph album at end of book.

In 1172 the third baron paid £6.10s scutage (a legal form of taxation during the feudal system, where a knight could pay a fee in lieu of military service to the Crown), to excuse himself from joining Henry II's conquest of Ireland. He gave Newminster's monks the use of the granges (historically the term relates to outlying farms with tithe barns) in the parish of Highlaws, and of Horton in the parish of Ponteland. To the nuns of Halystane he gave the wood called Baldwinswood, afterwards called Nunriding. Roger married Ada Morville, daughter of Sir Simon Morville and Ada Engaine, heiress of Burgh-By-Sands, Cumberland, and they produced a son William.

4th Baron Sir William II Bertram (c. 1157-1199)

In 1196 as son and heir Sir William II Bertram had to account to the sheriff for his barony which consisted of the parishes of Greatham (County Durham), Felton, Mitford and Ponteland. He continued his father's commitments and confirmed all the grants made to the monks of Brinkburn Priory. He died before his son Roger could inherit so he established wardship and custody of his lands during his son's minority to William Brewer, until he came of age, as recorded by John Hodgson 1832.

With regard to William Brewer's wardship, there are two versions, the version recorded by Burke's Peerage 1883 where wardship was given to Peter de Brus for a sum of 300 marks. It would appear that Burke has perhaps confused father and son. Having analysed many records, the more accurate version is recorded by John Hodgson in his History of Northumberland 1832. William married Alice, daughter of Robert de Umfreville, Baron Prudhoe and heiress to the villages of Great Babington and Kirklawe. Their son Roger became the next baron.

5th Baron Sir Roger II Bertram (c. 1180-1242)

In 1215 Roger joined the northern barons to force King John to sign the Magna Carta. As a result the village of Mitford was burnt to the ground and all the villagers burnt alive in Mitford Church. All of Sir Roger's lands were seized by the King and given to "an iniquitous minion of the Crown" Philip de Ulcotes who at the time held the post of sheriff of Northumberland. He remained sheriff for six consecutive years due to his links to King John. Luckily, when King John died in 1216, Bertram made peace with the new government and together with royal favour, a fine and payment of £100, all his lands and castle were restored to his ownership. Thereafter the baron of Mitford enjoyed peace and goodwill, he was frequently employed in state affairs of considerable importance as follows.

He was one of the English barons who swore to see Henry III's obligation to marry his sister Joan of England to King Alexander II of Scotland, carried into effect. In August he was a witness to the convention between Henry III and Geoffrey de Marisco, when the latter was appointed Justice of Ireland. In 1225 Sir Roger, along with Robert Lexington, Roger Gilbert Umfreville, Roger Merlay and Jordan Hayron became the itinerant justices at Newcastle upon Tyne.

In 1228 Gilbert Umfreville, Roger Merlay, Sir Roger II Bertram and other northern barons had a mandate to meet Alexander, King of Scotland, at Berwick to give him safe conduct to a conference between him and the King of England at York. In 1237 he was a witness to the agreement made before Cardinal Otto, the Pope's representative at York, regarding the differences between England and Scotland. Appointed by Pope Gregory 1X, Cardinal Otto oversaw The Treaty of York, a peace settlement between the kings of Scotland and England achieved at York on 25 September 1237. Cardinal Otto is also remembered for the reformatory statutes he laid out for the Benedictine Order, promulgated in November 1237 and held at St Pauls.

Due to ill health in 1242 and being unable to attend to the King in Gascony Sir Roger was obliged to pay a fee of 30 marks, the year Sir Roger III Bertram died. He married Agnes de Emmely (c. 1195-1253) and they produced a son and heir, also called Roger.

6th Baron Sir Roger III Bertram (c. 1224-1272)

In 1257 Roger obtained a grant of privileges in Mitford, Felton and Kirkley. Rights of privilege were rights given by the Crown to an individual, for example permission to hold a market. During the following year, along with other northern barons he was commanded to march into Scotland with all the force each of them could raise, to rescue the young King of Scotland, the King of England's son-in-law, out of the hands of his rebellious subjects. Like father like son. This proved that Roger was a person of daring spirit and courage but in the same breath - he also challenged the arbitrary measures of Henry III. In March 1264 he was summoned to be at Oxford, but regardless of the royal mandate he chose instead to join Simon de Monfort, Earl of Leicester who had also summoned him, to be at a convention in London to 'quieten the differences between king and nation'. This meeting marked the beginning of the Second Barons' War (1264 – 1267). A civil war led by Simon de Montfort against Royalist forces led by Prince Edward (later Edward I) in the name of Henry III. As with any adventure or battle, money is needed to support the troops and these costs are expensive. Apparently, Roger accepted a lump sum in lieu of future rent payments on his lands.

Sir Roger III fought alongside Roger Godberd, one of Simon de Monfort's captains and finally in the company of his neighbour Hugh Gubium, Lord of Shilvington, he was taken prisoner at the siege of Northampton 3 April 1264. This adventure shattered the fortunes of the Mitford barony. Not only had Sir Roger III sold off considerable portions of his estate without licence to raise battle money, he was now totally broke. He had also sold two of his grandmother's estates Bavington and Ottercops to the Earl of Leicester. The Earl was so well liked and respected in England that when he died, John Vescy, Lord of Alnwick, chopped off one of his feet, and presented it to the abbey in Northampton, which was enshrined in a shoe of pure silver, becoming the relic of a holy martyr. Simon Monfort had fought for the monks and this was their attempt to canonise his memory.

After Sir Roger III's capture at Northampton, his castle at Mitford and all his Northumberland estates were given into the custody of William de Valence, the King's half brother and were held for many years until finally restored after the payment of a heavy fine for his pardon and ransom.

After Sir Roger III's temporary loss of his castle and Northumberland estates the Mitford baronial decline was rapid. In 1264 Roger Bertram III rode proudly forth from the walls of Mitford Castle to strike a blow against the government – in favour of rights and liberties of which he and his vassals, lands and people had been deprived. He never returned as Baron of Mitford. Around fifty years later, his once proud castle, in the hands of a freebooter Sir Gilbert Middleton was destroyed. For over 900 years, time and circumstance have dismantled its once massive walls. A few remains of the walls crown the rocky hill to show how powerful the family had been. They provoke us to think back to our indebtedness to the Mitford barons and the other barons of kindred spirit who gathered together to force King John to sign the Magna Carta. Those rights became a source of the pride, freedom, happiness and prosperity of England and Great Britain to this day.

Roger married Joan and they had two sons Roger and Thomas, the latter son is believed to be illegitimate and 4 daughters, Agnes, Isabella, Christian and Ada. Thomas was given the Throphill property which he promptly sold to Hugh de Eure. Agnes married Thomas Fitzwilliam, Lord of Elmeley and Sprotborough in Yorkshire and later became a co-heiress of Roger Bertram. Their son William married Agnes, daughter and heir of Thomas, Lord Grey of Codnor. Isabella married Philip Darcy (a co-heir) and later became with her sister a co-heiress.

7th Baron Sir Roger VII Bertram (c. 1282)

Sir Roger VII took over the castle and Mitford village along with property held in Molesden, Felton, Framlington, Overgaree, Bichfield and Kirkly. He married Eva and they produced an only daughter Agnes who became the heiress to the Mitford barony. This is where the Bertram barons end and the line runs out when it joins with the Fitz-William family of Wentworth Yorkshire.

8th Baron Agnes Bertram (c. 1311)

Agnes married Thomas Fitzwilliam of Sprotborough & Emley, son of Sir William Fitzwilliam and Ela Plantagenet de Warenne. Agnes amazingly sold the barony to Eleanor, dowager Queen of England (Born in Aix en Provence 1122-1204 and married to

Henry III & mother of Edward I). Eleanor, in turn, then sold the Mitford barony to Alexander de Balliol). Eleanor, later married Robert Stutteville. Agnes and her son William were the last blood heirs of the castle and barony.

9th Baron William Fitzwilliam (c. 1195 - 1312)

William married Maud daughter of Edward Lord Deyncourt and via a sister was later to be found as the last blood heir of the Bertram barons of Mitford. From this point onwards the barony is no longer held by the original Bertram family and the succession passes through the families of Valence, Balliol, Stutteville, Cumin, Strabolgie, Percy and Borough until several centuries later, when it is handed back to the Mitford family of Mitford by royal decree.

The Fitzwilliams acquired extensive holdings in the south of the West Riding of Yorkshire, largely through strategic alliances through marriage. In 1410, Sir John Fitzwilliam of Sprotborough, who died in 1421, married Margaret Clarell, daughter of Thomas Clarell of Aldwark, the descendant of a major Norman landholding family.

Sir William Fitzwilliam (c. 1460–1534) was an Alderman and Sheriff of London acquired the Milton Hall estate in Peterborough in 1502. His grandson Sir William FitzWilliam served as Lord Deputy of Ireland from 1571 to 1575 and from 1588 to 1594.

Ownership Of The Barony & Mitford Castle

Via the families of Valence – Balliol – Stutteville – Comyn – Strabolgie – Percy & Burgh

1 William de Valence – 1st Earl of Pembroke (c. 1225-1296)

William was the son and heir of Hugh de Brun and Isabella Angoulême, the beautiful widow of King John, half brother to Henry III and uncle to Edward I. William had two brothers Richard Chilham, illegitimate son of King John, sometimes called Richard of Dover and John de Balliol, Lord of Bywell and Barnard Castle who married Dervaguilla, daughter of the Earl of Huntingdon and brother of William the Lion, King of Scotland – founder of Balliol College, Oxford.

After Roger Bertram's capture at Northampton, Henry III ordered that Mitford Castle and its lands be seized and placed in the custody of his half brother, William de Valence. Otherwise known as the Earl of Pembroke, he was buried in St Edmunds chapel in Westminster Abbey, where his monument remains today. William married Joan, only daughter of Warine de Munchensi and they produced three sons, John, William and Adomar and two daughters, Isabella and Agnes. Agnes married Maurice Fitzgerald, Baron of Offaly and then secondly she married Hugh de Balliol, brother of John Balliol, King of Scotland.

2 Adomar de Valence – 2nd Earl of Pembroke (c. 1275-1324)

John died young and the barony passed to his brother William who was killed in a fight with the Welsh in 1282. His brother Sir Adomar de Valence then inherited the castle and barony of Mitford. The 2nd earl of Pembroke (c. 1270-1324) was a tall, sallow faced fellow which caused the arrogant Piers de Graveston to call him "Joseph the Jew". A vile and evil man – Pembroke was an instrument of atrocious deeds and submitted to the mandates of the Crown, contrary to the dictates of honour, humanity and justice. He sat in judgement on Thomas, Earl of Lancaster and unjustly acquiesced in his sentence. He played a prime role in apprehending the famous Scottish patriot, Wallace of Craiggy in 1035 arranging his capture by corrupting his close friends and by the treachery of his most intimate associates along with Sir John Monteith and others.

Adomar de Valence was married three times. The third marriage ended when he was "accidentally" killed in a tournament on his wedding day. It was around 1318/20 that Mitford castle was taken by King Alexander of Scotland who dismantled and removed all the fortifications so no-one else could make use of this once mighty stronghold between England and Scotland.

Now in ruins the Mitford barony and royalties then passed to the widower of Adomer de Valence and her husband's heirs via the female line.

3 John Cumin (or Comyn (c. 1325)

John Cumin and Robert the Bruce entered into a secret agreement proposed by Robert the Bruce as follows – "I will give you my estate if you support my title to the Crown and you give me your estate if I support your title to the Crown". But Cumin went and revealed the secret to the King of England.

It was in the Chapel of Greyfriars Monastery on the 10th of February 1306 in Dumfries that Robert the Bruce met John Comyn, Lord of Badenoch and Lord of Lochaber, also known simply as the Red Comyn. John had links with the royal house of England as he was married to Joan de Valence, daughter of William de Valence, 1st Earl of Pembroke, an uncle of Edward I. John Comyn, was Bruce's chief rival for the throne of Scotland.

As Cumin and Robert the Bruce walked towards the high altar, Robert the Bruce challenged Comyn with having betrayed him by revealing matters they had mutually pledged to keep secret. There was a confrontation and Robert the Bruce stabbed Comyn in the heart.

John Strathbolgie, 10th lord of Athol who supported Robert the Bruce was sentenced to be hung, but due to his royal blood was not drawn as traitors usually were. Strathbolgie was put on a horse then hung from a 40 foot high gallows platform. His head was put on London Bridge and his body burnt. Soon after Robert the Bruce became King of Scotland. With John Cumin dead the Mitford barony went via Cumin's sister Johanna who married David de Strathbolgie, 12th earl of Athol.

4 Sir David de Strathbolgie (c. 1307-1326)

Sir David, 12th earl of Athol was killed at the age of 28, fighting for Edward III. His wife Katherine Beaumont was co-heiress to her uncle Aymer de Valence, Earl of Pembroke and owned Merdesfen, Ponteland, Little Eland, Calverdon, the castle of Mitford and lands in Molesden. The lands all went to his son and heir, also called David. Following the brothers and sisters along with sibling rivalry, it is not an easy task to keep track of all that happened. Apart from family feuds and jealousies there are records of John Balliol, lord of Bywell and Barnard castles in England and of Galloway in Scotland, heir to his brothers Hugh, Alan and Alexander, who was crowned King of Scotland 20 November 1292 and died in France in 1306.

5 David de Strathbolgie (c. 1332-1375)

The 13th and last earl of Athol David de Strathbolgie was three years old at the time of his father's death. He later sold Molesden to John Mitford in 1369, when de Strathbolgie died in 1375 aged 43 he owned Mitford Castle plus various properties and land in other counties. He was summoned to parliament in 1366 to 1369. He also participated in the Hundred Years Wars of France with the Black Prince. The ward and marriage of David's two daughters was given by Edward III to Earl Percy, who married them off to two of his own sons, brothers of Hotspur.

6 Sir Thomas Percy (c. 1364-1388)

Sir Thomas Percy was the second son of Henry, first earl of Northumberland and Mandy de Lucy, heiress of Cockermouth and uncle to Sir Henry Percy (Harry Hotspur). He was usually styled as Sir Thomas Percy of Athol. He married Elizabeth and via his wife had rights to lands held by Mary St Paul, Countess of Pembroke. He died in Spain around 1388.

7 Sir Henry Percy (c. 1393-1433)

Sir Henry Percy was the governor of Alnwick Castle under his grandfather, Henry 1st Earl of Northumberland during 1405. He chose not to join his grandfather in his rebellions against Henry IV, and escaped the ruin of the family. When he died he was in ownership of the manor and castle of Mitford, along with the rents from east Aldworth, Molesden and North Milburne, the manor of Ponteland and lands in Little Eland, Callerton-Valence and Merdesfen. He married Elizabeth Bruce and they produced two daughters. The first daughter Elizabeth was a co-heiress to the castle and manor of Mitford, she married Sir Thomas Borough of Gainsborough.

8 Sir Thomas Burgh (c. 1420)

Sir Thomas Borough of Gainsborough was a witness to Henry Percy taking the oath of fealty (oath of loyalty) to Edward IV in 1461. Ten years later in 1471, together with Sir William Stanley they rescued Edward IV, from confinement in Middleham Castle, in the custody of the archbishop of York.

When Edward IV returned from exile he was joined by Sir Thomas Burgh and many others and Edward gave Tom Burgh licence to waiver half of the barony of Mitford. This saved Sir Thomas having to find £384 (a discount) for wages for himself, men at arms and archers for an expedition to France to sign the truce between England and France on 13 August 1475, in a field beside the village Seyntre. Thomas married Elizabeth Percy they produced a heir, another Thomas Borough.

9 Sir Thomas Borough (c. 1431-1496)

Sir Thomas Borough of Gainsborough was made knight of the garter by Richard III and summoned to parliament from 1 September 1487 to 14 October 1495, and was witness to the Treaty of Picquigny between England and France signed by Richard III and the Duke of Brittany. He married Margaret, daughter of Lord Thomas Ross of Kendal and their son Edward became heir. He was buried at Gainsborough in 1496.

10 Sir Edward Borough (c. 1463-1528)

Sir Edward 2nd baron of Gainsborough was never summoned to Parliament and married Anne, only daughter and heir to Sir Thomas Cobham of Sterborough. They produced two sons, Thomas and Henry Burgh. Edward was declared a lunatic in 1510. The Mitford barony passed to Lord Thomas Borough.

11 Lord Thomas Borough (c 1480-1549)

Lord Borough, baron Burgh of Gainsborough, baron Cobham, and baron of Strathbolgie, was bodyguard to Henry VIII and summoned to Parliament from November 1529 to September 1552. Thomas was Lord Chamberlain to Anne Boleyn and later summoned to the trial of Anne Boleyn. Thomas married Anne (Agnes), daughter of William Tyrwhitt of Kettleby in Lincoln and they produced a son, another Thomas.

12 Sir Thomas Lord Borough (c. 1522-1584)

Sir Thomas married Alice who survived her husband then remarried to Edmund Rokewood. The Mitford barony is mentioned in both her first husband's will and her own will dated 24 March 1558. The barony is then passed to their son and heir.

13 Sir William Burgh (c. 1557-1597)

Henry Burgh died young and did not marry. Everything he owned then passed to his younger brother who became Lord William Burgh. William married Catherine Clinton, daughter of the Earl of Lincoln. Anthony and Cuthbert Mitford laid claim to the lands in Callerton, Ponteland, Mersfen, Framlington and Mitford. Lord Burgh sold these lands for £525 back to the Mitfords in 1557 however, the transaction document states that Lord Burgh kept Mitford castle and the royalties for himself. From here we go to his son and heir.

14 Sir John Burgh (c. 1562-1594)

Sir John, killed Sir William Dury in combat in the kingdom of Navarre (The Kingdom of Navarre, originally the Kingdom of Pamplona, famous for running of the bulls. This was a Basque kingdom that occupied lands on either side of the Pyrenees, alongside the Atlantic Ocean between present-day Spain and France). A little later aged 32, Sir John was killed during his successful capture of a rich and well loaded Spanish ship on 7 March 1594. All his family possessions went to his younger brother Lord Thomas Burgh who like his forebears, was summoned to Parliament which he attended from 1563 to 1597. He became Ambassador to Scotland and Lord Lieutenant of Ireland in the year he died.

15 Sir Robert Burgh (c. 1625)

Robert died an infant and Mitford castle became property of the Crown in the reign of James I. Later during the reign of Charles II (1660-1680) Mitford Castle was granted by his majesty by royal decree to Robert Mitford (1612-1674) the 19th Squire of Mitford. After 580 years, Mitford Castle and royalties joined back to the original, mainline Mitford family of Mitford, Northumberland and once again the estate became whole.

The succession of the lords and squires of Mitford up to the 21st century (2002) are detailed in a later chapter...

Chapter 4

Kidnapping The Bishop

Lawlessness, treason and scandal

Despite the lawlessness and isolation of the border land between England and Scotland, Mitford Castle was at one stage standing empty. It was in a good strategic position to garrison soldiers to control the area. It was placed under the guardianship of Sir John Evers, who passed then the responsibility and job to Sir Gilbert Middleton, based at Berwick in 1315. In turn, Gilbert and his brother John decided to make some easy money and took over the castle as part of their plans to freeboot, kidnap and collect ransoms. In fact, their treasonable activities against the king caused an uproar and panic within England and Middleton ended up - hung, drawn and quartered.

As a result, Edward II, in his fury gave the order to have Mitford Castle and the village destroyed. However with the wars and continuous feudal pillage and destruction along the English-Scottish borders, with Robert the Bruce and later King Alexander III of Scotland, it is probably more likely that the castle was finally demolished and dismantled around 1320.

Born about 1279, Sir Gilbert Middleton served in the army of Edward 1 during the Scottish invasion of England under the banner of John of Balliol. The Scots had ravaged the north western counties of England and much of Northumberland. The English counter-attacked via Berwick, but William Wallace defeated them at Stirling Bridge in 1297 and invaded Northumberland. Edward 1 responded and defeated Wallace at Falkirk, but irregular bands of Scots still pillaged the English borders. In 1305 Edward I conquered the Scots and created a constitution. Robert the Bruce headed a rebellion and assassinated the then leader of the Scots

William Wallace. He stabbed John Comyn of Badenach in church at Dumfries and was crowned King of the Scots in 1306. Edward I died in 1307 and his successor, Edward II, was too preoccupied with political squabbling and the barons' war in London to bother about his northern territories. For England, it was back to square one; the northern territories continued unchecked and were left open to pillage and lawlessness.

After Edward II's principal favourite Piers Gaveston had been murdered, Edward II realised that he had needed to address issues in the English Scottish borders and took an army to Scotland. With his ill-disciplined, clumsy and blustering army of over 20,000 men and 3,000 cavalry, that had seen little success in eight years of campaigns Edward II was defeated at the Battle of Bannockburn, by Robert the Bruce of Scotland in 1314. This freed Scotland from English control and Robert the Bruce continued to raid unchecked throughout northern England and Yorkshire.

It was not only the Scots who made life a misery to the Northumbrians, the king's servants and soldiers were almost as bad. To add to all this total wretchedness there was a dreadful summer in 1315; floods swept away crops and cattle so that the following year people were reduced to eating cats, dogs and horses - starvation and disease swept the region. The flooding situation got so bad that many of the locals joined the Scots because the English king was so useless and his servants so greedy.

One of the "servants and soldiers" was Gilbert Middleton, now in charge of Mitford Castle. He was captain of the garrison at Berwick, were he was accused of being almost worse than the Scots, taking food, horses and cattle without payment and even kidnapping people then holding them ransom. Those hostages for whom no ransom was paid were simply killed and thrown into the Tweed River. Petitions to the king for supplies and money to pay servants went unheeded. This dreadful state of affairs in Northumberland was a perfect breeding ground for the rebellion that was to follow.

In 1316 Pope John XX11 was elected and Edward II sent ambassadors to Rome to persuade the Pope to send papal letters to Britain to try to arrange peace between England and Scotland and once and for all bring an end to the border wars. Two Italian cardinals were appointed, Gaucelin Deuze and Luca de Fieschi. They arrived in England with a great flourish amid a large retinue of assistants, consultants and many generous gifts and presents which were to be given to influence discussion in forthcoming negotiations.

Also, to add to the complications and stir things up, the Bishop of Durham died in 1316. His successor by law should have been elected by the canons of the cathedral. However, Queen Isabella, daughter of Philip IV of France, asked that her cousin Lewis Beaumont should be appointed. Nudge-nudge, scratch my back and I'll scratch yours? Talk about stirring the pot, there is never a dull moment, and it gets worse…

The Bishop of Durham's job was much more than just a senior churchman. The status was akin to being a very powerful prince and like a viceroy of the north, able to impose taxes, control ships, raise armies and make truces. It was a vastly important appointment. The monks, preferring to vote for God's man, rather than the King's, elected Henry Stamford, Prior of Finchale, a very well educated fellow. But Isabella, backed by the King of France, pleaded for Lewis and the Pope, who had the final word, confirmed that the post went to the King's candidate Lewis, on payment of a very large sum of money to the court of Rome.

This naturally caused uproar. In the eyes of the clergy of Durham, not only was he illegally appointed but he was greedy, extravagant and did not know a word of Latin. Above all, he was not even a priest… even of a humble, lower order. In fact, everyone was against Lewis Beaumont, his two rather elegant Italian cardinals were warned that it was unwise to go further north than York. As we well know…tell someone not to do something and they tend to do it. Anyway, off they went. (Back to Monty Python and the Holy Grail) clip-clop, clippity-clop, clippity-clop…. onwards and upwards to York they went.

On the 31st of August 1317, it is recorded that the entourage slept at the market town of Darlington, which lies on the river

Skerne, a tributary of the river Tees. The following day, they continued along the Great North Road until they came to the hamlet of Rushyford. Here they were stopped by a large party of armed men... headed by Sir Gilbert Middleton and his brother John.

A report states "Gilbert attacked them with a multitude of armed men and all were despoiled. Lewis Beaumont and his brother Henry were taken as captives to Mitford Castle. Gilbert was warden but not lord of Mitford Castle. The two cardinals were given horses and were allowed to go free". Other reports claim that they were robbed of all their treasure and Lewis and Henry Beaumont were held to ransom until a great sum of money was paid over to Gilbert and his men.

Apparently, a local dignitary, The Earl of Lancaster kindly gave the two, highly upset and agitated Italian cardinals an escort from York to London, however with not much sympathy as they had not taken the advice to go no further north than York. Poor chaps, it must have been quite an ordeal, from the warm and sophisticated climate of Rome to the wilderness of northern England. Meanwhile, back at Mitford castle, Gilbert Middleton was having a whale of a time and continued his freebooting career while the Beaumont brothers were kept prisoners in the dungeons of Mitford Castle (I can assure you, they are awful as I have been there).

The local townsfolk, nobles and countrymen became increasingly worried about Middleton and his villainy so formed a group to deal with the matter. Under the guise of making a payment of money that was secretly hidden in the town, permission was given for access and exit in order to fetch it. At the castle gates they attacked the guards and let in an armed group of men hiding outside. Gilbert Middleton was captured, bound in iron chains and taken to Newcastle. From Newcastle he was put on a ship to London, where he was tried. Found guilty and condemned to be dragged through the city to the gallows, hanged alive, then whilst still alive to be torn apart then beheaded. His body was then cut up in four pieces and sent to the four points of the Kingdom.

Six years later the reign of Edward II ended when he was brutally murdered at Berkeley Castle in 1327. His son Edward III became king.

Mitford Castle was pulled apart. From the remains of this stronghold of the north, all the precious old stones became convenient, ready cut… take away, building blocks for village walls and farmhouses. Something like a medieval builder's supermarket; just drive in with your horse and cart and help yourself. As already mentioned, the Mitford family then built Mitford Manor House (1637) and Mitford Hall (1828) from the stones of Mitford Castle.

Now, all that is left of the castle are parts of the north wall, including one that bears an impressive arch looking towards Mitford Church, and the foundations of the keep, one of the only two pentagonal keeps in England. There are two vaulted chambers in the basement of the keep, which became the castle dungeons, as incised in one wall are the words "captivus morior 141" "Captive I die". Going by the date, the vaults were still used as a prison long after the main area of the castle was destroyed.

Chapter 5

Legend Of The Mitford Crest

A headless boar and a boarless head

The arms of the Mitford family – consists of three moles, as can be observed in the top left hand corner of the shield, taken from the early days when the family seat was Molesden and not at Mitford. On top is the family crest of a boar's head pierced by a sword. It is reproduced in the plate section. This shield was drawn by Admiral Mitford around 1825. The moles and crest can be seen on Mitford Manor tower, in Mitford Church, All Saints Church in Hunmanby, Yorkshire and on the old stone well which was situated between the Inn and the Smithy in earlier days. Hugh Mitford, holds the original stamp of the crest and family motto (used for estate letters and documents in earlier years). [see plate section.]

According to a manuscript written around 1879, legend has it that the Mitfords came upon their dramatic crest in a very curious way. Much of the county was forest inhabited by an enormous and savage boar which devastated the countryside. Many armed people, heroes and casual travellers, fell victim to the brute, until the King offered a reward for anyone who could kill it and bring the head as proof, to the court. Likewise, the Bishop of Durham, who then lived at Bishop Auckland and had also suffered from the boar's devastation, added a second reward for the same deed.

As the story goes, Egbert, a brave and gallant young man took on the job. In the woods where the boar had its lair, he climbed a large and stout beech tree and from this safe vantage point, scattered a great quantity of rich food on the ground, calculated to knock out the most suspicious old boar. Hidden by dense foliage he then waited patiently. The boar eventually arrived, paused, snuffled, and tucked in to eat a hearty meal. Soon the rich banquet was over and a gorged and sleepy boar tottered off towards its den for a snooze. Egbert cautiously followed, chose his battleground and attacked. The fight was fierce and long, but in the end the exhausted Egbert killed his foe, severed its head and placed the tongue in his carry bag before lying down beneath his beech tree for a well-earned sleep. When he awoke, to his dismay his fine trophy - the boar's head - had gone. Poor Egbert sought out his horse and proceeded to present the boar's tongue to the Bishop. The Bishop, who was about to sit down to dinner, was pleased and told Egbert that however much land he could ride around while the Bishop dined would be his.

But what happened to the boar's head? Well, it was a Mitford, on his way to London, who came upon the woodland scene, the sleeping Egbert, and the boar's head. Knowing of the Royal reward, he tied the head to his saddle and rode happily on to London, the palace and the King. He received the reward and also permission to take as his crest, a boar's head transfixed by a sword.

(Author unknown & edited by HMR)

Notes

As far as can be ascertained the largest wild boar found in England weighed 518 lbs or 234 kgs and the largest found in Scotland 420lbs or 190 kgs. Boar hunting is popular in many countries around the world. A world record was shot in Fayette County, Pennsylvania, USA, it was 9 foot long and weighed 1,100 lbs/498 kilograms.

Chapter 6

Mitford Church and Chapel

Burnt and demolished by King John

William Bertram, Baron of Mitford built Mitford Church in 1135. William is also the founder of Brinkburn Priory, and his son Roger, is buried at Brinkburn Priory with his tombstone inscribed with "Hic Jacet Rogervs Fundator". In 1306, Edward I, on his journey from Scotland via Carlisle, took ill and was welcomed at Lanercost Priory by the Prior between Newcastle and Carlisle, where he was nursed - he and his entourage were looked after for six months until he recovered and was able to continue on his journey. He died a year later at Burgh on Sands.

In gratitude for the kindness and care and appreciating that his stay had depleted the stores and reserves of the Priory, the King bestowed upon the Priory the great tithe of Mitford (a tithe is a tenth part of an annual income contributed or due as a tax, especially for the support of the clergy or church). In a letter to the Pope, King Edward explained the reasons for his generosity as his long stay, compensation for the damage done by the Scots and the devotion he felt for St Mary Magdalene. Hence Mitford church was named St Mary Magdalene.

Remembering that the Mitford barony extended over the parishes of Meldon, Ponteland and Felton in Northumberland and Greatham in Durham, the size of the estate enabled the first Bertrams to establish a Priory, erect a massive castle and stronghold and build a splendid church. This large church would be required to accommodate the vassals, retainers, freemen and villagers of this extensive barony. Back to the time when the church was first built it was the scene of processions and spectacles – when the baron and his knights met to receive the blessing of the Church before setting out to war for the King of the time and on return, when they were welcomed home with hymns and great celebration from battle.

The restoration of the church that can be seen today was begun in the early summer of 1874 by the 27th Squire of Mitford, Lt Col John Philip Mitford, my great-great uncle. Portions of the church rival the antiquity of the ruins of the old Norman castle still standing opposite just across the road. This distinguished and elegant church has shared with its neighbouring castle, the prosperity and decline of the barony – both suffered alike from the wars and turmoil of the Middle Ages.

King John, in pursuit of his northern barons who had forced him to sign the Magna Carta at Runnymede in 1215, burnt and reduced the church, the town and castle of Mitford, to ruins in 1216. The castle was partly rebuilt as a smaller stronghold but never fully restored. The church further suffered over following generations of neglect, apathy and poverty.

The list of serving vicars is long and distinguished. The record shows the average duration of incumbency to be around 14 years. Inserted in the north wall of the nave there is a brass plaque mounted on oak wood grown on the Mitford estate made by Messrs Hardman and Co of Birmingham and London. This is engraved with the 43 names of all the vicars from 1200 AD till 1880, the first being "Richard, son of Baldwin, chaplain to Roger Bertram A.D. 1200 & King John".

It is noted by Archdeacon Robinson of Newcastle in the minutes of his parochial visitations in 1758 "The vicar of Mitford, George Gordon, is I believe the oldest clergyman in the diocese being above 87 years old and able to perform all parochial duties". The Rev. Isaac Nelson, an uncle of Horatio Nelson succeeded George from 1759 to 1772. He managed to raise funds and had a vicarage built (subsequently replaced by the new vicarage in 1973, with the old stables becoming the parish hall as you see today). Sadly, while crossing the stepping stones across the River Wansbeck, he fell in and drowned.

Many churches fell into semi-ruinous condition during the eighteenth and early part of the nineteenth century, as did

Mitford Church, evidenced by the 1812 etching (please refer to the plate section). Mitford Church was described as "dark, dingy, damp, dilapidated and patchy".

The extracts from parochial visitations given in Hodgson's "History of Northumberland," record that during the greater part of previous centuries the church was constantly in need of repair. In 1826 Archdeacon Singleton wrote – "The church is venerable and spacious, but the roof of the chancel has had its leaden covering exchanged for one of grey freestone slate, and is steep and decaying. The south porch and chapel, belonging to the Mitfords of Mitford, is also in bad condition. I pressed for immediate restoration where necessary. It would appear that the proprietors and parishioners had made no consistent effort to put the church into a satisfactory condition. They had refrained from doing anything as long as they could, and when forced to do something they had done as little as possible".

In 1868 some donations were received from various members of the Mitford family but these went towards the vicarage and not church building repairs. The same principle appeared to have been at work in the parish up to 1874. It was only under instructions from the squire Lt Col John Philip Mitford, that the Newcastle architect Robert James Johnson (1832-1892), was asked to begin the work of restoration. Up until recently, the Mitfords had no money to pay for anything let alone restoration of a church. Funds had recently become available from the Hunmanby estate. In James Fergusson's book "Mitford Church – Its History, Restoration and Associations" published in 1884 by Andrew Reid, Newcastle, there is detailed description of the church before and after its restoration.

"As it now stands, the church consists of a chancel, with a small organ chamber on the north; a nave with a south aisle, a tower connected to the nave and spire; and two aisles or transcripts, north and south, at the junction of the nave with the chancel, whereby the building is rendered cruciform in plan. The new portions of the building are the organ chamber, the south aisle, a new south porch for the Mitford Chapel, the tower and spire, and the clerestory in the nave.

A new chancel arch had to be built, as well as one for the north transept, and the arcade of Norman arches and pillars latterly forming the south wall of the nave was taken down, and rebuilt with the old stones, so as to form the arcade for the new south aisle. Before 1874, there were only three of these arches standing. A fourth has been added in order to lengthen the nave. Also constructed beneath the north transcript or vestry was a furnace and boiler to supply hot water to the new heating system. Each feature has been scrupulously retained, while every element of spaciousness has been increased by many degrees. It is a building at once old and new – the old untouched by modern hammer or chisel, the new designed and executed in the spirit of the masters who built the ancient landmark".

The chancel is 51ft, 2 inches long and 19ft, 3 inches wide; the nave is 60 ft 7 inches long and 19ft, 3 inches wide and nearly 40ft from the floor to the top centre of the roof. Including the south aisle the church measures 30ft, 9 inches from the south wall of that aisle to the north wall of the nave, while across the transepts it is 54ft. The tower is 14 ft, 6 inches square inside. From the east wall of the chancel to the west wall of the tower the length is 130ft. The tower which measures 21ft by 21ft externally, and spire rise to a height of 130ft and features prominently in the surrounding landscape.

No expense was spared to ensure everything in and about the church as totally solid, substantial, efficient and in keeping with the original design. For acoustic properties the chancel is fitted with a semi-circular roof encased with wood. The altar steps and most of the chancel floor are laid with old encaustic tiles. The choir stalls are of carved oak. The floor of the nave consists of a thick coating of cement, upon which are laid a floor of wood formed entirely of oblongs about the same breadth and thickness as bricks, just a little longer, ensuring comfort and noise reduction.

The custom-made oak benches providing seating with kneeling boards were designed with comfort in mind. At the church altar, the beautiful reredos (ornamental screen behind the altar) is made from Belgian oak and the groups of figures from Turkish boxwood depicting the Annunciation, the Cross and the Nativity. These were made by Buckley, Thompson & Co. of London & Bruges. The Mitford Chapel is separated by a carved oak screen of similar elegant design and workmanship.

The ground floor of the tower forms the baptistery and a new font was installed. The first floor of the tower consists of a floor area and staircase in oak fitted much later. In the bell tower loft, a new peal of bells was fitted. The thirteen bells are fixed in pairs up on two wooden frameworks, which are placed with a slight inclination to each other as they reach the roof of the loft. The bells are saucer shaped and are fastened into cross beams of wood. Each bell has two hammers, the reason being so that the same note can be struck more than once in succession. If there was only one hammer it could not, after striking its note, return into its position sufficiently quick enough to repeat the note rapidly to maintain the time of the tune played.

On the floor below the bells there was a set of intricate machinery, which was set in motion by means of a weight, like an eight-day clock. On the top of the machine there was a key board, similar to that of a piano, consisting of 26 keys – one for each hammer. When the machinery is put in motion, and one of these keys is pressed it displaces one end of a lever to the other end of which is attached a wire rope which is fixed to one of the hammers above, and holds it also by means of a lever, in a position ever ready to fall. The moment the catch holding the lever is displaced, the hammer falls on the bell. That done, the lever is automatically repositioned and the hammer is once again held in suspension ready to strike the next blow. By this means, the musician can play any tune within the range of the finger board and bells. As an added benefit, the faces of the hammers were fitted with wood, to provide a fine softness of tone.

If there is no skilled musician available, music can still be played without a musician. For this, all is needed is a barrel with pins or studs, like those on a musical box or a barrel organ, placed within the machine, and it will displace the levers even more deftly than the fingers of a pianist. With no one to touch or even look at the machine, chimes can be rung, along with wedding bells, funeral dirges, and many popular hymns and psalms.

The machine has a total of four barrels which can play fourteen tunes, using ten, eight and three bells or the monotonous funeral march to the grave. Some of the set tunes are – Come all ye Faithful, the Wedding March, God Save the Queen, Home Sweet Home and The Evening Hymn, there are many others. When fully wound up it plays for one hour.

With time this system became troublesome and out of tune. The steel cable holding it all in place broke and the bells came crashing down through the tower. Luckily the Mitford family were at hand and in 1899 a new system of 8 bells rung by one person was installed. This was also the time when my great-great grandfather had the exquisite painting of a dove, that he had painted, secured at the top of the bell tower, as it is today.

Over 150 years later this picture of the dove is also printed on the cover of the reprint of the book, 'British Policy in the Middle East and the Creation of Israel". Written by Hugh Mitford Raymond's great-great-grandfather in support of the Jewish nation, published in 1845 by Hatchards of Piccadilly, London and presented to minsters at Westminster Parliament.

The bells were cast by Messrs Taylor, Loughborough, and were installed with the machinery made by Messrs Lund and Blockley of 42, Pall Mall, London. Masons – Messrs J & G Waterston of Morpeth, Joiner – Mr Gradon of Durham, Slater – Mr Athey of Morpeth, Engineers – Messrs Dinning & Cooke of Newcastle and Plumbers – Messrs Barclay & Wilson of Newcastle.

The stained glass windows were made as follows. The west window of two lights is by the famous German stained glass design and manufacturing company, based in Munich, Germany, Franz Mayer & Co. and the chancel windows are by Messrs Clayton and Bell. The Mitford aisle or "Dorcas" window was made by William Wailes (1808-1881) of Newcastle, a student of Franz Mayer & Co.

With reference to Peter Else, Chairman of the Mitford Historical Society, starting in the chancel the small oval window has the Agnus Dei, the Lamb of God, standing on a rainbow. Below the central window shows the crucifixion with Saint Mary Magdalene kneeling below – the left shows the Virgin Mary and to the right, Saint John. The inscription below reads "behold the

Lamb of God, which taketh away the sins of the world" and at the bottom of the central light is the Mitford motto "God caryth for us."

The six tall windows in the south wall of the chancel are, from left to right – Saint Peter, holding the keys to the kingdom of Heaven – Saint Matthew with his symbol of a man or angel – Saint Mark, with his symbol of a lion – Saint Luke, with his symbol of a cow – Saint John, with his symbol of an eagle and writing the Book of Revelations, and Saint Paul, with his sword.

Interestingly, there is a little window in the Mitford Chapel where lepers could see and also take mass without entering the church. (See photo plate section).

The stained glass windows in the Nave are as follows. On the left walking into the church is Saint John the Baptist. In the west wall of the tower is the splendid Mayer & Co. window of the Resurrection and the Ascension. In the north wall of the Nave you'll find - The Good Samaritan, Saint George and the dragon - The Good Shepherd, and The presentation in the Temple.

In the south wall is a window showing scenes from the life of Saint Mary Magdalene. (Please refer to the plate section)

All in all the Mitford family paid £14,000 pounds (approximately £1.4 million today) for the complete restoration and furnishing, which includes the entrance gate and archway into the churchyard and the sturdy stone wall around the churchyard.

After three years of building, restoration and refurbishment a number of well attended ceremonies took place at Mitford Church. A church once consecrated does not require the ceremony to be performed again. However, due to the extensive and almost total restoration project done, it was considered fitting that the church be re-dedicated to the service of God with Episcopal authority.

In 1881 a re-dedication was performed by the Right Rev. the Lord Bishop of Durham and in 1889, the Right Rev. Dr Wilberforce, Bishop of Newcastle presided over the dedication of the elegant new church entrance gate and the consecration of an additional piece of land, also a gift from the Mitford family to the Church of England, in addition to the existing churchyard. This was enclosed by a substantial stone wall with iron railing.

Not often seen and kept in the bank for safe keeping is the magnificent silver communion cup inscribed with "Mitford Church 1699" it is used only for special occasions, Christmas and Easter. This cup was donated to the church by Squire Robert Mitford (1662-1707) squire for 34 years from 1673 to 1707.

In contrast to the new bells, there hangs an old one, which was removed from church use in 1862, when Admiral Robert Mitford presented two new bells to the parish, before the bell tower was built. The old one is an interesting relic – believed, by competent authorities in the history of bell-founding, to be over 800 years old. It is now positioned inside the entrance of the church. [See plate section.]

With the ancient importance of Mitford, the size of its church and its contiguity to Newminster Abbey close by, which unfortunately did not survive the Middle Ages – Mitford enjoyed the status of an established town before the Normans set foot in England. It could even boast of miracles performed by the relics of the Great Saxon Saint of Northumbria.

Apparently, as the story goes, in the year 1006 AD, an old man named Urdar obtained his living by carrying about with him a collection of holy relics, for the sight of which he received the alms of the faithful. He was neither priest nor monk, but had been a servant to a friar of Durham. A rather crafty servant I would imagine. In going about his travels he arrived one day at the town of Mitford, and was told that there was an old woman who had been blind for six months and who believed she would recover her sight if she could get an eyewash in which some portions of Saint Cuthbert's clothes had been soaked.

Of course Urdar had in his collection the required article in the shape of a piece of cloth that had formed part of the wrappings in which the saint's body had lain for 418 years. The drinking cup of a neighbouring well was filled at the spring and the rag dipped into it twice, three times, and again. But the water had no power to wet the sacred relic. Noticing the miracle, Urdar instantly gulped down this amazing water and was forthwith healed of dysentery from which he had suffered for over ten years. He however, like a businessman, left sufficient water to bathe the old woman's eyes. Once done, she quickly had her vision restored. Urdar and his tribe worked with people of very simple faith and knowledge.

In front of the row of houses next to the old blacksmith's shop in the village of Mitford there was a well with a covering of hewn stone - in the top of the covering is a small recess cut out for the reception of a drinking cup. Many years ago there was a constant supply of water in the well and a cup lay inverted in the niche for the use of the thirsty villager or traveller. When people used the well they retold the story of Urdar's miracle and have kept the story alive for many generations. People were always keen to have a cup of Mitford water!

Alas, to this day there remains a small stone recess with a tap in the centre and the Mitford crest above, but no water. Some flowers take its place.

Urdar's story bears witness to the existence of a Saxon town or village at Mitford. . The old kingdom of Northumbria, along with Kent was the first of the Anglo-Saxon kingdoms to gain sovereignty. It is said that in King Edwin's day (c616-32), he had bronze bowls placed at springs along roadsides so travellers might refresh themselves. Perhaps the cup at the Mitford well was in memory of Edwin's good deed, later Saxons chose to keep alive to maintain peace, calm and goodwill to others.....along with the occasional miracle.

After devoting many years of his stewardship of Mitford to the complete restoration of Mitford Church the parish of Mitford thought it fitting to make a presentation of their appreciation to Lt Col John Philip Mitford. The words of this address have been edited from old English by the author as follows.

"Sir, - We, the undersigned Vicar, Churchwardens present and past, and other members of the parish of Mitford, on behalf of all other parishioners and ourselves, would like to express our heartfelt thanks for the great work you have accomplished to the enrichment of the parish - the restoration of the ancient church of St Mary Magdalene - the fine wood carvings therein – the magnificent bell tower containing thirteen bells and crowning it with a lofty spire, which can be seen for miles around in

Wansbeck's lovely vale. And yet still further, the more recent gift of additional land to the church and surrounding all this with a massive stone wall, centred with a most excellent entrance gate. This, we trust, through this simple testimonial, shows our deep-felt gratitude; while it also conveys to you our hearty appreciation of this excellent work. May the blessing of God rest upon you and the Mitford family".

Signed by the Committee and engraved with the Mitford arms & crest by Messrs Reid of Newcastle in 1889.

To this day, Mitford Church is kept in pristine condition by the Mitford Trust for the goodwill of all at Mitford for future generations to use and enjoy.

Chapter 7

The Squires Of Mitford

Line of succession from 1066 to 2002

The Domain of Mitford was granted to the Mitford family as an Earldom by King Edward the Confessor in 1042 AD. The records of the Mitford family of Mitford and branches are preserved in the archives of the College of Arms, London and by the early Heralds' Visitations 1530, 1615 & 1666.

In old England, land ownership determined the social order. Gallant knights and brave warriors not only fought for king, queen and country but also became landowners. From age old custom - appreciation and gratitude was rewarded with solid and tangible assets - land. Along with the Church and Crown land owners became the ruling class.

From the Middle Ages, a squire was typically a teenage boy training to become a knight. The squire would sometimes carry the knight's flag into battle with his master. Later the squire's rank came to be recognised in its own right and a squire became a village leader (if he owned an estate) and lord of the manor.

Possession of land generated revenue from rent and taxation and also gave control over community activities, labour, welfare and village life. Landowners were the lords. Over time through wars and generations hereditary status slowly declined along with the squires practical prowess and skill as gallant warriors. Back in the early days of the Mitford family, the Barons of Mitford fought tooth and nail for democracy and as a result got everything they owned sold and confiscated... not once – but twice, by English kings..

With persistence and goodwill later generations recovered lost assets to the mainline Mitford family. Tracing the background of 33 generations of Mitford squires – they all served the Crown – and worked in the military, church and civil service and upon retirement managed the Mitford estates. The exception being the two squires who became lawyers who created and organised the original family wealth. Holding onto what one has for over 960 years is no easy task. Through the succession this extraordinary family dynasty ended in perfect indifference with no heir to be found. The last foothold of the Mitford family in Mitford was sold in 2006, severing all formal ties with Mitford, after nearly 1,000 years.

The original Mitford crest used by my great-great grandfather Edward Ledwich Mitford can be seen illustrated in the plate section. He passed on this crest on to his youngest son, the South African novelist Bertram Mitford FRGS, it was then passed to his son Major Roland Mitford, then to his wife, the late Princess Djoumkosvsky and then on to myself.

The Mitford Coat of Arms (the dynasty shield) pictured on the back cover and illustrated in the plate section was originally hand drawn by Admiral Mitford 26th Squire of Mitford. Robert Mitford was a noted scientific bird illustrator and was taught art and drawing by the celebrated bird artist John James Audubon (1785-1851) during his visit to England and wood engraving by Thomas Bewick (1753-1828) of Newcastle. However, this artistic talent was no doubt influenced by his brother-in-law John Selby (1788-1867) the famed ornithologist and a master of bird art, to help illustrate his ornithology art books. Incidentally, in 2010 at Sotheby's, John James Audubon's "The Birds of America" a first edition in four volumes sold for £7,321,250.

The explanation of the Mitford Coat of Arms is covered in the section The Squires of Mitford - 26th Squire. The Mitford family tree is displayed in the Mitford Family Chapel, inside Mitford Church and the Mitford Coat of Arms and Crest is also displayed in the magnificent stained glass windows above the altar, likewise in All Saints Church, Hunmanby, Yorkshire.

Here follows the family history tracing the Mitford line of succession from 1060 into the 21st century.

Mitford line of succession

1 John Mitford c. 1060
2 Matthew Mitford c. 1065
3 Nicholas Mitford c. 1100
4 Peter Mitford c. 1135
5 Eustace Mitford c. 1170
6 Hugh Mitford c. 1205
7 Adam Mitford
8 Roger Mitford
9 Gilbert Mitford c. 1310.
10 Sir John Mitford MP (1346-1409) Knight
Keeper of the seal to Edward, Duke of York
& High Sheriff of Northumberland 1401
11 William Mitford MP (1369-1423)
High Sheriff of Northumberland 1415 — Son of John
12 John Mitford (1402-1437) — Son of William
13 John Mitford (1433-1461)
Killed at the Battle of Towton — Son of John
14 Bertram Mitford (1455-1493) — Son of John
15 Gawen Mitford (1480-1550) — Son of Bertram
16 Cuthbert Mitford (1520-1594) — Son of Gawen
17 Robert Mitford (1544-1625) — Son of Cuthbert
18 Cuthbert Mitford (1582-1613) — Son of Robert
19 Robert Mitford (1612-1674)
High Sheriff of Northumberland 1650 — Son of Cuthbert

From Robert's third son, John Mitford (1643-1720) sprung the branch, Mitfords of Exbury. This is where the "Mitford Sisters" hail from, daughters of the 2nd Lord Redesdale.

20 Humphrey Mitford (1632-1677) — Son of Robert
21 Robert Mitford (1662-1707)
High Sheriff of Northumberland 1697 — Son of Humphrey
22 Robert Mitford (1686-1756)
Married Mary Osbaldeston

High Sheriff of Northumberland 1723 Son of Robert
23 Robert Mitford (1718-1784) Son of Robert
24 Bertram Mitford (1748-1800) Son of Robert
25 Bertram Mitford (1777-1842)
High Sheriff of Northumberland 1835 (no children)
Son of Bertram
26 Admiral Robert Mitford (1781-1870)
Twice appointed High Sheriff of Yorkshire (only daughter)
Brother of Bertram
27 Lt Col John Philip Mitford (1809-1895)
High Sheriff of Northumberland 1878 (no children)
Cousin of Robert
28 Edward Ledwich Mitford FRGS (1811-1912)
(5 sons & 4 daughters) Brother of John
29 Capt Robert Cuthbert Mitford (1846-1924) Son of Edward
30 Bertram Lane Mitford (1876-1939)
(no surviving children reverted back to 28 & 3rd son)
Son of Robert
31 The Rev Edward Mitford (1853-1948)
3rd Son of Edward Ledwich
32 Lt Col John Philip Mitford (1880-1970) Son of Rev Edward
33 Brigadier Edward Cecil Mitford (1908-2002)
Last Squire of Mitford (no children)
Only Son of John Philip

Mitford Castle & Estate Sold 1993 & in 2006 (old manor tower)

Hugh Geoffrey Mitford Raymond
Great-great grandson, great nephew and cousin to the last 7 Squires

Mitford Squires From The Conquest & 1066 to 2006

At the time of the conquest in 1066 Sir John Mitford was Lord of Mitford. The Mitford family was established 24 years previously in 1042, on lands granted by Edward the Confessor. Sybil Mitford, his only daughter was heir to his estate.

As was convention marriage joined important families together, John's only daughter and sole heir was married off to Richard Bertram, son Lord of Dignan in Normandy, by William the Conqueror around 1080. The marriage of Sybil Mitford to Richard Bertram marks the beginning of the succession of the feudal barons of Mitford (as detailed in a previous chapter).

Sir Richard Bertram and Sybil Mitford produced two sons, William and Roger Bertram. The eldest William succeeded to the barony created by Henry I, in the service of five knight's fees. Baron William Bertram and his wife Hawyse, daughter of Sir William Merlay of Morpeth, with his sons Roger, Guy, William and Richard, founded the priory of Brinkburn, where he lies buried with his inscription "BIC Jacet Rogervs Bertram Fyndator" as can be seen today. Brinkburn Priory, a medieval monastery built on a bend of the River Coquet, some 4 miles (6 km) east of Rothbury in Northumberland. He also gave lands to the abbey of Newminster, close to Mitford, which alas, the abbey did not survive the generations of conflict and feudal wars.

Sir John Mitford also had a brother Matthew, born around c. 1065 whose his son (and Sir John's nephew) Nicolas Mitford born around c.1100. It is from this time that the source of different lines of the Mitford family can be followed; the Mitfords of Mitford, and the branches - Mitfords of Benhall, Suffolk; William Mitford, of Pittshill, Sussex and Lord Redesdale, the Exbury branch (Mitford girls).

According to John Hodgson's book, "A History of Northumberland", printed in 1832, Lord Redesdale states that "the original possessions of Matthew, brother of John, Lord of Mitford, whose daughter Sybil married Richard Bertram, are not mentioned in any statement of the barony, in inquisitions or other documents, because they were not part of the barony. They belonged to the younger brother under the Saxon government".

When William the Conqueror gave Sir John Mitford's land along with his daughter in marriage to Richard Bertram, he required Bertram to hold the lands by the service of five knight's fees, as all Normans who acquired lands in the same way were required to do by providing military services to the Crown. The lands held by Matthew Mitford (John's brother) were not part of the Conquest, therefore not subjected to military tenure. As such, Mathew Mitford's land is not recorded in any documents detailing the property of the Bertram family, or subsequent owners.

As previously mentioned, during the medieval feudal times "in the service of knights' fees" was the law of the ruling monarch. Five knight's fees means that a knight's fee was a measure of a unit of land deemed sufficient from which a knight could derive not only sustenance for himself and his esquires, but also the means to furnish himself and his equipage with horses and armour to fight for his overlord and king in battle. It was effectively the size of a fee (or "fief" which word is synonymous with "fee") sufficient to support one knight for one year in the performance of his feudal duties of knight-service to the Crown.

A barony was held by military service to the Crown. This meant that the barons had to be able to put into the field five fully armed, equipped and provisioned knights with their attendants. These warriors had to serve the king for a fixed period of each year. (Military training and conscription continued in its various forms for hundreds of years).

Knights were tenants to the baron and paid most of their rent by supplying military service. Other tenants paid their rent by supplying arrows, saddlery and so forth, which equipped the baron and his knights. Matthew Mitford, John's brother, was also a tenant, holding various lands in and about Mitford, for which he paid the baron one pound of pepper annually. John was not unduly affected by the Norman Conquest and he and his descendants prospered quietly throughout the storms and conflicts which raged around the Bertrams. In the end, his line outlived the Bertrams and when the barony collapsed Robert Mitford (19th Squire, see page 78) recovered the castle and royalties by grant from Charles II.

When Sir John Mitford died, Henry IV, as chief lord of the fee, seized Mitford, the surrounding villages and other lands. An inventory was taken of all the property of Matthew & Sir John Mitford, who died in 1409.

As stated, Matthew Mitford, brother of Sir John & Nicolas Mitford, son of Matthew and heirs were not included in the barony and their land holdings were separate.

Their line of succession from Matthew followed through to…

4. Peter c. 1135, 5. Eustace c. 1170, 6. Hugh c. 1205, 7. Adam, 8. Roger, & 9. Gilbert c. 1310, to his son…

10th Lord of Mitford – Sir John Mitford (1346-1409) Knight

Landowner & squire for over 38 years
(accumulated the original family wealth)

It is written in Parliamentary records, "Sir John was one of the most successful administrators to represent Northumberland during the Middle Ages. John Mitford enjoyed a remarkable career covering almost every facet of local government. Over a period of almost 40 years he not only sat in at least 13 Parliaments, but also served as a tax collector, crown commissioner, sheriff and diplomat while also holding a variety of stewardships and constableships for such eminent figures as Henry, Earl of Northumberland, Edward, Duke of York, and Sir John le Scrope.

The 10th Lord's achievements were largely those of a self-made man, although his family was not without influence, especially in the port of Newcastle upon Tyne, where his father Gilbert, held office in the 1350s collecting of customs and weighing wool.

He was a trusted businessman and lawyer, with a rapidly growing circle of clients in the north. Further expansion followed, when David, Earl of Atholl, granted him 'all his lands and tenements in the village of Molesden in Mitford, thus providing him with a sizeable territorial base. It was perhaps also at this time that the Earl settled upon John and his brother, Alexander, additional holdings in the Lincolnshire village of Gainsborough, which John passed on to his descendants.

In February 1370, Henry, Lord Percy, made John steward of his manor of Corbridge on the river Tyne, an appointment which John retained for almost 38 years until shortly before his death. His connection with the Percys remained continuous until their rebellion against Henry IV in 1403, John was also the steward of the Percy's manor of Morpeth, for a brief period in the early 1380s, John served on many commissions and embassies to Scotland with his patron Lord Percy, who was created Earl of Northumberland in 1377. Sir John Mitford acted as a feoffee (in feudal law it is a person to whom a grant of freehold property is made), for Lord Percy Earl of Northumberland and his second wife, Maud, Baroness Lucy, holding in trust at various times their castles at Warkworth (Northumberland) and Cockermouth (Cumberland), and large areas of property in Northumberland, Cumberland, Yorkshire and Sussex.

The Earl of Northumberland's son, 'Hotspur', employed John Mitford's services as a mainpernor (in feudal law this is a legal surety declaring that a prisoner will appear in court) on at least one occasion, and it seems likely that John's popularity with the electors of Northumberland was due, in part at least, to the support of the powerful baronial Percy family. John Mitford first entered Parliament in 1372, not long after being given a seat on the Northumbrian bench.

Over the next few years John Mitford began to consolidate his estates even further by a process of leasing, purchase and exchange which brought him extensive land holdings in local areas. Sir John le Scrope, a kinsman by marriage of both Sir Aymer (a colleague) and the Percys, gave John Mitford additional land in Mitford. Scrope evidently valued his neighbour's services very highly, as in 1396 he made John keeper of Mitford castle for life and also awarded him a fee of 100 shillings. 'for his counsel and advice'. The two men had previously been involved in the settlement of a boundary dispute between the inhabitants of Mitford and Morpeth, where John's legal expertise had clearly been put to good use.

Not surprisingly in view of his great industry and diligence in the field of local government, rewards eventually began to come his way from Richard II. In 1383, for example, John Mitford obtained the wardship and marriage of the late John Belasise's next heir; and in March 1393 Richard II promised him an annuity of £20 for life. This grant was made specifically 'for his good services as a messenger and on treaties in the north', although it was conditional upon his foregoing the right to any further reward in future. Often together with his friend, Sir Gerard Heron, John Mitford took part in over 30 diplomatic missions to negotiate for peace with the Scots, and he was regularly out of pocket as a result. However, if he had to help finance these embassies, in the short term at least, there was no lack of funds with which to do so.

In addition to the revenues from John Mitford's estates, and profits from a flourishing legal practice, he could rely upon a substantial return from trading ventures along the coast from Northumberland to Yarmouth and London. He maintained close links with the mercantile community from whence he came, evidenced from his appearance with Sir Gerard Heron in February 1394 as a mainpernor (old legal term or surety declaring that a prisoner will appear in court) for a group of merchants from Berwick-upon-Tweed.

Moreover, in the following July, a cargo of coal, which John Mitford was shipping south from Newcastle was confiscated without reason at Yarmouth. His son, William, offered sureties of £300 on his behalf; and the consignment was restored, pending an official inquiry. Although John Mitford received formal letters of pardon from Richard II in 1398, it seems likely that he remained aloof from the political struggles which beset the last years of the century.

Being first and foremost a conscientious bureaucrat, concerned with the smooth running of local government, John Mitford transferred his allegiance without protest, in 1399, to the newly crowned Henry IV, whom he served as loyally and diligently as he had his predecessor, Richard ll. The Lancastrian regime made great use of John's long and varied experience, and although he must have been at least sixty years old, he was immediately put to work on the border, negotiating with the Scots. Having confirmed a royal annuity of £20, Henry IV entrusted John Mitford with a sum of 100 marks to make good any losses sustained by the people of Northumberland during recent battles.

An altogether more generous employer than Richard II, Henry lV also gave him and his two colleagues (one of whom was, once again, Sir Gerard) a similar sum by way of recompense for the 'time and labour' they had previously devoted to Scottish affairs. Naturally enough, John was among the representatives from Northumberland summoned to attend a great council at Westminster in the summer of 1401, and at some point a few months later was knighted for his services to Crown and country.

During the course of John Mitford's 13th and last Parliament, in the autumn of 1402, he was made sheriff of Northumberland, and thus came to play an important part in suppressing the rebellion staged by the Percys and their adherents the following year. Notwithstanding his long and fruitful association with the Earl of Northumberland, he gave unstinting support to the government, and was even present, on 25 Sept. 1403, at a council meeting at Durham Priory where plans were made for the surrender of the Earl's castles. In the company of his old friend, Sir Gerard, he took control of Warkworth, to which, ironically, he already possessed a legal title as one of Northumberland's most trusted feoffees or legal stewards".

John Mitford and Heron (for whom he had previously done surety as a collector of customs at Berwick-upon-Tweed) were rewarded with a royal grant of the ward ship of the late Thomas Heron's estates, which they shared along with William, Sir John's son. William who was by then married to Sir Aymer Atholl's granddaughter, Margery, had already begun to follow an enterprising career of his own as legal advisor to such prominent members of his wife's prolific family as Sir Henry Percy of Atholl, Lord of the Manor of Hunmanby in Yorkshire, while also assisting Sir Aymer in various capacities. Hunmanby would later become part of the Mitford estates by marriage.

By the time of John Mitford's death, on 16 July 1409, there was, then, no doubt that the estates which he had so carefully built up over the previous three decades would remain safe in the hands of his male descendants. On the very day that he died, an assignment of £20 was made at the Exchequer to cover the cost of his most recent visit to Scotland as a Royal Envoy, so it would appear he remained active to the very end.

John Hodgson writes, "Sir John was a person of considerable note and a distinguished gentleman during his time. He held the deeds to property around the area of Mitford and Newcastle, by grant from David Stratbolgie, 13th Earl of Athol, of all the lands to him and his male heirs".

The Scotch Rolls or Ragman Rolls (collection of deeds and documents by which the nobility and gentry of Scotland subscribed allegiance to Edward I of England), from 1383 to 1407, contain over 40 documents in which Sir John's name occurs in mandates, writs or commissions empowering him to act in matters of a civil or diplomatic nature between England and Scotland.

John Mitford's name also occurs on numerous treaties and embassy documents. A lawyer by profession he was also keeper of the seal to Edward, Duke of York. John Mitford attended parliament for Northumberland in the reigns of Edward III, Richard II and Henry IV, and in 1401 was High Sheriff of Northumberland.

It was during Edward III's reign (1327-1377) that various English institutions took recognisable form. Parliament was divided into two houses, Lords and Commons. Edward founded the Order of the Garter (1348) and English gradually replaced French as the "official" language of England.

Richard II (1377-1400) is believed to have invented the handkerchief and was passionately interested in culture and cookery. The books of Geoffrey Chaucer, William Langland and John Gower were written during his reign. Possibly Henry IV's greatest achievement was to leave his son Richard ll, a kingdom that was peaceful, loyal and united.

The Mitford estate then passed to John's son and heir William Mitford.

11th Squire Sir William Mitford (1369-1423)

Squire for 14 years from 1409-1423

Sir William was 40 years old when his father died and in 1410 was made a Commissioner of Array against Scotland. A Commission of Array was a commission given by English royalty to officers or gentry in a given territory to muster and organise the inhabitants - to maintain them in 'condition' for war (presumably this would have required archery training and practice plus other appropriate skills), it would also have been necessary to employ soldiers ready for military service. In 1415 William Mitford was High Sheriff of Northumberland and attended Parliament during the reign of Henry V in 1414 and 1421.

Henry V (1387-1422) was King of England, Duke of Normandy and Regent of France. He was the last of the medieval warrior-kings. He made England once more a continental power.

William Mitford married Margaret, daughter of Sir Robert Lisle, of Woodburn & Felton and they produced two sons John and Alexander. Much later, after her husband's death, Margaret gave the town of Bucliffe, and half the hamlet of Portyet, in Hexhamshire, to her friend and lover Gerard Woderington. One could say, a rather generous lady. The second son, Alexander Mitford is from where the branch, Mitfords of Ponteland descend.

William inherited a large estate consisting of the manors of Molesden in Mitford, Newsham and Espley, as well as extensive holdings in Newcastle and over 10 Northumbrian villages, all accumulated from the 1370s onwards out of the profits of government office and a lucrative legal practice. Although less active in the property market than his father, William still continued his father's policy of buying up any available tenements and plots in and around Mitford. As well as attending parliament in London with the long and arduous journey from Northumberland to London, William found time to follow an active career in local government, while also holding stewardships on the estates of both Sir John le Scrope's widow, Elizabeth, and the Prior of Tynemouth.

William Mitford was on close terms with Nicholas Turpin who faced charges of being an accessory to murder in June 1421, he named William as one of his mainpernors (stand surety/bail). William continued the family bond of friendship with the Percys when the young earl of Northumberland made him bailiff of Morpeth. William Mitford died on 7 March 1423, just four weeks before his son and heir, John, came of age.

The Crown asserted its rights of wardship and Thomas Holden, steward of Thomas Langley, bishop of Durham, paid £20 for the young man's marriage. John Mitford eventually took as his wife Constance, the daughter of Sir Robert Ogle, thus continuing the alliance forged by his father some while before. The widowed Margaret Mitford obtained the customary third share of her late husband's estate, which she occupied for over 25 years and as mentioned she settled land in Hexhamshire with her 'beloved friend', Gerard Woderington around 1452.

12th Squire Sir John Mitford (1402-1437)

Squire for 14 years from 1423-1437

Sir John, was born in April 1402 and baptised at St. Nicholas Church, Newcastle (now Newcastle's St Nicholas Cathedral). His grandfather, Sir John arrived too late to witness the ceremony, but caught up with the nurse in the churchyard, kissed the child and with a touching display of sentiment gave it a grandfather's blessing. He simply wanted to see his grandson, to reassure himself and be in no doubt that the estates which he had so carefully built up would remain safe in the hands of his male descendants. Little did the 9th squire know that his estates would continue for 32 generations and 600 years.

John was an only son aged 21 when he inherited his father's and grandfather's estates and in 1425, gave some land and tenements to St Nicholas Church in Newcastle, and the monks of Newminster. He married Constance, daughter of Sir Robert Ogle and they produced two sons John and Bertram and a daughter Margaret.

13th Squire John Mitford (1433-1461)

John was just 24 years old when he inherited the Mitford estate. He joined up with Richard, Duke of York and was killed at the battle of Towton in 1461. The Battle of Towton was fought during the English Wars of the Roses on 29 March 1461, near the village of Towton in Yorkshire - 28,000 died on the battlefield. Two monarchs fought for the Crown of England.

Edward IV displaced Henry VI as King of England, driving the head of the Lancastrians and his key supporters out of the country. Contemporary accounts described Henry VI as peaceful and pious, not suited for violent dynastic civil wars, such as the War of the Roses. This conflict began in the 1450s and was a war between the red rose of Lancaster versus the white rose of York. Beginning as a revolt against a weak government, it became a challenge to the throne when Richard, Duke of York (1311-1360) formed an alliance with the powerful Earl of Warwick. York won the battle of Towton and Richards's son became Edward IV.

The estate then passed to his only son, Bertram Mitford, and held in trust.

14th Squire Bertram Mitford (1460-1493)

Lands held in Trust

All Bertram's lands in Newcastle and Mitford, Molesden, Espley, Morpeth, Cowpen, Mersfen, Bebside, and Newbiggen by the sea, along with all his lands in Gainsborough, in Lincolnshire were held in trust for Bertram and his son Gawen.

In 1459, William Caxton invented the printing press with movable type and this was the start of printing with books in English and Latin. Henry VIII (1509-1547) created the Church of England, dissolving all catholic monasteries. A new class of land ownership was created.

15th Squire Gawen Mitford (1480-1550)
Squire for 32 years from 1518-1550

All the lands aforementioned were released to Gawen in 1518. In turn, it's recorded that Gawen gave his lands in High Callerton, three houses in Newcastle and a tenement in Mersfen for life to George Parkinson and Margaret, his wife, being Gawen's sister.

It's recorded that in 1525, John Fitzherbert wrote a book of husbandry which offers the following advice.

When thou art up and ready, then first sweep thy house, dress up thy dish-board, and set all things in good order within thy house; milk thy kine (cows), feed thy calves, sile (strain) up thy milk, take up thy children and array them, and provide for thy husband's breakfast, dinner, supper, and for thy children and servants, and take thy part with them.

And to ordain (organize) corn and malt to the mill, to bake and brew withal when need is. . . Thou must make butter and cheese when thou may; serve thy swine, both morning and evening, and give thy pullen (fowl) meat in the morning, and when time of the year cometh, thou must take heed how thy hen, ducks and geese do lay, and to gather up their eggs; and when they wax broody to set them thereas no beasts, swine or other vermin hurt them. If that wasn't enough to keep the dutiful housewife occupied there is more!

In the beginning of March, or a little before, is time for a wife to make her garden. And also in March is time to sow flax and hemp and thereof may thou make sheets, board-cloths (table cloths), towels, shirts, smocks and such other necessaries!

16th Squire Cuthbert Mitford (1520-1594)
Squire for 44 years from 1550-1594

Family intrigue and family rivalry persists through Cuthbert Mitford's era. Cuthbert married Anne Wallis and inherited a large estate of many thousands of acres. In 1557, Cuthbert along with his younger brother Anthony Mitford of Ponteland decided to increase their land holdings around Mitford and bought 2,300 acres of land in High Callerton, Ponteland, Mersfen, Framlington and Mitford for £525 from Lord William Burgh. Cuthbert took the northern share and Anthony the southern share. Mitford itself fell to Cuthbert. When Cuthbert died in 1594, Anthony attempted to claim the estate by stating that Cuthbert's son and heir, Robert, and his three sisters, Isabel, Jane and Margaret were illegitimate. Sir Isaac Heard who investigated this matter, found that the documents had been altered and proved that Robert Mitford was indeed the legitimate son and heir. With the collapse of the barony Mitford's population was down to 380 people.

It was during this time that the union of England and Wales was formalised by two Acts of Parliament in 1536 and 1543. During 1555-1558 more than 300 people were burned at the stake, most of them in the south east of England, the north and west were still heavily Catholic.

In 1558, the Spanish Armada set sail to invade the England of Queen Elizabeth 1.

17th Squire Robert Mitford (1544-1625)
Squire for 31 years from 1594-1625

Robert married Jane, daughter of John Mitford of Seighill and produced eight children, four daughters and four sons. Records show that on the 13th of December 1598 he was called-up by the archdeacon for not attending evening prayers. During 1558-1563 William Cecil (later Lord Burghley), the Queen's closest advisor, assists Elizabeth in passing laws making the monarch the head of the Church, the English prayer book, and generally laying the foundations of the Anglican Church as we know it today. Shakespeare died in 1616. In 1604 King James declared England & Scotland a united monarchy to be known as Great Britain and the Union Jack flag was created.

18th Squire Cuthbert Mitford (1582-1613)

Cuthbert married Mary, daughter of Christopher Wharton of Wingate Grange and Offerton in Durham. She was a great niece of the celebrated northern apostle, Bernard Gilpin. Mary and her husband both died on the same day at Mitford in 1613, and were succeeded by their son Robert Mitford.

In 1603 Queen Elizabeth died at Richmond, Surrey , aged 70, after a 45-year reign. The new king (son of Mary Queen of Scots) is the legitimate heir to the thrones of both England and Scotland; colonies are founded; the Pilgrim Fathers leave; the English Civil War breaks out; a king is executed, and England is governed by a military dictatorship. The population of England is estimated at 4 million. In 1605 the Gunpowder Plot, led by Guy Fawkes, a Catholic plot to blow up the King, heir (Prince Charles) and Houses of Parliament. Bonfire Night, of 5th November is still celebrated to this day.

19th Squire Robert Mitford (1612-1674)

Robert Mitford married Philadelphia, third daughter of Humphrey Wharton of Gillingwood in Yorkshire. The arms of Mitford impaling Wharton "argent, a maunch, sable" may still be seen carved on a shield above the entrance to the porch tower of the old Manor House, in Mitford village with the date 1637. The tower section is of a more modern style and was perhaps added as an entrance to the older more rustic, bastle house at some stage.

By closer inspection it is possible to notice the date 1637 – the upper part of the figure 6 was broken off making the date 1037 and a piece has been added to form the 6. It has been said that the stone bearing this inscription was recovered from another site, pretending to a date before the Conquest. The figure 6 has since been restored (1834). However its true antiquity is debatable.

Robert acquired Mitford castle and royalties by grant from Charles II. The castle had reverted to the Crown from the Burgh family some time before. Thus the original Mitford family of Mitford regained their ancestral lands some five hundred years after the Norman conquest. The estate once again became whole. Robert was made High Sheriff of Northumberland in 1650. In 1663 his estate consisted of Mitford, Newton-Underwood, Molesden, Newton-East-side, and lands at Espley, which altogether were assessed upon a rental of £510 a year.

They produced six children, with Humphrey Mitford being the eldest son and heir. The second son, Cuthbert (1639-1662) was senior fellow of Calus College, Cambridge and rector of Ingram in 1662. The third son, John Mitford (1643-1720), married Sarah, daughter and co heir of Henry Powell, a London merchant – from which the Mitfords of Exbury and John Mitford, Baron Lord Redesdale are descended. Later, in 1886, in order to inherit substantial estates in accordance with the Will, their family name was changed to Freeman-Mitford. This is where the Mitford Girls descend, daughters of David Freeman Mitford, 2nd Lord Redesdale.

It was around 1642 that England was plunged into civil war. Fought between the Royalists (Charles 1) and the Roundheads, it spilt friends, families and the country down the middle. At the battle of Naseby in 1645, Cromwell's army defeated the Royalists and Charles was beheaded in 1649. Cromwell abolished the monarchy in 1653. In 1665 the Bubonic plague erupted in London - spread to humans by fleas living on infected rats. This was followed by the Great Fire of London in 1666 that killed the rats and fleas that had spread the plague. To clean up and revive London, Christopher Wren was commissioned to build St Paul's Cathedral.

20th Squire Humphrey Mitford (1632-1677)

Squire for 3 years from 1674-1677

Humphrey married Frances, daughter of Sir George Vane of Long Newton in Co Durham. Humphrey was an attorney at Gray's Inn in London. They produced 3 sons and 8 daughters.

His will reads as follows. "Appraised by Mr Thomas Burrell, George Batchlor, John Charleton and William Heaton, to be exhibited by his relict Frances Aldford and Widdow, administrix".

It's interesting to note the Will of a successful Gray's Inn lawyer in the 1600's contained the following items.

A cast iron pot with handles and three feet. Called a 'yetling'
A small bowl with handle used for liquids such as soup. Called a 'porrenger'
A "caudel" cup used for a warm drink made from wine/ale, mixed with eggs/bread/sugar and spices - usually taken when you are unwell.
Household equipment, furniture, linen, carpets, etc £89.10s
Purse & apparel £40
Books - £10
Kitchen & parlour - £10.5s
2 geldings - £10
3 cows - £8 10s
70 sheep - £20
Hay in the field - £5
Cart and wheels - 15s
2 saddles and bridles - 15s ... Total value £194.15s.

21st Squire Robert Mitford (1662-1707)
Squire for 30 years from 1677-1707

Robert married Anne Ashton (13th great granddaughter of Edward I) and was High Sheriff of Northumberland in 1697 renewed annually for one year during the reign of William III and of Yorkshire in 1702. His third brother, William Mitford of Petworth, Sussex, also produced a son William, who became a clerk of the treasury for the county of Sussex and father of Charles Mitford of Pitshill. The family of Mitford of Pitshill in Tillington is descended from Robert's youngest son, William (1699-1777), who arrived in Sussex and started the Pitshill branch.

Robert's fourth brother John, married Anne, daughter of Sir George Mertius, and became an independent banker and goldsmith in London around the year 1645 when the proceedings of parliament confounded all social order that merchants could no longer trust the crown banking system with their cash. This is where the Hampstead branch of the Mitford family hails from. It was via the Ashton family that the Mitfords became acquainted with East Riding in Yorkshire and to later join with the Osbaldeston family.

In 1694, the Bank of England was created - the model on which all central banks in Europe and later the USA was replicated. The year Robert died in 1707; the Act of Union between England and Scotland made Queen Anne first sovereign of the United Kingdom. Though the Scots lost their Parliament they retained their own religious and legal systems. Robert and Anne Ashton produced 5 sons and one daughter.

22nd Squire Robert Mitford (1686-1756)

Squire for 49 years from 1707-1756

Robert married Mary, daughter of Sir Richard Osbaldeston, grandson of Sir Richard Osbaldeston (1691-1764) who was Attorney-General of Ireland. Mary became co heiress with her brother Fountayne Wentworth Osbaldeston to Hunmanby Manor and estate, in Yorkshire. Her great-grandson, Bertram Mitford would later inherit the Osbaldeston estates in 1800.

Robert was High Sheriff of Northumberland in 1723 for one year and had interests in Heaton Colliery in 1738. Robert and Mary produced 4 sons and 3 daughters. One of their daughters Philadelphia Mitford married the Rev John Wickens of Petworth and was mother of Geo Wickens, who upon inheriting the estates of Hutton Buscell, in Yorkshire, took the name Osbaldeston, and was the father of the celebrated sportsman "Squire Osbaldeston". Details of his remarkable life are contained in a later chapter.

23rd Squire Robert Mitford (1718-1784)

Squire for 28 years from 1756-1784

Major Robert Mitford married Anne, daughter of John Lewis from the ancient family of Lewis of Harton House in Radnorshire and Jamaica and produced 4 sons and 2 daughters. Bertram, the eldest son went on to inherit the Mitford estates and was the father of Admiral Mitford, and Lt Col John Philip Mitford, both of whom later succeeded to the Mitford and Hunmanby estates as you will read. One daughter Mary married Thomas Bullock of Spital-Hill, near Mitford.

24th Squire Bertram Mitford (1749-1800)

Squire for 16 years from 1784-1800

Bertram married Tabitha, daughter of Dr Francis Johnson, MD of Newcastle. They produced three sons. Bertram his heir born in 1777, Robert born in 1781, a captain in the Royal Navy, who would also become an admiral and squire of Mitford and Hunmanby and Joseph George born in 1791 who served in the military service of the East India Company.

It was during this time in 1784, that the first volumes of William Mitford's History of Greece were published. Due to diminished health the last volumes only appeared in 1810. His patron was Hugh Percy, 1st Duke of Northumberland. William's life and times are to be found in a later chapter of this book. Also, in 1797 Mary Russell Mitford, aged ten years won the lottery and received £20,000, a fortune in those days, which her father promptly spent. Read her story in later pages. The Mitford estate then passed onto his son Bertram.

It was during the early 1700s that the industrial revolution took place in Britain before spreading throughout the world.

There was also a national wheat shortage and Bertram, in February 1796, along with other Northumberland justices of the peace were instructed to enforce a reduction in consumption of wheat by one third of the regular quantity consumed in ordinary times.

In 1799 William Pitt the Younger introduced Britain's first income tax – two pence in the pound, rising to two shillings for incomes over £200. This was an attempt to pay for the crippling costs of the Napoleonic Wars. This was in addition to the taxes on land, servants and animals.

25th Squire Bertram Mitford (1777-1842)

Squire for 42 years from 1800-1842 aged 23 years.

A lawyer. Established the Mitford's Estate Act and Trust to perpetuate the family wealth and built Mitford Hall.

In 1832 John Hodgson, author of A History of Northumberland wrote – "*the present township of Mitford comprises the ancient manor of Mitford, situated in the tongue of land which lies between the Wansbeck and Font Rivers. The whole township consists of about 1733 acres, and belongs to Bertram Mitford, Esq.*"

Bertram inherited not only the Mitford Estate but also Hunmanby Estate situated in East and West Riding in Yorkshire. Due to lack of Osbaldeston male heirs the Manor of Hunmanby and estate passed to Bertram Mitford whose great grandmother was Mary, daughter of Sir Richard Osbaldeston. This very distinguished Osbaldeston family goes back to another Sir Richard Osbaldeston (1585-1640) who was Attorney-General of Ireland and yet another Richard Osbaldeston (1691-1764) who was Lord Bishop of London from 1762 to 1764 when he died in office.

Bertram married Frances Fabiola, daughter of Francis Johnson, M.D. of Newcastle. Originally educated as a lawyer he never practised law, but later became Justice of the Peace for Northumberland and was High Sheriff of Northumberland in 1835. He was a benevolent and kindly man who often gave money to the prisoners in Morpeth. He inherited a profitable and well organised estate. At the age of 23 he was one of the youngest squires to inherit. The next three squires would experience the tragic loss of their second family home and country "seat" Mitford Manor House (built 1637) as it was gutted by fire and later pulled down (around 1813). Just the turret tower remains and the kitchen wing was developed into a new modern home.

Bertram Mitford inherited from Humphrey Brooke Osbaldeston, as Humphrey did not produce a male heir. Humphrey Brooke had been required to take the additional name Osbaldeston and was the eldest male descendant in direct line to Fountayne Wentworth Osbaldeston, under whose Will he inherited the Hunmanby estate. Humphrey, during his time as Lord of Hunmanby Manor, consolidated the estate into separate independent areas in 1791. Three independent commissioners were officially appointed to ensure fair play.

The agrarian revolution was the transferring from the old farming system using strips to open crop management with enclosed fields. After successful enclosure and registration Bertram then enclosed the remainder of the Hunmanby Manor and estate in 1809. Both enclosures were surveyed and mapped by Joseph Dickenson, a noted surveyor. Humphrey Osbaldeston established himself as the largest land-owner in and around Hunmanby and the coastal village of Filey, Boundaries and roads were clearly defined, and remain much the same today.

The large Hunmanby house was extended by adding a north and south wing to become Hunmanby Hall Park. The outlying farms formed the Hunmanby agricultural estate. The entire manor and estate were both financially and socially stable.

Not so for Mitford.

Several issues needed attention. What should be done about the lack of male heirs and funds to pay for a new Mitford family home? At this stage the Mitford family had no family seat. The castle was in ruins and Mitford Manor house was, apart from the kitchen wing, reduced to charred rubble. Bertram did two things. Firstly, he commissioned the well known Newcastle architect John Dobson, to build Mitford Hall in 1810. John Dobson (1787-1865) was one of the leading architects in the north of England. He designed more than 150 homes and churches and perhaps best known for designing Newcastle Central Station and developing the centre of Newcastle in the neoclassical style.

All the old stones from the castle and manor house were brought up to the new building site overlooking the River Wansbeck: stone was cut from the local quarry and river bed.

The beautiful white sandstone used for the outside walls was obtained from a stratum of rock which forms the bed of the River Font, between the Newton Park and Nunriding properties - once a wild and romantic spot, with steep river banks covered with bilberry plants and undergrowth. The first building to go up was what was then called Mitford Hill House. A small, neat, pillared house where the Mitford family lived during the building of Mitford Hall. This building is now known as the gatehouse or butler's house and stands at the imposing entrance gates to Mitford Hall.

It took 18 years to build Mitford Hall, with a further 10 years to build and finish all the surrounding outbuildings and coach house. Along with other family members and his brother Robert, Bertram was able to oversee the building of Mitford Hall and further acquisition and development of lands around Mitford Hall. Building was finally completed with the roof going on, on the 9th December 1828, celebrated with a dinner party and drinks for all. It was only two years later that Bertram and his family actually moved into the hall - celebrated with another party for all the workmen, tenants and staff on Saturday 30th August 1830. Charles Darwin visited in 1839 and planted a camellia tree to celebrate the final construction of the hall, the camellia is still growing to this day. Darwin became fascinated with the work of John James Audubon and John Selby. John James Audubon was a visiting American ornithologist and painter, John Selby was an English ornithologist, botanist who married Tabitha Mitford. and during Darwin's visits to Newcastle met the Mitford brothers Bertram and Robert in time becoming friends.

I'm inclined to think the lengthy time taken to build Mitford Hall was not entirely due to labour problems, no train or labour strikes in those days, or lack of suitable building materials (plenty of old stones from the old castle, manor house and quarry), but rather a cash flow problem as Bertram suspended work in 1825. Debts were building up. One notion suggested by a local Mitford resident, with the Napoleonic Wars drawing to an end, was that "in war time prosperity, Bertram Mitford decided to build his new mansion and in post war depression, he found it necessary to progress slowly, in step with the receipts from his tenant farmers"! Either way, to ensure continued succession and income it was necessary to make a decision.. There was only one way. Sell land. So it was decided to sell off a section of the profitable Hunmanby estate in order to pay off debts and source the large sums of money needed to construct Mitford Hall and buy additional lands around Mitford.

As such, and according to the laws of the land and manorial property, Bertram registered his last Will in 1838, and drew up the Mitford Estate Act which came into being (see page 226) which was enacted by parliament, and given Royal Assent in 1854. The schedule of 5,000 acres of land sold in Yorkshire, as listed in the Act, paid for the building of Mitford Hall (and much else around Mitford see 26th Squire), increased family land holdings in Mitford and established a trust to continue for 900 years. The consolidation of assets in Northumberland had the potential to be a turning point for the Mitford family, if managed properly.

The prime objective of the Mitford Estate Act 1854, was to ensure succession, to provide descendants and beneficiaries with additional estate income, stability and continuity. At the time of the Mitford Estate Act, apart from service to the Crown by way of civil, military and church careers with salaries and pensions earned from positions held, the only other source of income available to the squires of Mitford was from careful and astute estate management of the lands rented out to tenant farmers.

When an emergency arose and extra funds were needed (there being no reserve capital funds with interest accruing) the only alternative at hand was to sell off land – a farm here and a farm there, in order to raise funds. Not the best way of financial management. However, for the Mitford family, it was the only way. Or, marry money. The act was to hopefully clarify issues relating to succession.

Britain was doing well in the 1850s with exports to the rest of the world booming. With careful financial management and investment the act should enable the family to have financial stability and an estate income for generations ahead.

Sadly, one morning on the way to Newcastle, Bertram suddenly took ill and died aged 65 . With no male heir the Mitford and Hunmanby estates passed to Bertram's closest relative, his brother. Bertram's wife Frances, suffering diminishing eyesight received an annuity of £1,300 for life and stayed on at Mitford Hall until her death in 1868. This arrangement was agreed between the brothers as Admiral Robert Mitford preferred Hunmanby Hall to that of Mitford. Francis left her diamonds in her will for the Vicarage of Mitford expressing that the Ecclesiastical Commissioners would meet that with a similar grant. The diamonds were sold for £1,000 and with the money Consolidated Bank Annuities at three percent were purchased and transferred to the Church Commissioners who made a grant of £32, twice a year to the Vicar of Mitford, the details were announced in the London Gazette of 15th April 1870.

From the 25th squire onwards due to the Osbaldeston inheritance, the family was obliged to add the name Osbaldeston to Mitford.

During Bertram's time as squire of both estates a scandal [The life and times of 'Jack' Mitford is detailed in a later chapter, John (Jack) Mitford (1782-1831)] involving "Jack" Mitford, Lady Viscountess Perceval and the Princess of Wales in 1814 was reported in the London press.

Another member of the family, John Mitford became editor of the "Gentleman's Magazine" from 1833 to 1850 and he edited the works of English poets, Milton, Swift, Parnell, Young, Lamb, Wordsworth, Byron and Thomas Grey. *[Please see later chapter].* In 1805 Admiral Nelson won the Battle of Trafalgar – celebrated with Nelson's Column in Trafalgar Square. As previously mentioned, Rev. Isaac Nelson, an uncle of Horatio, vicar of Mitford Church from 1759 to 1772 never got to learn of his nephew's great success as he unfortunately fell into the river at Mitford and drowned.

26th Squire Admiral Robert Mitford (1781-1870)

Squire for 28 years from 1842-1870 aged 61 years

Squire of Mitford & last resident Lord of Hunmanby Manor & Estate, Yorkshire.

The Admiral Robert Mitford, younger brother of Bertram, lived through the reign of three kings - George III (1761-1820) George IV (1821-1830) & William IV (1831-1837) and was 19th in direct descent from Edward I of England. Robert Mitford was born in Mitford and joined the Navy as a boy aged 13 in 1794.

He received his commission as a Lieutenant in 1802 and as Post-Captain in 1813. He rose to the rank of Rear Admiral in 1846; Vice-Admiral in 1855 and Admiral in 1861.

Taking over both the Mitford and Hunmanby estates in 1842 aged 61, Admiral Robert Mitford, RN. Admiral of the Red, (highest rank that an Admiral could attain) was a fine, benevolent Lord of the Manor. He was highly regarded by his tenants and was the last true Lord to reside in Hunmanby Hall. He was twice appointed High Sheriff of Yorkshire, but preferred to remain in retirement and pay £500 towards the salary of a substitute.

The running of the Mitford estate was left to the estate manager and agent at Mitford. The Admiral took part in the restoration of the Hunmanby parish church in 1845 and contributed the gallery, organ and three large windows on the south side. The village population peaked in 1861 with 1425 residents. Like all the Mitfords he enjoyed outdoor sports of hunting, shooting and fishing and kept a kennel of top bred greyhounds. A particular talent lay in art and drawing, as he painted the Mitford shield and recreated a new version of the crest. Altogether a remarkable and talented man.

Robert married Margaret Dunsmure, daughter of James Dunsmore M.D. of Edinburgh. Their only daughter Margaret Susan Mitford born 1835, married her childhood sweetheart William Tyssen Amhurst (Lord Amhurst 1835-1909) M.P. of Amhurst, Kent, Diddlington Hall in Norfolk and Hackney Middlesex – great-great grandfather of Sir Henry Cecil, the Newmarket racehorse trainer, in 1856. With the unlimited Tyssen funds and the Admiral's keen knowledge of Egypt, they travelled extensively and went on to create one of the largest collection of Egyptian artefacts in England. This collection was housed at Didlington Hall in Norfolk. It was here that Howard Carter began his lifelong fascination of Egyptology, as Carter's father was employed as an artist by Lord Amhurst at Diddlington Hall. The Amhersts sponsored his first visit to Egypt.

Part of this collection is now at the Metropolitan Museum in New York. In turn, their daughter Mary Rothes Margaret Tyssen-Amhurst OBE, Baroness Amhurst, married Lord William Cecil

CVO, linked to the Vanderbilt family and George Washington. Thus, after over seven hundred years of direct descent in the male line, the house of Mitford descended to an only daughter and cousin.

These marriages linked the Mitfords with some of the most prominent families of England as evidenced by the hatchment (heraldic achievement, being a full display of all the heraldic components to which the bearer of a coat of arms is entitled). The admiral was also a talented artist and as already mentioned took lessons from celebrated artists John James Audubon and John Selby. Robert created the hatchment shortly before he died, it links together six prominent families of England- namely Mitford, Ashton, Osbaldeston, Wentworth, Fountayne and Monckton. The Raymond family was added in 1877 (of Exmouth, Devonshire, a leopard sejant per fess collared and chained and spotted counter changed). The Raymond family records date back to the early 1600's and creation of the East India Company. Hugh and John Raymond were both boat owners, captains and directors.

The shield displays the arms and crests of the six families – 1st Mitford, argent, a fess, between three moles, sable; 2nd, Ashton, arg. a mullet, pierced sable: 3rd Osbaldeston, arg, a mascle, sable, between three ogresses; 4th Wentworth, sable, a chevron between three lions' faces, or; 5th Fountayne, or, a fesse gules, between three elephants' heads, erased, sable; 6th Monckton, sable on a chevron between three martlets, or as many mullets of the first, impaling Dunsmure, vert three garbs, or, banded sable. On a wreath of the colours is the Mitford crest – a dexter and sinister arm, proper, supporting a sword, in pale, argent, pierced through a boar's head and below, on a ribbon the Mitford motto 'God caryth for us".

Two great and well documented occasions were celebrated at Hunmanby Hall. The first in June 1856, was the marriage of William Tyssen Amhurst of Didlington Park, Norfolk and of Hackney, Middlesex, to Margaret Susan, only child of Admiral Mitford. With a central theme depicting the four seasons, spring, summer, autumn and winter, massive and magnificent flower displays were on show everywhere. A total of 300 guests were invited and large parties also dined in all the local pubs, the

Buck Inn, Black Horse Inn and the White Swan (which is still operating today).

Two grand balls were hosted - one for all the tenants within a large marquee erected on the lawn in front of the mansion, and a special party for the 145 village children. For all the festivities, the Admiral appeared in his full naval uniform - quite something to behold. He was not a large imposing fellow, in fact quite the opposite. Cheerfully, short and round.

This entire ceremony was repeated in Mitford. A spacious marquee over one hundred feet long and sixty feet wide was erected in a field alongside the road. The marquee was totally fitted out with all ballroom amenities attached. On entering the village everyone had to pass under a massive triumphal arch of evergreen branches bearing large shields and banners with the arms and crests of the Mitford and Amhurst families.

During the evening, the event was fully illuminated with oil lamps. On entering the marquee the first sight was a stunning representation of the ancient castle of Mitford, complete with towers and bastions. On the ramparts floated the national flags of England, France, Turkey and Sardinia. The battlements were occupied by figures in military costume. Knights in armour, bringing to mind the romance of the ancient chivalry – the highland chieftains, "whose clan would follow where he led", and the heroes of times past.

The artist who created this was none other than Admiral Mitford himself. His detailed and delicate artwork may still be seen today in his many colourful paintings of exotic feathered birds (see plate section). In John Selby's major work, the book entitled 'Illustrations of British Ornithology' published in 19 parts between 1821 and 1883 there are 222 plates etched by Selby with the assistance of his brother-in-law Admiral Robert Mitford. An orchestra occupied the first parapet of the castle and was guarded on each side by sentinels in full military uniform. The entire occasion was organised by a leading French decorator, based in Edinburgh. It was on this occasion that the Admiral introduced his successor, he clearly stated "Do not let John Philip come here without my tenants knowing that he will step into my shoes".

Further speeches and toasts were proposed to George Brumell and family, the well known and highly respected Morpeth legal firm, hoping George as well as his father would long continue to perform the duties of solicitors to the Mitford family. Everyone – from local gentry to tenants, labourers, tradesmen, cottagers together with their wives and children were invited. For those in the closest town Morpeth a grand banquet was given at Mr Braithwaite's White Swan Inn.

Back in Hunmanby, not to be outdone, the coastal village of Filey also organised much celebration with banners and flags everywhere, even from the mast at the coast guard station. A salute was fired by Captain White and the Filey Coast Guards; dinner was provided for everyone at the Pack Horse Inn by the Admiral.

Another celebration took place on the 26th February 1867, it was Admiral Mitford's 86th Birthday. The programme of the day's proceedings included a procession of the Admiral's tenants through the village to the Hall, a presentation of a memorial of congratulations and a dinner in honour of the day. The whole village turned out to express their heartfelt warmth and affectionate greetings of respect to a kind landlord, beloved benefactor and friend. The Admiral was presented with a signed copy of a specially prepared birthday card from the tenants with the following text.

"To Robert Mitford of Mitford, in the County of Northumberland, and Hunmanby in the County of York, Esquire Admiral of the Red; of the Barony of Mitford, in the county of Northumberland and of the manor of Hunmanby, Filey, Muston, Reighton, Wold Newton, Fordon and Foxholes in the county of York...with an illustration of the arms of Mitford quartering Ashton, Osbaldeston, Wentworth, Fountayne and Monckton, and impaling Dunsmure, surmounted by the crest, helmet and mantling and bearing the family motto of God careth for us".

"We the undersigned tenants of your farms in the parishes of Hunmanby, Filey, Reighton, Muston, Wold Newton, Fordon, Foxholes, Langloft, North Burton and Thwing, present ourselves to you to acknowledge with grateful feelings the many kindnesses which you have conferred upon us. The event before us causes us to look back upon the many years you have been resident amongst us, during which we have learnt to appreciate and respect you as an English gentleman, a kind hearted landlord and a generous benefactor to your fellow creatures. We as tenants, can boast of a landlord who is not only beloved by his tenants but by all who knew him and who, while in the services of his country distinguished himself by his bravery, energy and kindness. We trust that the life of rectitude and virtue displayed by you will cause your name to live long in the memory of future generations and be an example to your successors".

After this speech, the Admiral was so overcome by emotion he had to ask his son in law Lord Amhurst to present his reply...

"My good friends, I thank you most heartily for the address you have so kindly presented to me this day. You allude to the time I spent in my youth in the navy, in the service of my country and I trust that I not only endeavoured then to follow the example given by one of England's greatest heroes, "that every man is expected to do his duty" but that since I left the active service I have striven with God's blessing to do my duty towards my tenants and neighbours". Robert Mitford.

The original document was signed by all the tenants dated 26 January 1867 Hunmanby Hall. Sadly, the original has been lost through the generations. Lithographed copies of this document were framed and presented to each tenant. The Admiral hosted a dinner party at the Hall and the White Swan (owned by a Mr Dodd at the time) until the early hours of the following morning. It is recorded that many glasses were raised with the "greatest enthusiasm!"

As previously mentioned, the coastal village of Filey and surrounding lands was once part of the Hunmanby estate and owned by the Mitford family. With the introduction of the railway in around 1847 Filey expanded and developed as a Victorian seaside resort, A local entrepreneur, John Wilkes Unett drew up plans to create a seaside resort. It extended southwards from Queen Street, eventually incorporating Murray Street and West Avenue, and the complete sea frontage west of the Ravine.

To progress his development land had to be bought from the Lord of Hunmanby Manor, Admiral Mitford.

Admiral Mitford sold off five separate areas of land, retaining the prime sites to be sold at a later date. Local legend has it that the Mitfords, being huge landowners, when they sold off large sections of land, would always keep a few prime sites back which could be later sold at much higher prices. For example, in 1870, before the beginning of a slump, farm land had been worth on average about £53 an acre. During the worst of the inter-war depression, its selling price was at rock bottom somewhere between £23 and £28 an acre. In the years ahead, the price began gradually and firmly to rise to £73 an acre by 1959, to £98 by 1961 and £114 by 1963. Those families who had managed to hold onto land found themselves much better off.

In addition in Northumberland, via the Act of Parliament set up by Bertram, the Admiral was able to increase family land holdings adjoining Mitford Hall by acquiring the large and valuable estates of Newton Park, Newton Underwood, East & West Throphill and Pigdon .

The Admiral was indeed quite a character... perhaps charmingly eccentric. He chose to build a relic! With no gatehouse or entrance gate to Hunmanby Hall and Park, the admiral built a massive entrance gate and archway which looks like the drive in entrance of a battered castle. It has lancet windows and a massive, gated, Gothic archway. At one stage it was covered in plants, growing out of every nook and crack, adding to its "relic status". To build this "relic" the admiral took stones from Filey Bay and had his knuckles rapped – being severely criticised by his tenants for doing so.

It was at Hunmanby that Archdeacon Francis Wrangham (1769-1842), the great classical historian during his time as Vicar of Hunmanby parish wrote most of his works. One of his quests was to end slavery. Hunmanby Hall also hosted the annual Staintondale and Derwent Hunts.

With no son and male heir and as stated in Mitford's Estate Act of 1854 [*see later chapter*], the estates of Mitford and Hunmanby were to be passed to Robert's next in line, his cousin John Philip

Mitford (1809-1895), the grandson of Captain John Mitford, a brother of the Admiral's father, Bertram Mitford. In turn, should he have no son and male heir, the estate was to pass to his younger brother Edward Ledwich Mitford (1811-1912), my great-great grandfather "and his said infant sons, and their respective issue male, and of any other issue male, that Edward Ledwich Mitford may hereafter have".

In addition, two of my great uncles are likewise nominated in the Act of Parliament. As you will read later, they all became Squires of Mitford and Hunmanby. Robert Mitford left £35,000 with three codicils, clothing and fuel allowances to the poor of Hunmanby. His wife received a rent allowance of £600 a year from the manor and lordship of Reighton, Yorkshire and use of an estate house for her lifetime.

27th Squire John Philip Mitford (1809-1895)

Squire for 25 years from 1870-1895 aged 61 years

(my great-great uncle).

Rebuilt and renovated Mitford Church

John attained the rank of Lieutenant Colonel in the regular army, aged 61 he took over in 1870. Emerging from military retirement, with a pension of around £800 a year, he found himself inheriting wealth and becoming lord of the manor, not only of Mitford but also Hunmanby in Yorkshire. He and the Admiral were the first Mitfords to enjoy the benefits of the inherited Osbaldeston fortune. (See Mitford Estate Act). John Philip Mitford did it well and spent a great deal of money, along with his cousin, Fanny Mitford also born in 1809, whom he married.

Three years before he took over the Mitford estates John undertook a tour of Europe. He produced a 260 page memoir and manuscript, illustrated with drawings, watercolours, photographs and postcards which gives an insight to his character. It was sold at auction by Anderson and Garland on the 23rd March 2010 (lot 366) with a reserve of £600, to quote and described as follows.

"On 30 January 1867, John Philip Mitford left London for

France accompanied by his wife Fanny and a female relative, together with a maid and an Italian courier, Signor Carenco. His account of the journey is divided into eight sections: the first about the journey to Rome, the second about Rome itself, with further sections about Naples, Florence, Venice, Milan, Turin and the return journey including Paris. The journey to Rome includes descriptions of Paris, Marseilles, Cannes, Menton ('one of the loveliest spots in Christendom'), Savona, Genoa, Pisa, Livorno and Civitavecchia, while the section on Naples includes descriptions of Pompeii and Mount Vesuvius.

As well as lengthy accounts of the buildings and works of art, there are descriptions of the lottery being drawn and gaming in the streets of Rome, of eating frogs' legs for the first time in Turin, 'We made a desperate attempt to enjoy it, but it was "no go". We tried to persuade ourselves that it was like baby chickens, ducks or rabbits... but frogs is frogs and nothing else, so, revenons à nos cotelettes". Meaning… best to return to the meat you know!

The frog leg episode is accompanied by a watercolour of 'poor froggy' losing his legs, one of a number of similarly humorous illustrations. There are also several watercolour views, including the English cemetery in Rome and Vesuvius, and a few fine early albumen prints of peasants and their animals. The tour ends in Paris not long after the opening of the Exposition Universelle, which they visited on several occasions and oversaw the setting-up of the stand of 'our Cheltenham brother".

Mitford concludes his journal with a section on the expense of the trip, which came to a total of £550, but explains how the same journey could be made more cheaply. He cautions against expecting home comforts, 'if they expect that the wretched 'bûche' is to warm them up like the coal from Newcastle on Tyne... they will assuredly be disappointed', and ends by comparing three table d'hôte menus in Milan and Rome with one at a 'first rate English country house', Alnwick Castle.

On becoming squire one of the first events John Philip hosted in October 1871 was the entertainment of the permanent staff of the Northumberland Militia, of which he was Major (at that time), at Mitford Hall. The party arrived from Alnwick by train to waiting carriages in Morpeth. The officers took the carriages, the sergeants and non-commissioned officers, accompanied by the militia band and bandmaster created quite a flurry of activity as they marched through Morpeth and onto the village of Mitford to the sounds of "Guy Mannering, English Rose, Gems of Ireland, Colegian and Galop". The latter being a delightful gallop, and only known band work by Arthur Bird. It reflects a clear, buoyant and humorous lightness. Rather fitting for a country walk to Mitford Hall.

The champagne and squire's speeches flowed with statements like "England expects every man to do his duty, and I have two champagne toasts to propose – toasts which I call by that name because they are worthy of the liquor!

My first toast is "Our Sovereign Lady the Queen." I know that in these days disaffection stalks abroad almost unchecked, such is the mild rule under which Englishmen live; but we soldiers are the sworn protectors of our Queen and constitution with swords ready to leap from their scabbards, and their bayonets to come down to the "charge" against the foes of our Queen and country, at a moment's notice, be they Prussian, French – or… any other treasonable plotter.

What I say is… confounded be all the Queen's enemies and… "God save the Queen." The second toast I wish to propose is the health of his Grace the Duke of Northumberland, Colonel of the regiment and our noble chief. When we older hands, shoulder our crutches to show how fields are won." And so it carries on, endless hail hearty speeches with toast after toast being drunk.

Another of his speeches in 1871 included the following.

"The constitutional monarchy under which we live has fallen upon happy times. By character, conduct, and domestic experience, the Queen has obtained a place in the hearts of the people, without any time exciting feelings of distrust, still less of hostility. A queen must be a dear good queen indeed, when an open enemy speaks thus of her. The Queen is the apex of the constitution, the key stone, as it were, of the estates of the realm.

Top is the Mitford Coat of Arms and shield with the Mitford family motto.
Above is the original Mitford family crest shown here on the old printer's stamp, negative on left and positive on right.
Photograph below is the road sign at the entrance to Mitford village.

Above, lithograph illustration 'Remains of Mitford Castle.

Opposite page, right and below are photographs of Mitford Castle. Clockwise from top right; archway looking out to Mitford church, 2 photos of ruins of wall to inner keep, dungeon window, castle cellars, stairs leading down to castle dungeon.

Above, Mitford church in 1874 and below after being rebuilt by the family – as it is today.

Opposite page clockwise from top right. Painting of dove on the ceiling of Mitford church bell tower, painted by Edward L. Mitford, 1898. Stained glass windows, family chapel, old bell and lepers window and stained glass window of Mitford crest and arms in Mitford church bell tower.

GOD
FOR
CARYTH

Come hither
the Lambs wife.
Let us be glad and rejoice, and
give honour to him for the marriage

Above, Mitford Manor tower before renovation.

Below, after renovation entrance to Mitford Manor showing the Mitford Coat of Arms above the arch with ANDO 1637 and the three Mitford moles.

Opposite page. Top, Mitford Hall as it is today. Centre, Mitford Hall entrance and Butler's house.

Bottom, Ordinance Survey of 1885 of Mitford Hall (with kind thanks to Woodhorn Archives).

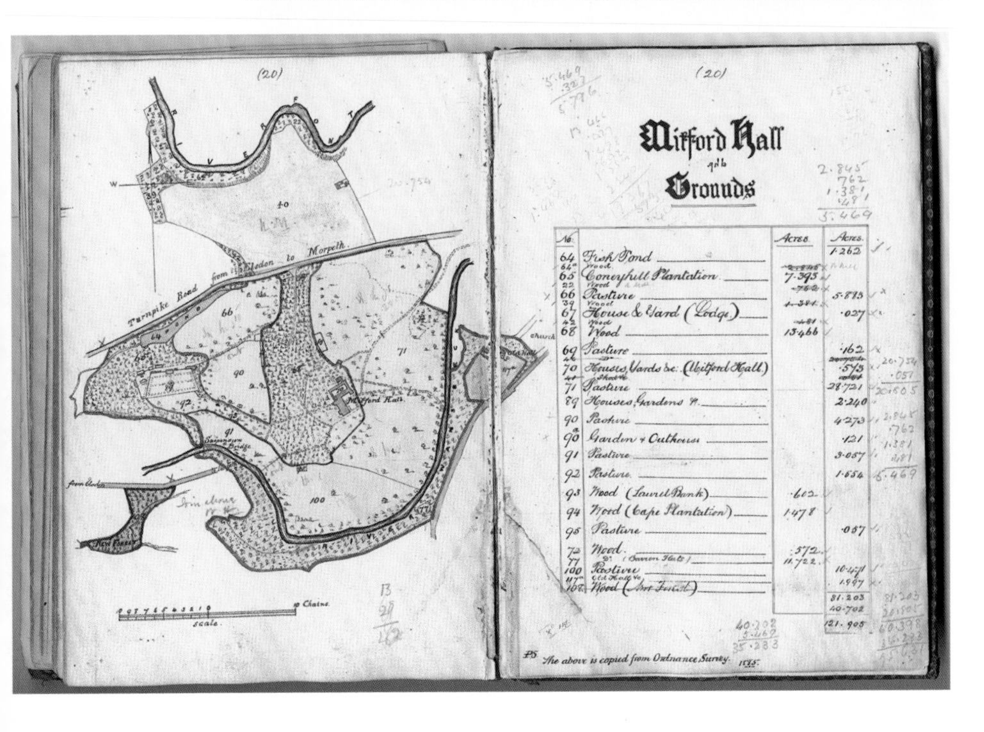

(20)

(20)

Mitford Hall and Grounds

No.		Acres	Acres.
64	Fish Pond		1·262
64a	Wood	~~2·846~~	
65	Coneyhill Plantation	7·393	
22	Wood	~~·762~~	
66	Pasture		5·883
39	Wood	~~1·381~~	
67	House & Yard (Lodge)		·027
42	Wood	~~·481~~	
68	Wood	13·466	
69	Pasture		·162
70	Houses, Yards &c. (Mitford Hall)		·573
71	Pasture		28·721
89	Houses, Gardens &c.		2·240
90	Pasture		4·273
90a	Garden & Outhouse		·121
91	Pasture		3·057
92	Pasture		1·654
93	Wood (Laurel Bank)	·602	
94	Wood (Cape Plantation)	1·478	
95	Pasture		·057
72	Wood	·572	
77	Do. (Barren Flats)	11·722	
100	Pasture		10·471
117a	Old Hall &c.		1·997
108	Wood ([illegible])		
			81·203
			40·702
			121·905

The above is copied from Ordnance Survey.

LOT.
87. Coup Cart.
88. Cart Harness.
89. Plough Chains.
90. Stable Barrow.
91. Wheelbarrow.
92. Cake Crusher.
93. Wire Netting.
94. do.
95. 2 Wood Sheep Troughs.
96. Old Hay Tedder.
97. do. Reaper.
98. Useful Ladder.
99. do.
100. Sack Barrow.

GRASS PARK, 29½ Acres (in Hay)

Will be Let at close of Auction Sale. Taker to make and carry away the hay and to have the eatage till Oct. 31st, 1912, and to find his own Herd.

CONDITIONS OF SALE.

1.—The Sale is for Ready Money.

2.—The Highest Bidder to be the Purchaser and if any dispute should arise between two or more bidders the Lot in dispute shall be put up again and resold.

3.—The Auctioneers shall regulate the Biddings, and no bid shall be retracted after having once been taken.

4.—Purchasers' Lots to be at their own risk after the fall of the hammer, and no Lot to be removed from the premises until it is paid for, when a Delivery Ticket will be given.

5.—Should any purchaser refuse or neglect to complete his purchase, the Auctioneers shall have full power to resell the Lot or Lots, either publicly or privately, and any loss that may arise from such second sale, together with all expenses and charges incurred by the same, shall be made good by the Defaulters at this present sale, and be recoverable as and for Liquidated Damages. This condition is without prejudice to the right of the Auctioneers to enforce the Contract made at this Sale.

6.—Five per cent. Commission to be paid by the Purchaser to the Auctioneers.

7.—The whole having been on view and subject to any examination prior to Sale the Auctioneers will not hold themselves responsible for any misdescription or otherwise of any Lot.

8.—No Cheques accepted from strangers without approved reference.

9.—All Lots to be removed at the Purchasers expense by 5 p.m. on Thursday, July 25th, 1912.

These Conditions will be strictly adhered to and no deviation therefrom allowed.

THOS. WATERS & SON, Auctioneers.

MITFORD HALL,

2¼ Miles West of Morpeth.

CATALOGUE OF HORSES, CARRIAGES, HARNESS, IMPLEMENTS, &c.,

To be SOLD BY AUCTION at the STABLES,

ON

WEDNESDAY, JULY 24th, 1912,

By Order of the Executors of the late RICHARD LEDWICK OSBALDESTON MITFORD, Esq.

SALE at 2 p.m. prompt.

ON VIEW July 23rd, 1 till 4 p.m.

Terms - Cash and No Reserve.

THOMAS WATERS & SON,

AUCTIONEERS.

MOTOR CHAR-A-BANC will leave the Market Place at 1 p.m. for the Sale.

SALE OFFICE:
75 Newgate Street,
Morpeth.

Top, auction catalogue from 1912.
Bottom, photograph taken in 1910, driving the carriage is Robert Gill. The Brougham with the match pair – two superb grey geldings, 'Peter & Paul' were well known in Mitford village during the time of Squire Edward Mitford FRGS. (Photograph with kind thanks to Richard, Vallerie & Helen Gill).

The Queen is head of a limited Monarchy, a form of government which has proved, after centuries of trial, the best guarantee for the liberty of the subject, the safety of the person, and the property of the people; and when I speak of liberty, I do not talk of licentiousness, of every man being allowed to follow his own devices, whether good or evil. No! Liberty clearly, distinctly, and properly defined by Blackstone (Judge & Politician) is this, the "being governed by good laws". I call upon you to drink this toast with a will, because, for some 35 years, during which the Queen has held the sceptre, we have been godly and quietly governed. To the health of Victoria, by the grace of God, Queen."

The pomp and circumstance was tolerated by other members of the family, especially his younger brother, heir to the Mitford estates, who had no need to wave ceremonial flags. Sibling rivalry persisted.

A little later in 1878, John Philip became High Sheriff of Northumberland. To mark the occasion a grand fancy dress ball was hosted at Mitford Hall with 150 invited guests. The ball room was decorated in white, blue and amber wall hangings and flowers, representing the heraldic colours of the family. The orchestra podium was ornamented with quilted fabric, the arms of the Mitford family and the weapons used by Colonel Mitford in the first China war were draped with two Chinese flags. The first China War (1839-1842) was also known as the Opium War and was fought between the British and the Qing Empire. With memories and weapons of war it sounds rather bizarre for a grand social occasion and fancy dress ball where everyone is expected to relax and have fun? The ball started off with a loud blast from the Sheriff's trumpeters and the dancing, led off by Lt Colonel Mitford and Lady Louisa Hamilton (1812-1905), continued until 5 am in the morning. Where was Fanny?

Lt Colonel Mitford's wife Fanny Mitford, also born in 1809, was the daughter of Charles Mitford of Pitshill in Sussex. They had a common ancestor in Robert Mitford (1662-1707) as mentioned previously - Robert's fourth son settled at Petworth and changed their name to Townley-Mitford, thus the Sussex branch of the family became known as the Townley-Mitfords of Pitshill.

Altogether, Colonel Mitford saw 42 years of military service, mostly in the regular army. He was devotedly attached to Mitford and when he succeeded as lord of the manor, he lived all year round at Mitford Hall. For many years he was chairman of the Bench for Morpeth. He was an exceedingly generous man and the great work of his life as Squire of Mitford was the restoration of Mitford Church.

Having been aware of the process and costs during the successful construction of the new Mitford family home, Mitford Hall and several other projects around Mitford, John decided to continue and totally rebuilt and renovated Mitford Church in 1874/77, costing upwards of £10,000 (see Mitford Church), this extended to £14,000, around £1.4 million today. An amazing act of generosity to the village and community of Mitford. These funds originated from the sale of the profitable, Osbaldeston Hunmanby estate lands.

Col Mitford's generosity continued. In 1881 the Hunmanby estate covered some 7,000 acres and he permanently reduced all rents by 20 percent. In 1885 a further reduction of 10 per cent was made, giving a total of 30 per cent reduction to all tenants. With a generous nature and a fortune in the bank he was not very astute with estate and financial management. This created and fuelled continuing sibling rivalry between the families. It was at this stage my great grandmother Mary Margaret Mitford (1860-1943) mindful of her father's succession to the Hunmanby, Yorkshire and Mitford, Northumberland estates, to be followed by her brother Robert, confronted her uncle John about his extravagant generosity and management of the Mitford estates.

John's generous approach created further frictions and opened a rift that would never heal until his death. In 1887 Mary Margaret married Walter Raymond (1861-1929) a graduate of Cirencester Agricultural College and a leading golfing personality who owned a part of the west side of Hayling Island. He did much for the Hayling Island Golf Club, that still can be seen today, the honours board at the golf club is maintained for the Walter Raymond Trophy, presented by Walter's wife, Margaret Mitford Raymond in 1930.

John celebrated his golden wedding anniversary on the 30th May 1894, a year before he died. Consistent with his personality as a popular and generous landlord, a great many private and public gifts were distributed. To quote from his speech at the anniversary dinner party.

"We cannot find words adequate to express our thanks to you all. We take no credit for doing our duty in the position in which providence has placed us – it would have been utterly disgraceful had we done otherwise. We are only stewards and whether we are entrusted with two talents or with ten, I know that in a short time we must give an account of our stewardship"...

He could not have said it better. The cupboard and table were to become bare.

His pastime was photography, a very expensive hobby. The local publication "Tyneside" holds several examples of his skill as a photographer, namely a reproduction of a photograph of himself which was his own work and a photograph of Mitford Church, which you see on the cover of this book. Above all, he was larger than life, an ardent churchman and vigorous upholder of church and state. Every local cause of a benevolent, philanthropic or intellectual character received generous financial support. His funeral was attended by the Bishop of Newcastle.

He had no children and the Mitford and Hunmanby estates passed onto his younger brother Edward, my great, great grandfather. In his will, the Mitford family reserves amounting to £46,000 (around £5 million today) were entrusted to his wife Fanny Mitford including a "suite of diamonds". She promptly left Mitford and moved to the south of England, Chichester. The funds in Fanny's control passed out from the Mitford family of Mitford, and started the domino effect towards the breaking up of the estates and Mitford inheritance. A mighty blow from the grave as it were.

After donations, gifts and trusts totalling £20,000, Fanny Mitford made another will and when she died, 7 years later in 1902 aged 83 years, she left the remainder of £26,000. With various bequeaths to her relations and charities, the will provided £5,000 to her nephew, Charles Lloyd Mitford, and to her sister-in-law, the Hon Margaret Emily Townley Mitford, the income of £7,000 for life and a life grant to Lt Colonel William Kenyon Mitford of Pitshill, Petworth.

It was during John Philip Mitford's era that in 1871 Algernon Freeman-Mitford published "Tales of Old Japan", which is still considered to be an interesting introduction to Japanese culture and history. It includes Algernon's eyewitness accounts of a selection of Japanese rituals, ranging from marriage to hara-kiri, detailed in a laterlater chapter. In 1886 another Mitford the Right Hon. John Thomas Earl of Redesdale died leaving his numerous estates amounting to upwards of £195,000 to various members of the Exbury branch of the family stating that the person who succeeds to the Batsford estate was to take the name Freeman. This is where the Mitford girls grew up.

28th Squire Edward Ledwich Mitford FRGS (1811-1912)
Squire for 17 years from 1895-1912
(my great-great grandfather) aged 84 years.

Last of the great squires of Mitford. He inherited the family estates from his older brother, with not a penny in the bank, except his annual, civil service pension.

Edward, was a boy of four years old during the Battle of Waterloo and lived through nine years of the reign of George III, and all the reigns of George IV, William IV and Queen Victoria (1819-1901).

With the Hunmanby and Mitford estates still intact and owned by the Mitford family, Edward took control at the grand old age of 84 years. A tough job, as every farm and building fell under the responsibility of the squire. Looking through family letters, it's clear to see that Edward, after his amazing life and earlier career, was true to form – and readily able to rise to the daunting challenge of managing the Mitford and the Hunmanby estates, not to mention coping with family politics. One can only imagine what the relationship was between the two brothers…and the Fanny problem, with 'family money going sideways'.

One brother was of humble nature, a practical and an accomplished celebrated author, artist, poet, Arabic linguist, reformer, middle east politician – specialist and doyen of the Foreign Office and Colonial Service and father of 8 talented & successful children, all managed on a civil servant's government agent - consular salary and pension. The other brother served in the regular army with active duty in the China war being his most significant life-time event (remember the fancy dress ball) and his pastime of photography.... who inherited wealth, with no children and heirs... it's quite easy to reach a conclusion.

John Philip lived high and enjoyed his privileged position of being a generous, benevolent and philanthropic squire, landlord, and friend to all. With access to the ample funds from the profitable Osbaldeston estate via the proceeds of Mitford's Estate Act [*see later chapter*] he could well afford to develop his new lifestyle accordingly, with energy and largesse.

When Edward and his sons and family inherited the stewardship of family estates only to discover that the "cupboard was bare" and the family reserves had "gone south", with Fanny, it must have been a very bitter pill indeed for the 84 year old, squire of Mitford and his heirs to swallow. Later, "the Fanny problem" would lead to the breakup of the Mitford estates, provoking bitter family feuds.

With no capital reserves or money in the bank, Edward faced running an undercapitalised estate and struggled hard to hold the estates together with income from tenants, evidenced by his letter to all the tenant farmers dated 1896 as follows.

"Due to the embarrassed position I find myself in with having to pay the exorbitant taxes and death duties in succeeding to the Mitford and Hunmanby estates from my brother, I am unable to continue with his exceptional liberality and generosity in the returns and reductions of rents. Last year, the late Colonel Mitford returned over £1,380 to tenants. The whole year's rental of both estates will not cover the taxes. With no income and funds in the bank, I will have to borrow money at a high interest rate. I am further, unable to incur any expense which is not absolutely necessary. To this end, I have shut up Mitford Hall, and only by the most rigid economy will I be able to tide over the present crisis in the affairs of the family".

His only other income was his annual government consular pension of £1,200. The burden of the estate was to eventually pass to his son, Robert Mitford (my great uncle), who was eventually forced to break up the Mitford estates and inheritance. A few more farms had to be sold.

Meanwhile as stated, his brother's wife Fanny, who had outlived her husband, was busy settling into her new home in Chichester, in the south of England, with the family wealth of £46,000, from the Hunmanby estate and the family diamonds. However, a few years later a disaster happened that sent Fanny rushing back to Mitford. One can imagine her cry to the coach driver, "To Mitford, and don't spare the horses". It was the summer of 1899 and Mitford village was in full bloom, all was quiet and peaceful amidst the rolling green hills and idyllic scenery….. until the Mitford Church bells came crashing down through the bell tower due to a broken steel cable.

The bells would have remained on the church floor for a long time as no one had any money - no church trust fund and clearly it had not been insured. Fanny hastily paid for all the repairs and the installation of a new set of bells, eight in number. She went to great pains to do everything as quickly as possible and keep everything as discreet as possible. This confrontation was a little awkward, as she and my great-great grandfather, his wife and my great grandmother were not on speaking terms. Naturally, she stayed at Mitford Hall, which was at least, large enough for the relatives not to bump into each other. In circumstances like this, butlers (Mr Jobson was butler at the time)…. are absolutely essential. They keep everything running smoothly.

With Estate Manager, Mr Hodgson, who lived in Redesdale Cottage on the Mitford Estate, Edward developed an excellent relationship. He realised that without the long term experience of the skilled and trusted estate manager, things would deteriorate even further. To quote the thoughtful old squire that he was – from one of his estate letters "Dear Mr Hodgson, I have been thinking over your position and come to the conclusion that you are underpaid. I have decided that I will pay you £200 a year to date from the 1st of January last". This letter was hand written at the age of 92 and dated 5 July 1903.

The Mitford estate consisted of 35,000 acres or approximately 130 square kilometres at this time, with over 26 tenanted farms and around 600 village residents. Likewise, Edward became squire of the Hunmanby estate in Yorkshire. Luckily, at this time Hunmanby Hall was rented out to Lord & Lady William Cecil, who often hosted their great friend Princess Henry of Battenberg. The much needed rent money helped pay the bills! Edward also found time to help and assist at Hunmanby and contributed to their church renovation projects and other community activities which is evidenced by various plaques.

Canon Roderick Charles Macleod became resident Vicar of Mitford Church in 1897. He was a very keen photographer and took hundreds of photographs of life in and around Mitford, all well preserved in the Woodhorn Archives, thanks to George Brown. His original home was Dunvegan Castle in Skye, Scotland. He was an excellent musician, along with his daughter Brenda who became wife of Bertram-Lane Mitford, the 30th squire. His younger daughter Ela, formed the Mitford Orchestra and Choir.

It was during this time (1909 to 1911) that Filey Bay, part of the Mitford & Hunmanby estate became the scene of pioneer flying in England. The great Yorkshire aviation designer Robert Blackburn founded the Blackburn Aeroplane Company and Flying School at Filey Bay. The entire beach in Filey Bay belonged to Edward Ledwich Mitford who possessed full Lordship rights. This included all of Filey, Hunmanby and Reighton sands. There existed an age old tradition to establish this right for the Lord of Hunmanby Manor… a chosen horseman rode out into the water and threw a ceremonial javelin out to sea. Everything landward of the javelin was the property of the Hunmanby Lord.

This was ceremoniously acted every year until the Hunmanby Manor and lordship was sold in 1922.

Long before taking over the Mitford Estate, Edward had enjoyed a remarkable and celebrated life. He married Janet Bailey, daughter of the Archdeacon of Ceylon, Benjamin Bailey and they produced 9 children, five boys and four girls, the first son died of an infection. Edward, during his bachelor days, at the age of 28 years was the first person to travel 10,000 miles and ride 7,000 miles on horseback from London to Ceylon (now Sri Lanka) and later, wrote a fascinating book of his early adventures "A Land March from England to Ceylon" 7,000 miles on horseback. A synopsis is contained later in this book.

He also wrote "An Appeal In Behalf Of The Jewish Nation" in support of creating a Jewish state, one of the first government officials to propose the creation and establishment of Israel. His plan was influential and was followed leading to the Balfour agreement and British mandate over Palestine from which emerged the State of Israel. Along with his book of poems he left an exquisite painting of a white dove (see Mitford Church) which can be seen on the ceiling of the Mitford church bell tower to this day. It was placed there after Fanny had the new bells installed. Fluent in Arabic and many dialects, he was considered a specialist on the Middle East and was actively engaged in London politics.

Two of his sons became heirs and squires of Mitford and his fourth son Bertram Mitford FRGS was the first person to travel around South Africa to interview survivors of the Zulu War at Isandlwana, the worst British defeat during the Victorian era. All great uncles of mine. Bertram was also well acquainted with mining baron and pioneer Cecil John Rhodes (1853-1902) and the creation of Rhodesia. Bertram spent 25 years in South Africa and wrote 43 bestselling novels. Together with his contemporary and friend Rider Haggard, they are among the founders of South African literature. Bertram's life and works are contained in a separate chapter.

It was during this time in 1909 that Lloyd George, the Chancellor of the Exchequer produced his famous People's Budget. In addition there was to be a complete survey and valuation of all land throughout the country. All landowners were targeted by the government.

Edward with older years and assisted by his son and heir Robert, had the presence and countenance to run the estate with careful thought and detail right up to when he received a congratulatory message from the King on attaining his 100th birthday (the telegram sent from Sandringham is on display in the Mitford family chapel, within Mitford church). He was a fine old man and his figure was well known on the Bench of the Northumberland Magistrates at Newcastle upon Tyne. His remarkable life is detailed in a later chapter.

Edward was interested in legal issues, one of the main concerns up to the last moments of his life concerned a law case at the time that had occupied the minds of judge and jury for many days. Edward expressed sadness that a daughter should have been called upon to give such damaging evidence against her parents as to have led to the condemnation of one of them. This drew his mind onto a subject that had pre-occupied his thoughts for years and his views on capital punishment worth crediting on record as a remarkable proof of his energy of mind and purpose. He said he wished to he could meet the Member for the Borough of Morpeth, with whom he had already corresponded on the subject, that he might prevail on him to bring forward a Bill urging the immediate abolition of capital punishment for women. It was pointed out that this law was seldom enforced at the time, but that did not suffice. He maintained that it was a blot on the statute book that such an Act should still be retained.

Edward's gravestone in Mitford churchyard has the following inscription "There the tears of earth are dried – there the hidden things are clear". A provoking statement of perspective and insight.

Edward left an estate valued at £8,495 and net £7,372 to his widow Ella Elizabeth. The estates at Mitford, Northumberland and Hunmanby in Yorkshire, then passed to Edward's eldest son Robert, my great uncle.

29th Squire Robert Cuthbert Mitford (1846-1924)

Squire for 12 years from 1912-1924 aged 66 years
(my great uncle).

The manors and estates of Mitford and Hunmanby having passed from Lt Colonel J.P. Mitford and thereafter to Edward

Ledwich Mitford FRGS, were in desperate need of money to keep the estates going. Part of the family capital reserves had been depleted from the building of Mitford Hall, increasing land ownership in Mitford and rebuilding Mitford Church. Plus, the main part of the inherited wealth and capital funds had passed out of the family. The Hunmanby Manor House and estate was still rented out to several tenants. Robert was faced with a desperate situation.

As a future squire he was one of the few Mitfords to attend Eton and follow on to Sandhurst. An army Captain, Robert married Annie Lane, daughter of Major-General Charles Stuart Lane and great granddaughter of Lady Jane Fisher who apparently helped Charles II, disguised as his groom, escape to France in 1651 after his defeat at the battle of Worcester. (Incidentally, before the battle Charles II contracted Worcester Clothing Company to outfit his army with uniforms but was unable to pay the bill of £453. In June 2008 Charles, Prince of Wales paid off the 357 year old debt (less the interest of £47,500).

Robert at 66 years was the last of the all powerful Mitford squires as every house and farm was owned by the squire. However, when Robert took over both estates from his father in 1912, with taxes, charges, expenses and death duties he was forced to review and enter into new agreements, terms and conditions of tenancy with all the farmers in order to make ends meet. His letter to all the tenants was as follows (see original Tenants Letter). Not a pleasant time for the Mitford family and tenants.

Holding onto a family estate is something only a few will know. It's a very strong bond held over from medieval days when people were given or bought a piece of land due to their goodwill to the crown or lord, be it half an acre or 30,000 acres. Through the generations, it's the understanding of what one has and finding a way to hold onto it, which counts. Checking through family letters (kept by my great grandmother) and the estate records and accounts over several generations it's quite easy to see that the Mitford squires were all kindly and benevolent landlords to their tenants. Ready and available to help find a solution to any difficulty that cropped up. There was no welfare state and social security in those days. Everyone was dependant on the squire for everything.

Robert was in desperate need of funds to cover taxes and expenses. To this end, shortly after his father's death, he held a public auction sale at Mitford Hall on the 24th July 1912 (see catalogue and photographs in the first plate section) and sold the Mitford carriages, horses, farm implements, even household furniture, family silver, the wine cellar, and yes ... his father's gold watch for a total of £728 (around £72,000, today). A tough decision to make, there was nothing else to sell to bring in the much needed cash.

But never the less, times were changing with the introduction of the motor car and modern farming methods. The carriages would soon be collecting dust and would become expensive family relics to hold onto. World War I was two years away (1914-1918). All this could have been averted had the family wealth and reserves remained secure, remember the… "Fanny problem?"

Shortly after the Mitford Hall contents sale, Robert put an advertisement in The Yorkshire Post newspaper to sell off some land at Filey. "Consequent upon the succession of Captain Robert Mitford of Mitford, to the Mitford estates in Northumberland and Yorkshire, a portion of the Hunmanby Mitford estate at Filey is to be offered for sale by public auction at Victoria Hall, by Messrs Cranswick and Cranswick". The property offered comprised freehold building plots, land and house property, old pasture grass, arable allotments and accommodation land.

The lands sold covered – 27 Acres with 975 feet frontage to Muston Road for £1,100, 3 acres of old pasture alongside the railway station for £300; 8 acres of old pasture land with right of way from West Avenue for £400; Seadales Field, 7 acres of arable land adjoining West Avenue and Filey Golf Course for £1,000, and Manor Farm House with a frontage of 53 feet to Queen Street and 53 feet to Mitford Street; a total of 1,550 square yards was sold for £500. The old and trusted family firm of Brumell and Sample of Morpeth acted on behalf of Robert Mitford. This brought in a total of £3,300 (with an approximate average of £83 per acre) to keep the Mitford flag flying and the wolf from the gate… for the time being.

An additional source of income was land rights on the Yorkshire coastline. Robert as Lord of the Manor held the rights over the Filey sands. He was entitled to take one-half of the net profits resulting from the letting of sites and stands on Filey sands, allowing by arrangement the Filey Council to take the other half in return for the work of letting out, controlling the sands and collecting rents. Robert was also Lord of the Manors of Hunmanby and Muston, whose sands are a continuation of those of Filey. He also held a similar arrangement with the Council for the Muston sands.

Robert had also inherited Mitford Hall with over 12 staff members. Junior members of staff changed frequently, but the older and senior staff members such as the butler, housekeeper, chauffeur, 4 gardeners, gamekeeper, rabbit catcher, drainer and joiner were in lifelong employment until they retired and kept their house, rent-free until they died. Robert was desperate to keep it all going and hold everything together. Fanny was far away, enjoying her new home in Chichester.

During this time, from 1895 to 1914 Hunmanby Hall was rented out to tenants, the most notable being Lord William Cecil. Princess Beatrice and her daughter, the Queen of Spain, were frequent visitors to the hall. With the turn of the century, Col. Sir Henry Dennis Readett Bayley (1878-1940), rented Hunmanby Hall. He attended the Royal Agricultural College at Cirencester and had inherited a vast coal mining fortune. He became High Sheriff of Yorkshire and chose Hunmanby Hall as his 'seat'. Clearly, I think he realised the desperate financial state of the Mitford family so simply hovered on the sidelines, biding his time. Baroness Angela Bardett-Coutts (1814 – 1906) heiress to Coutts Bank and the wealthiest woman in England also rented Hunmanby Hall from my great-great grandfather during 1898.

During later years around 1920 another prominent person who enjoyed the hospitality at Hunmanby Hall was Herbert Smith, the President of the Yorkshire Miner's Association, who was the guest of Sir Henry at a moment of great tension in the British coal industry. Sir Henry owned a large Nottingham colliery and it was said at the time that the quiet heart-to-heart talk the two had during that eventful weekend saved the situation. Not so for the fate and demise of Wentworth House and the Fitzwilliams in Yorkshire, when the grounds of the largest ancestral palace in England were dug up by order of the government, totally desecrating the landscape around Wentworth House after the open-cast mining.

With no other options available, there was only one thing left to do, Robert sold the entire Hunmanby estate in Yorkshire to Sir Henry, complete with the Lordship. Sir Henry in turn sold off all land and properties to his tenants with suitable financial arrangements for all, and departed from Hunmanby Hall in 1922. In 1928 it became a girls' school with 400 pupils. *[See Chapter Squire Osbaldeston, Yorkshire.]*

Some years later, speaking in the House of Commons in 1924, Edward Wood said there was "a silent revolution in progress". He was right. In the years before and after the First World War, some six to eight million acres, one quarter of the land in England, was sold by gentry.

Apparently, the Mitfords were not cut out for any type of commercialism or financial property wrangling. Considered... "infra dig". After this, with no financial problems, times naturally became more enjoyable for all concerned on the Mitford estate. The Mitfords continued their annual holidays in Torquay, Devon, playing golf at Hayling Island with the Raymond family. The Fanny problem was buried. The profitable Hunmanby estate was sold.

Robert and Annie performed an enormous amount of social work within the village community and readily allowed the use of the ballroom for any fund raising events. For local sporting activities, especially after the 1914-1918 war, the Mitford Cricket Club needed a new cricket field and Robert readily made available part of Mitford Park, alongside Mitford Hall, for a nominal rental of £6 per annum in perpetuity. He also provided the small red-roofed, timber pavilion that still can be seen today (at time of writing). A new pavilion alongside has recently been added in

2013, funded from local grants and money raised by the members of the Mitford Cricket Club.

Robert was quite a character, or in the English sense, somewhat eccentric. After patching up a disagreement with Canon Macleod, the Vicar of Mitford Church, the regular Sunday morning church services must have provided some amusement for the local villagers. Robert took a large alarm clock to Sunday morning church services to time the Vicar's sermons. After ten minutes it went off… those having a snooze woke up… or nearly fell off their pews, while others jumped up to sing the last hymn. Robert's son would later marry the Vicar's daughter.

Another amusing glimpse into Robert's character is evidenced by a letter he wrote to the editor of The Newcastle Journal in 1914 – headed Disrespect for the Dead. "Sir, - I think the following facts ought to be made public….

While driving back to Morpeth on Friday, when a few miles out from Newcastle, I passed an abandoned hearse standing in the road, outside a public house. Inside the hearse was a coffin. The horse had been removed from the shafts. The body was entirely unattended and not a human being was in sight. They were presumably drinking in the public-house. The time was 12.20 pm. Such a scandalous state of things, I hope, will be taken notice of by the relatives of the deceased, at any rate".

Coffins usually have a lid and are normally closed? I wonder, did he actually open the coffin to see if there was a dead body inside? Thinking of another Mitford, Jessica Mitford, one of the Mitford girls who wrote "The American way of Death" one can assume that this coffin could have been empty… on delivery for a funeral or being recycled for another body?

The estate then passed to Robert's son, my cousin.

30th Squire Bertram Lane Mitford (1876-1939)

Squire for 15 years from 1924-1939 aged 48 years *(my cousin).*

With the family financial stability partly restored from the sale of the Hunmanby estate a period of relative calm ensured. Aged 48, Bertram was one of the youngest squires to inherit the

Mitford estates and the only one not following a military, religious or civil service career. He was brought up by my great uncle with the sole purpose of managing the estate. Sadly, it all ended with a series of tragic events.

Bertram married Brenda McLeod, the eldest daughter of the vicar of Mitford Church, Cannon Roderick Macleod of the Macleod Clan at Dunvegan Castle in Skye. Dunvegan Castle on the shores of Loch Dunvegan was once entirely encircled by the sea, and is the oldest continuously inhabited castle in Scotland. First opened to the public in 1933, it has been the ancestral home of the Chiefs of Clan MacLeod for 800 years.

Brenda was an accomplished pianist and violinist, a playing member of the London Symphony Orchestra. Bertram and Brenda did much for the Scout movement and were appointed Scout Commissioners for the Northumberland Cubs, Scouts & Girl Guides movement, providing tents, uniforms and camping gear and free use of the billiard room and grounds at Mitford Hall, along with use of a car and chauffeur for transport. On one grand occasion Lady Baden-Powell came to inspect the parade of Scouts and Guides at Mitford Hall.

In 1936 when the Duchess of Northumberland attended a Guides event at Mitford Hall, Brenda Mitford, made an interesting speech on the aims and objectives of the Guide movement – highlighting the fact that "uniform is a great leveller, rich and poor girls could work together in absolute equality, as they were all dressed alike".

The first tragic event to take place was the death of their only child Humphrey, son and heir, at the age of two and a half years. It was apparently due to a local flu at the time; some say the nurse overdosed him – we shall never know. A rumour circulated that Bertram, with his good looks and roving blue eyes had an affair with a member of Mitford Hall staff and sired an illegitimate child, the spitting image of himself.

The second tragic event took place in 1939, the year WW2 was declared - Bertram dropped dead of a reported heart attack at the aged 63. Brenda, having lost her son, then her husband and then her home, with WW2 ahead was left totally and utterly devastated. Brenda, sadly returned to her family home Dunvegan Castle in Skye. Through this period and especially when war was declared, the name Mitford was constantly featured in many British newspapers. "Peer's daughter coming from Germany - Detention of Unity Mitford, Home Secretary Will Not Say In Advance – Unity Mitford, Secretary for War to be Asked a Question – The Mitfords, No disquiet Over Island Home, says Mr Eden, War Minister – Miss Mitford Married to Nephew of Winston Churchill"...the list goes on. This alarming and constant flow of publicity caused quite a stir in those days.

Quite something for any family to take on board. The Victorian times represented paradox and power and with the "British stiff upper lip" adverse publicity was frowned upon. Many were caught up in the ripple effect.

During the early 1930s, there was the scandal and controversy with the British Royal Family. Edward VIII (1894-1972) ascended the throne in 1936 but was never crowned King due to his relationship with Wallis Simpson, an American divorcee, that provoked a constitutional crisis. It ended with his abdication, and he was created Duke of Windsor in 1937.

The Duke and Duchess of Windsor lived most of their lives just outside Paris, as neighbours to Diana Mitford and Sir Oswald Mosley. The Mosley's bought a villa called Temple de la Gloire, overlooking a small lake, after having spent three years interned in a house in the grounds of Holloway prison. Diana wrote an intimate and detailed account of their lives together in her book entitled "The Duchess of Windsor". Edward's younger brother George VI (1895-1952) continued as King. "Keep calm and carry on".

Bertram Lane Mitford left an estate of £4,007, around £200,000 today. The succession of the Mitford estate reverted back and passed to my great-great-grandfather's third son, my great uncle Rev, Edward Mitford.

From here onwards with WW2, general economic conditions and changing times the estate suffered badly and took a steady downhill slide towards its last chance of revival when the last squire of Mitford took over in 1970.

31st Squire The Rev Edward Mitford (1853-1948)

Squire for 9 years from 1939-1948 aged 86 years
(my great uncle)

The Reverend Edward Mitford attended Winchester College and St John's College, Cambridge. He married Annie Price and produced one son and five daughters. He was the only Mitford sibling and squire to have attended Winchester public school and Cambridge University – all the rest (except Bertram) chose a military career. Reverend Edward was ordained in 1878 and was Vicar of Hunmanby from 1888 to 1919. Later he became Rector of Acrise and retired in 1923. At the good old age of 86 years he inherited a dilapidated hall and much run down estate. He held the estate for only 9 years which included WW2 so not much could be done or enjoyed. All that he could do was attend to the task of putting all the beautiful walnut furniture, oil paintings and pictures into storage which were later, sadly sold off at Morpeth in 1947. Mitford Hall was commandeered by the army and around 400 personnel were stationed there in corrugated iron huts across Mitford Park.

A vast amount of damage was done to the house and grounds. Bren gun carriers and armoured tanks trained in the grounds and around the castle and by the time it was handed back to the Mitford family it was a heart breaking sight. Alongside Mitford Cricket Club, there remains a large section of concrete which was specially built for armoured tank training, to train drivers or pilots how to manoeuvre and do fast armoured tank turn abouts. Perhaps rather distressing for the estate gardener and gamekeeper. In 1948, the Northumberland Education Committee planned to purchase the Hall and turn it into a special, residential school for handicapped children, but the family decided to move back into the Hall.

The constant wave of alarming publicity surrounding the Mitford girls, a branch of the family based in southern England continued. Some took it on the chin, but in those days people were mainly conservative with a small 'c' and opposed to blatant frivolity.

In June 1940, Churchill received from the Home Secretary, names of one hundred and fifty prominent people who had been arrested under the new Defence of the Realm Regulations. Two of the first three – Lady Mosley (Diana Mitford then Guinness) and George Pit-Rivers, were in fact relatives to Churchill. With war life was disrupted and for many, lives were changed never to return to pre-war normality. For the Mitford girls the war had a domino effect as they all became separated. Nancy Mitford's marriage broke up, and she eventually settled in Paris after the city was liberated. Jessica immigrated to America – her husband joined up and was killed. She then married a lawyer from the Bronx and they both joined the Communist Party.

As a result of Diana's Nazi sympathies her father disinherited her. When Diana and Oswald were released from internment, Nancy and Jessica strongly and publicly protested, after the war they went into exile in France.

Unity, head over heels about Hitler, was apparently so distraught at the prospect of war between Britain and Germany that she shot herself in the head. She did a lousy job. The German and French press thought differently. *"C'est Himmler qui donna l'ordre de supprimer miss Unity Mitford"*. There was a great deal of one up-man-ship within the ranks, due to her intimacy with soldiers ranked close to Hitler and being British. It didn't kill her and she was brought back home, and lingered on in Scotland until she died in 1948, leaving an estate of £850, around £25,000 today.

A somewhat amusing incident took place some ten years before her death. Unity and her father Lord Redesdale attended court where she was fined £1 and her licence was endorsed for speeding on the main London road. In fact, she was driving at double the speed limit at 60 miles per hour. In her court statement she said "I have just come back from Germany, where there is no speed limit and I am afraid I forgot the limit when driving in England after so many months absence".

Their brother Tom, also a Fascist sympathizer, refused to fight the Germans, but joined up and was killed in the Far East, devastating the entire family and ending their line of succession.

Even their parents were caught up – they were divided as to which side to support, and their marriage ultimately collapsed with part of the family retreating to their island at Inchkenneth in Scotland.

Across Britain, the name Mitford represented scandal and embarrassment. Much later, even in a far away country, like the British colony of South Africa, where many went to create a new beginning after the horrors of WW2, the stigma continued. As I remember so well – whenever the name Mitford cropped up my parents said the name was "taboo". Being a youngster, christened with the surname Mitford it was a little difficult and rather confusing for me to understand. I only discovered the full story much later.

By the end of the war in 1945 the surviving Mitford girls were personally estranged and living in separate countries. It was only Deborah, married to Lord Andrew Cavendish who remained conventional and on speaking terms with all her sisters. I first met her in 2006.

As youngsters their lives were great fun but later it all turned rather bitter. The comfortable and cosy childhood that Nancy, Unity, Diana & Jessica had enjoyed, as reported across the press had disappeared for ever. As one can well imagine, non stop publicity created a major rift between families with the Mitford squires remaining totally indignant to all the media coverage. Every wave of publicity was taken with charmed and perfect indifference, as the Northumberland family shunned the lime light. Not us you know, it's that lot down south…. ! There was notably, no love lost between the families. The Mitford girls and other relatives follow in later chapters.

After the war, when Edward died, the estate passed to his only son, my cousin.

32nd Squire John Philip Mitford (1880-1970)

Squire for 22 years from 1948-1970 aged 68 years *(my cousin)*

Lt Colonel John Mitford D.S.O. attended Haileybury then served in the Indian army and Afghan War of 1919. John, married Edith Tytler, took over the estate in 1948 aged 68. His first and most depressing task was repairing all the damage done during the war, along with purchasing a complete new household of furniture for the Hall. He made various properties habitable for ex-servicemen and their families, as many had no homes to return to. Some land as detailed below, on the estate had to be sold to cover costs. Amazingly, it is also recorded in a letter dated 17th November 1949, that he sold the Fishing Rights on the Wansbeck River to the Tynemouth Corporation for £60.00. The area sold covered 960 yards on the north bank and 590 yards on the south bank and was subject to tenant right. A further condition was to encourage the propagation of trout, to exclude cannibal and course fish and to enter into a bond to pay a fine of £1,000 to the vendor if it be shown that salmon, sea trout and grayling or fry have been introduced into the water.

Shortly afterwards in 1951, approval was granted to the local council to construct 10 houses at a cost of £14,000 on the acquired Mitford property. The council then needed agreement to borrow the amount required, to actually do the job. Meanwhile, the construction of 40 houses at Pegswood, a local coal mining village had exceeded their budget of £53,500 by £1,580 due to the cost of supplies. More money had to be borrowed. Those were tough times?

You'll note through the Mitford succession, many squires through the generations served in the military and civil government. It was part of family culture. These trends continued right up to the end of the Mitford dynasty, from father to son - devoting their lifetime to military careers and inheriting the family estate upon retirement age. As such, evidenced over the generations the squires were ill equipped in venturing into entrepreneurial business ventures and alternative, additional revenue making activities to support running the Mitford estate. As mentioned before, when a crisis arose, a piece of land was simply sold off. The Mitfords never had money, they married it wherever possible.

My mother, a war time nurse and veteran of WW2, during trips from South Africa to England in the 1960's, met the 32nd squire and Edward his son. Their discussion naturally ended up with the Mitford succession and inheritance. I was at boarding school at the time and was kept advised by her letters via the "tuck boxes" from mother to son. The subsequent result was I would be contacted and will always have a home in England, as long as I hold a British passport.

In 1963, Ivan Mitford-Barberton a well known artist and sculptor, linked to a branch of the Mitford family created and gave Hout Bay's famous bronze leopard to Cape Town, a sentinel on constant guard since the last free leopard in 1930. *[See plate section].*

In 1970 John left an estate of £19,894 net to his only son and heir Edward Mitford with a prepaid estate duty of £4,617.

33rd Squire Edward Cecil Mitford (1908-2002)

Last Squire Of Mitford
Absent squire for 23 years from 1970-1993 & sold the estate (my cousin).

Brigadier Edward Mitford MC was awarded the Military Cross for bravery in action during WW2. After Sandhurst he joined the army and became an explorer of the Sahara desert before the war which led him to becoming one of the original members of the Long Range Desert Group, the forerunner to the SAS. He later commanded five armoured regiments (three in action) and an armoured brigade.

After Edward's final posting in Ankara as the military attaché at the British Embassy, he then served as the military assistant to the Commander-in-Chief, Eastern Command, until he finally retired from the army in 1966. In 1970, aged 62, Edward Cecil Mitford took over the 5,000 acre (16 km2) family estate at Mitford. Edward married twice. Firstly, to Margaret Greaves in 1937, she died in 1945, and secondly, to Patricia Kirrage in 1949 in Turkey. There were no children from either marriage.

With all this action and adventure in Africa and the Middle East, one can perhaps appreciate the difficulty in retiring to the countryside in northern England, to sheep farming, fishing and pottering about the estate. He chose to remain in London and his home in the Middle East, with visits to Mitford.

Unfortunately, Edward was to remain an absentee landlord as he and his wife Patricia preferred London's social life. They were members of the Roehampton Club with its 100 acres of magnificent park like grounds on the edge of London, with tennis and cricket, their country estate was far away and the journey tiring.

As a result, the estate continued its slow decline with no member of the family attending to the management, maintenance and day to day problems that only a landlord can do. For example with the estate management, apparently a cheque for the building of a bridge was signed, but the bridge was never built. The squire only discovered this during a visit some years later and no one will ever know the outcome. The old post office was sold off for £16,500 in 1977 and is now a comfortable private home. The squire did not take an active role in running the estate, like previous squires. Likewise, his wife Patricia did not enjoy country life or the long train and road journeys to visit Mitford. In fact, she positively disliked everything to do with the estate. Edward gifted her some Mitford property in July 1990 and she promptly sold it to a construction company in November 1990 for £40,368. As you may appreciate, she was not a strong woman suited to the role of 'lady of the manor'. However, Edward did do something surprising. He had Mitford Hall modernised and redecorated, each of the eight bedrooms were fitted with an en-suite bathroom and a lift was installed.

During a tour of one of the estate farms, one tenant did say to me, to quote "As you can see for yourself no renovations and repairs have been done since WW2". I also noticed the farm house had no central heating. No one seems to know why he went to the enormous expense of refitting the mansion except perhaps if someone was going to perhaps turn it into a small country hotel? From the sizeable grant of £20,450 made in November 1973 when the new highway was built through the estate he perhaps had nothing else to spend it on (apart from tenant needs) and used the funds to modernize Mitford Hall with en-suite bathrooms?

Someone did mention the motivation was perhaps entertaining his military friends and hosting reunions. One thinks to the old

British Empire and all the charming colonial jokes, camaraderie and banter as it goes..."When I was in India trundling about on my elephant... do have another gin old chap, and when I was in Africa on my camel" please pass the port etc.

After a lifetime and over 20 years of retirement Edward Mitford neither found a suitable heir and / or created a foundation or trust to consolidate the vast and amazing history of the Mitford dynasty, nor tried to establish or continue a family heritage project for future generations.

According to family opinion, he lacked the creativity and vision to preserve the family history. An only son with no children, he was a military man through and through – devoted to his military career. In fact the role of Squire became a burden around his neck. True to military form he simply handed the management of the estate to someone else and told them to get on with it. He was used to delegation and taking advice from others. Frosty and Victorian someone once described him. The last chance to revive the Mitford legend was lost, as with the money. As no heir could be found he chose to end his stewardship in 1992 and the estate was put on the property market to be sold. This received extensive local and international press publicity. As a result of this announcement, a curious incident took place in August 1992. The incident was reported in the Newcastle Chronicle on 5 August 1992,

"A team of what were referred to as professional burglars broke into Mitford Hall through the security system and the ground floor drawing room window and systematically stripped the home of its valuable possessions". This was only discovered in the morning when a member of staff arrived at work. "The thieves took silverware, plates with the family crest, candelabras, family jewellery and even the Squire's silver cigarette box". Apparently none of it was ever found. I would imagine the silver has perhaps been melted down and sold?

One excellent family souvenir presented to my great-great grandfather on his hundredth birthday by the Mitford and Hunmanby tenants is nowhere to be found. A huge, magnificent Georgian silver bowl made by Messers Reid and Sons of Newcastle is decorated with a series of bold double flutes around the base. It has carved, silver lions heads with pendant rings in their mouths as handles with four carved lions feet to support the bowl. It has my grandfather's name and date engraved with the Mitford arms, crest and motto.

Also, nowhere to be found is part of the souvenir collection collected by my great uncle, the South African novelist Bertram Mitford FRGS. A Matchlock rifle – once the property of the Emperor of Morocco; Zulu shields and assegais used in the Zulu war and the hoof of the only horse killed at the same time as the Prince Imperial Napoleon of France. On it mounted in silver is a replica of the cross erected on the spot where he fell. They must be somewhere?

As reported, six months later the Mitford Estate of 5,000 acres with 45 houses and 7 farms was sold in March 1993, for £2,850,000 bar the Mitford Manor tower and the ancient walled, kitchen garden lands, ending nearly 1,000 years of Mitford history. Finally - the last straw was an auction sale dispersing the left-overs of Mitford Hall. With no heir, no one cared or bothered.

The Mitford dynasty ended with the death of Brigadier Edward (Teddy) Mitford on the 16th July 2002 in London at 19 Ennismore Gardens, London SW7.

Chapter 8
Extraordinary Characters & Notable People

270 Years Of Mitford Ink

Peter Else, founder chairman of the Mitford Historical Society said...

"Ink (and scandal) forms part of the Mitford blood".

(i)William Mitford

(1744-1827)

History Of Greece

Leafing through the five volumes of William Mitford's History of Greece one can readily see what a massive amount of work was undertaken - a daunting task. However, living in a splendid country home on the edge of the New Forest with a fortune in the bank and early retirement, one needs to do something. William Mitford became a lawyer and member of Parliament with the assistance from his cousin the Duke of Northumberland and his life's legacy became the "History of Greece".

Born into the successful and well known Exbury branch of the Mitford family, his younger brother John (1748-1830) also a lawyer and politician became Speaker of the House of Commons and Lord Chancellor of Ireland. Another cousin The Rev. John Mitford was editor of the Gentleman's Magazine and compiled and edited a selection of work from the great English poets (covered in more detail in a later section). William was also the great-great-great grandfather to the Mitford sisters .

William attended Cheam School and went on to Queens College at Oxford. At a young age he inherited the Exbury estate and a comfortable fortune. Perhaps understandably he preferred amusement to study and he chose to marry and retire early. His wife died young and it was only when he took himself on a tour abroad and met some fellow scholars and friends in France that his interest and energy became focussed and devoted to writing the History of Greece. It was in 1784 that the first volume appeared in print and only much later in 1810, when his eyesight was diminishing, that the 5th and final volume was published. Amazingly, it is believed, he never visited Greece.

Written from a conservative point of view with a very strong political bias, it has been said that William wrote his History of Greece to prove that virtue was on the side of the aristocrats, and he has less sympathy with the leaders of Athens than he had with the leaders of revolutionary France. For many years, his work stood alone as the standard work on Grecian history. Opinionated and undemocratic in tone, William apparently aroused the generous indignation of some academics in particular Connop Thirwall (1797-1875) Bishop of St David's and his friend George Grote (1794-1871). Both these historians wrote their own independent version of the history of Greece.

Connop Thirwall was from an old Northumberland family and attended Trinity College, Cambridge. He studied and finished law then was ordained deacon in the same year. He travelled around Europe and was greatly influenced following his visit to Rome. Later his first volume of History of Greece appeared in 1835 with the last of 8 volumes published in 1847. He was buried at Westminster Abbey in the same grave as Grote.

George Grote was an English Politician and historian and his grandfather a founder of the bank Grote, Prescott & Co. in Threadneedle Street, London. He did not attend university and studied under various tutors covering history, metaphysics, politics and languages. In 1826 he published a commentary of William Mitford's History of Greece in the Westminster Review.

He too was struck by the anti democratic stance of William Mitford's work and on further examination wrote his appraisal based on misstatements of facts and understandings. After writing a critique of William Mitford's work he developed an interest in Greek literature; through the years he became devoted to Greek history and in 1842 he left his employment with the family bank and concentrated his energy to writing his version of the History of Greece. In 1846 the first two volumes of his History of Greece appeared and the remaining ten volumes were published between 1847 and 1856. In total it took him 30 years to produce History of Greece.

Of the three historians and their separate versions of History of Greece they have been characterised as follows. Thirwall was labelled academic, Grote's interpretation – philosophical and Mitford's bigoted. For balance and further insight I chose to include the following introductory pages from Grote. To quote:

"The first idea of this History was conceived many years ago, at a time when ancient Hellas was known to the English public chiefly through the pages of Mitford ; and my purpose in writing it was to rectify the erroneous statements as to matter of fact which that History contained, as well as to present the general phenomena of the Grecian world under what I thought a juster and more comprehensive point of view. My leisure, however, was not at that time equal to the execution of any large literary undertaking; nor is it until within the last three or four years that I have been able to devote to the work that continuous and exclusive labour, without which, though much may be done to illustrate detached points, no entire or complicated subject can ever be set forth in a manner worthy to meet the public eye.

Meanwhile the state of the English literary world, in reference to ancient Hellas, has been materially changed in more ways than one. If my early friend Dr. Thirlwall's History of Greece had appeared a few years sooner, I should probably never have conceived the design of the present work at all ; I should certainly not have been prompted to the task by any deficiencies, such as those which I felt and regretted in Mitford. The comparison of the two authors affords, indeed, a striking proof of the progress of sound and enlarged views respecting the ancient world during the present generation.

Having studied of course the same evidences as Dr Thirwall, I am better enabled than others to bear testimony to the learning, the sagacity, and the candour which pervade his excellent work : and it is the more incumbent on me to give expression to this sentiment, since the particular points on which I shall have occasion to advert to it will, unavoidably, be points of dissent oftener than of coincidence. The liberal spirit of criticism, in which Dr. Thirwall stands so much distinguished from Mitford, is his own : there are other features of superiority which belong to him conjointly with his age. For during the generation since Mitford 's work, philological studies have been prosecuted in Germany with remarkable success : the stock of facts and documents, comparatively scanty, handed down from the ancient world, has been combined and illustrated in a thousand different ways : and if our witnesses cannot be multiplied, we at least have numerous interpreters to catch, repeat, amplify, and explain their broken and half-inaudible depositions.

Some of the best writers in this department – Boeckh, Niebuhr, 0. Miiller – have been translated into our language ; so that the English public has been enabled to form some idea of the new lights thrown upon many subjects of antiquity by the inestimable aid of German erudition. The poets, historians, orators, and philosophers of Greece, have thus been all rendered both more intelligible and more instructive than they were to a student in the last century ; and the general picture of the Grecian world may now be conceived with a degree of fidelity, which, considering our imperfect materials, it is curious to contemplate.

It is that general picture which an historian of Greece is required first to embody in his own mind, and next to lay out before his readers ; – a picture not merely such as to enlighten the imagination by brilliancy of colouring and depth of sentiment, but also suggestive and improving to the reason not omitting the hints of resemblance as well as of contrast with the better-known forms of modern society, he will especially study to exhibit the spontaneous movement of Grecian intellect, sometimes aided but never borrowed from without, and lighting up a small portion of a world otherwise clouded and stationary, lie will develop the action of that social system which, while insuring to the mass of freemen a degree of protection elsewhere unknown, acted as a stimulus to the creative impulses of genius, and left the superior minds sufficiently unshackled to soar above religious and political routine, to overshoot their own age, and to become the teachers of posterity".

(ii) The Rev. John Mitford

(1781-1859)

Editor of the great English Poets

John Mitford's friends included William Wordsworth, Samuel Taylor Coleridge, Charles Lamb and Lord Byron. John Mitford was a remarkable individual of many talents who supported the best of eighteenth century literature. He was a highly accomplished and universally respected English writer and critic who edited and published the poems of Milton, Gray, Swift, Parnell amongst others. He was appointed editor of the Gentleman's Magazine in 1834 for 17 years. His numerous poems published in the magazine were simply signed JM.

He was a student of the Greek and Roman classics, well acquainted with Italian, French and German authors, deeply read in every area of English literature, a skilful ornithologist and botanist, he was also a passionate lover of painting, especially that of the Italian school. He travelled all over England and Europe in search of the perfect setting.

Descended from the original family of Mitford, Northumberland, John attended Tunbridge Grammar School under Dr Vicesimus Knox and then went on to Oriel College at Oxford under the celebrated tutor Dr Edward Copleton. He developed a close friendship with Reginald Heber and both contested for the English verse prize, which was won by Heber with his poem Palestine. Heber went on to become a poet and noted writer of hymns such as Holy, Holy, Holy; later becoming the Bishop of Calcutta. John Mitford attained his BA in 1804; he then proceeded to take holy orders and was ordained in 1809.

With the assistance of Lord Redesdale he was then appointed to the Vicarage of Benhall, Suffolk later moving to become Rector of Stratford St Andrew and of Weston also in Suffolk the churches united under his guidance. He married Augusta in 1814, daughter of Edward Boodle, of Brooke Street, Grosvenor Square, London and a year later they had an only son Robert Henry Mitford. This was an unhappy marriage and John devoted much of his time to his writing, spending time at his Sloane Street apartment. It was in London that John Mitford developed a long term friendship with Samuel Rogers along with many other well known literary personalities, Alexander Dyce, Dr William Beattie, Henry Luttrell, William Wordsworth, Samuel Taylor Coleridge, Charles Lamb and Lord Byron.

John Mitford loved gardening and planted a great variety of foreign and ornamental trees and shrubs, he created one of the most elegant vicarages in England. His other passion was his collection of books with his extensive and valuable library of English poetry. In his younger days he was a great cricketer and spent many enjoyable hours in conversation with William Fennex, a cricket veteran who worked in his gardens at Benhall. As a result much was written about cricket resulting in many newspaper articles, notes and a manuscript which he later gave the Rev. James Pycroft in 1836 who used his writings for his book entitled The Cricket Field (1851).

To quote some words…. "The pest of the hunting-field is the man always thinking of his own horse and own riding, galloping against MEN and not after DOG. The pest of the cricket-field is the man who bores you about his average - his wickets - his catches; and looks blue even at the success of his own party. If unsuccessful in batting or fielding, he shuts up - the wretch focussed on himself.

No! Give me the man who forgets himself in the game and missing a ball does not stop to exculpate himself by dumb show, but rattles away after it - who does not blame his partner when he is run out - who plays like play, and not like earnest - who can say good humouredly, - runs enough I hope without mine - If such a man makes a score, players remark on all sides - Our friend deserves luck for his good humour and true spirit of the game".

Following a discussion on the art of batting relating to William Beldham or "Silver Billy" due to his silver hair, Rev. John Mitford wrote " It was a study for Phidias, to see Beldham rise to strike; the grandeur of the attitude, the settled composure of the look, the piercing lightening of the eye, the rapid glance of the bat were electrical". He seems to have possessed the three gifts essential for the making of a fine batsman - strong nerves, a keen eye and supple limbs. He is said to have been the first batsman who went out to meet the ball – up to then batsmen had been content to wait for it.

The following is a list of his publications. 1. Agnes, the Indian Captive, with other poems by the Rev. John Mitford. 2. The Poems and Works of Gray which were afterwards reprinted forming a portion of the Aldine Poets. 3. The Poems of Spencer, Milton, Dryden, Butler, Prior, Swift, Young, Parnell, Goldsmith and Falconer. 4. The Life of Milton. 5. The Poems of Vincent Bourne. 6. Sacred Specimens, selected from early English poets. 7. The Correspondence of Walpole and Mason. 8. Miscellaneous Poems, published about 6 months before he died.

In a book written and compiled by John Bowyer Nichols entitled Nichols's Illustrations of Literature of the 18th Century, dedicated to Rev. John Mitford M.A. dated 19 Feb. 1848 where he includes the letters between Edward Ledwich (the father of my great-great grandmother) and Bishop Percy covering the Ledwich correspondence, John Mitford points out a misunderstanding made by Edward Ledwich and makes the correction as follows.

"Robert Mitford belonged to the elder branch of the Mitford family. Lord Redesdale and his elder brother, the historian of Greece, to the youngest. First branch (mainline), Bertram Mitford of Mitford Castle. Second branch, Rev. John Mitford of Benhall, Suffolk. Third branch, William Mitford, of Pittshill, Sussex and the fourth and last branch, Lord Redesdale, and his elder brother, the historian of Greece" (the Mitford girls)."

As it would appear, John Mitford was a truly remarkable individual, well respected by his friends and colleagues. His work provides an excellent insight for anyone studying 18th century poets and literary personalities The Rev. John Mitford's books, notes and manuscripts are kept at the British Library and Museum.

(iii) John (Jack) Mitford

(1782-1831)

HMS Victory and a London Madhouse

"But I don't want to go among mad people," Alice remarked.

"Oh, you can't help that," said the Cat. "We're all mad here. I'm mad. You're mad."

"How do you know I'm mad?" said Alice.

"You must be," said the Cat, "or you wouldn't have come here."

Lewis Carroll

One of the most eccentric and possibly charming Mitford characters was John Mitford, commonly known as Jack. His career in the navy and as a writer is truly extraordinary. His intelligence and talents were drowned in alcohol; he died of a chest infection, saying "if my soul was on one table and a bottle of gin was on another, I would sell the former to taste the latter".

He was born at Newton Red House at Mitford, Northumberland the son of John Mitford and Dorothy Young. His uncle Bertram Mitford was the squire of Mitford and he was a cousin to Admiral Mitford. The younger son of a younger son he joined the navy as a midshipman on HMS Victory under Nelson and fought in the battle of Toulon in 1795. Three years later he served under Captain Samuel Hood on HMS Zealous in the battle of the Nile in 1798. His last naval command was in 1811 as master of HMS Philomel in the Mediterranean. Honourable mention was made of his name many times as having performed gallant deeds.

Apparently he was called back home by his wife and Lady Perceval to secure a civil service job which turned out to be a hoax. Lady Perceval had other things in mind and employed him to copy and publish letters in support of the Princess of Wales, who was devoted to her cause and campaign to better her estranged situation in the public eye. Also known as the Blackheath Affair, Bridget Viscountess Perceval was a friend of Princess Caroline who had separated from the Prince Regent and was installed in a rented house in Blackheath, close to where Bridget lived. Distraught at being separated from her daughter Princess Charlotte, Caroline attempted to contact her daughter on a number of occasions. Lady Perceval and Caroline placed letters in the press in a campaign to appeal to the Prince and his supporters. John Mitford, Lady Perceval's cousin became drawn into the campaign, his role was to deliver a series of letters to newspaper editors in favour of the Princess's case.

The letters were so libellous that proceedings were instituted against the writers, whereupon Mitford perceived the brilliant idea of getting himself shut up in a madhouse - Warburton's in Hoxton. It appears that his brain had become temporarily deranged from excessive drinking – but it's not every crafty lunatic who could turn such a story around as John Mitford did. His uncle Admiral Mitford (then a captain), only found out after it had all happened!

With the help of London mental asylum owner Thomas Warburton, following a certificate of John's insanity being sent to the Admiralty, a naval surgeon called at the 'madhouse' to verify the matter. In turn, a hopeless lunatic was substituted as John Mitford, past master of HMS Philomel, while the real John Mitford calmly attended posing as an interested spectator. The Admiralty not only granted Mitford discharge from the navy but paid him a nice sum of money in arrears due up to the date of his discharge. Mitford spent nearly a year in the Hoxton madhouse. No wonder he needed a bottle or two.

Viscountess Perceval, the Princess of Wales, and others now tried their level best to shift the blame for the newspaper articles on Mitford. The Viscountess believed that he had, at her request, destroyed all her letters to him. Some two or three had been kept and these, when produced at his trial before Lord Ellenborough in the court of King's Bench, secured his acquittal.

Mitford then wrote and published a 123 page booklet in 1814 detailing the trial, and later in 1825 he wrote a further booklet of 64 pages in two parts that focus on the management of Warburton's madhouse. In this publication, which he dedicated to Lord Redesdale, Lord Chancellor of Ireland and Viscount

Sidmouth, Secretary of State, he presented a horrible and truly grisly account of his time spent in Hoxton and his intimate knowledge of the crimes, horrors and evils of what happened in that asylum. To quote "The scoundrel in charge" …'If a man comes in here mad, we'll keep him so – if he is in his senses, we'll soon drive him out of them'.

John Mitford presents a most eloquent account of his experiences and observations, he allowed his imagination and pen full licence in writing his report. A great many of the facts and circumstances related were indeed substantially true, as later investigations discovered. Mitford describes beatings, sexual abuse of the young and vulnerable, tying-up and flogging of the awkward and helpless, and generally dehumanising and degrading treatment. The conditions of Warburton's were beyond appalling. With insufficient beds for the number of bodies, "two must squeeze into one". Warburton would cram three into a bed when pushed.

With the management of violent lunatics of all classes he claimed that these patients could readily be controlled with a leg lock, manacles and even hobbles, used when milking a cow. John writes, "I sometimes ask myself, if I live and breathe – am of the same flesh and formed by the same hand which gave life to these monsters. This asylum will receive a man or woman under any excuse, and call it insanity. Amongst the many sufferers confined in these disgraceful places are a considerable number of naval and military officers whose openness of character has been taken advantage of by interested relatives".

In conclusion John Mitford writes. "The subject is well worth legislatorial attention – is there no Member of Parliament who will come forward? Establishments something on the plan of our excellently conducted and well regulated public hospitals should be built with separate facilities for males and females. They should be open to public inspection and no man ought to be consigned to them as a patient until a jury of twelve of his nearest neighbours have pronounced him insane. But this is only my opinion and would leave it to men of better and abler judgement than myself. I have done my duty".

In Mitford's book, Lord Sidmouth is accused of getting his demented son a Civil Service appointment, a sinecure worth £3,000 a year and then shutting him up in the madhouse. Sir Francis Baring (Baring Bank) is charged with having an extraordinary fancy for sending unfortunate bank clerks to the mental asylum. The Duke of Athol, Sir Henry Parnell, Orater Hunt and others are all circumstantially accused of indulging in the luxury of such revenge. The Hoxton Warburton Asylum continued to provide care for people from the south of England for many years after the Lunacy Act of 1845. It closed in 1902, when London County Council acquired the site and built a school. Today 34 Hoxton Street, a tall, four-storey late nineteenth-century house, is the only surviving part of the old Warburton Hoxton asylum.

At one stage of his extraordinary life, Jack was a respectable and classical scholar and gentleman. However, following his discharge from the navy, over the last 14 years of his life was a downhill slide to the poorhouse. One can perhaps appreciate his state of mind, especially with what he had experienced and what he was up against, particularly the crimes and horrors of living in a madhouse.

A relative, Lord Redesdale stood by him and made every attempt to keep him on the straight and narrow but to no avail. His wife and children were cared for, otherwise they too would have been reduced to the streets of London. Jack lived by chance on odd jobs and slept in the open air in various London parks when he chose to spend his money on booze rather than accommodation. A ragged, dirty and loathsome beggar, shunned by all.

As it happened, a kindly fellow Northumbrian took pity on him in his wretched condition and recognising Jack's talents took him home and endeavoured to make him decent. Jack managed to stay sober for a few days and then, after all attempts to fit him out with a new set of clothing, he broke loose once again and refused to conform to what his friends were trying to achieve. All this attention and encouragement enabled his host to get him writing again. Jack wrote for a local periodical called the Bon Ton Gazette.

To keep the work flowing Jack lived in his kitchen cellar only to emerge when the bottle was empty. He did go crazy at times and his shoes were removed to stop him running away. This was not a problem to Jack, he ran about bare feet to the local grog shop; and even sold his coat for half a pint of gin in the middle of winter. At one stage he had an excellent pair of Wellington boots, that had been given to him by a good Samaritan, which he then sold for one shilling. The chap who bought them sold them to a pawn shop for 15 shillings and in triumph waved the money in Jack's face. Jack's retort was, "Ah! at least you suffered the cold and inconvenience".

Before his drink problems he edited a satirical journal called The Scourge and at the time of his death was writing for another dubious publication called the Quizzical Gazette. The titles are sufficient to indicate the nature of the contents. He was also employed by some religious publishers, which curiously puts him at odds with the former from a psychological point of view. Likewise he was the author of a successful nautical novel titled 'The Adventures of Johnny Newcome in the Navy, a Poem in four Cantos,' first published in 1818 under the pseudonym of Alfred Burton with sixteen coloured illustrations. The illustrator of this book, Thomas Rowlandson (1756-1827) was much like Jack Mitford and enjoyed drinking and the good life. He was one of the most successful caricaturists and book illustrators in his time and worked on many of the great classics of eighteenth century fiction. Some examples of his work are included at the back of this book.

The publisher of the novel, recognising Jack's talent gave him a shilling a day until he finished writing it. Incredible as it may appear he lived the whole of this time in Bayswater fields, sleeping on a bed of grass and nettles. For forty odd days his daily meal consisted of bread, cheese and an onion – the rest of the shilling was spent on gin. When he needed clean clothes he washed his shirt and socks in a pond. A short time before his death, during the time the Duke of Clarence came to the throne as William IV, Jack wrote the song – "The King is a True British Sailor" to suit current tastes. He managed to sell the manuscript to several different publishers, earning himself an extra supply of gin! The song became very popular in local concert halls.

Jack ended his days in relative comfort and was admitted to Saint Giles's Workhouse via a naval colleague of his, James Green who had fought with him under Admiral Nelson. The following is a copy of the last letter he ever wrote, addressed to James Green and Lord Redesdale.

"Sir, I have been so changeable in my state, that sometimes I have not strength to hold a pen to thank you for the very great kindness I have experienced at your hands. The doctor is very humane and attentive, for I cannot forget what a wretched beggar I was for any of you to notice. My breath will never recover and I truly believe my lungs are decaying fast; but I hope to get round and live a few years on Lord Redesdale's generosity and my earthly saviour Mr Green's care. He said he would leave another sovereign – but I have no extravagances to gratify; fruits and other light things are all that I require and paper, pens etc. I wish to go as near the mark as possible as I place no faith in my future hopes. The nurse is truly honest and accounts for every penny. Some clothes to sit up in would I am sure would hasten my recovery. You mentioned an old dressing gown. If you sir can favour me with your assistance on this great point, it will be an additional obligation conferred on an improvident poor wretch, who had no hope of 24 hours life when you received him into this benevolent asylum. I am sir, your truly obliged and obedient humble servant, John Mitford".

(iv) Robert Mitford

(1783-1836)

Mitford Hospital, Dhaka, Bengal

Robert Mitford worked in the British civil service for many years; posted to India he served as a collector and later as a judge at the Provincial Court of Appeal in Dhaka. Judge, Sir Robert Mitford was shocked to see the meagre medical facilities available and how people suffered. Before his death he bequeathed his property to the government of Bengal to build a facility for the welfare of marginalised and sick people. He gave a vast sum of money which was used to build Mitford Hospital. It was inaugurated on 1st May 1854 with a total of 92 beds.

It is the oldest hospital in Bengal and also one of the first hospitals in the Indian subcontinent. The initiative for building the hospital was taken in 1820 by Sir Robert Mitford (1783-1836) the Collector of Dacca (now Dhaka) and also a long serving judge of the Provincial Court of Appeal. During his time, cholera epidemics broke out regularly, spreading at an alarming rate and killing hundreds of people every day in Dhaka . It was only through the goodwill of Sir Robert and the people of Dhaka that the hospital was established. Had he not bequeathed the funds to provoke the government of Bengal into doing something, nothing would have happened. His legacy upholds his values and his dedication to his work for all to follow and appreciate to this day. It was his vision and the few good people that supported him within the government of Dhaka that created what continues to be a major hospital for all in need of medical treatment.

Today, starting with the treatment of simple but prevalent diseases like cholera, diarrhoea, fever, anaemia, etc. it has expanded vastly. It now provides multi-disciplinary treatment facilities for all diseases. The hospital occupies an oblong area of 12.8 acres of land on the banks of the River Buriganga. The main hospital complex is an 8 storied building known as the surgery building. Two other 3 storied annexes include the King Edward VII building. The hospital serves both resident and out patients, as well as pathological and diagnostic services. It serves about 2,000 out patients daily. In 1999, it had a total of 600 beds. This hospital has featured in international headlines over recent years; it not only provides health care for Dhaka residents it is also a teaching hospital and centre for research.

The dramatic events, eventual funding and final building of the very first hospital in Dhaka is something you'll only find in an Agatha Christie novel and it only took shape 18 years after Sir Robert Mitford's death. It's all detailed in a codicil to the will of Sir Robert Mitford in the court proceedings with Reynolds versus Thrupp and the East India Company. (A codicil is an additional statement that amends, rather than replaces, a previously executed will).

The Judge, Sir Robert Mitford died in Paris leaving an estate of considerable value with family property in England and personal property in India. He also left a widow and a brother, the Rev. John Mitford (covered in a previous chapter) with Mrs Reynolds his only next of kin. In 1829 Sir Robert separated from his wife and gave her an annual settlement for life. This was increased in 1835. The will dated 20 July 1835 was not disputed and the executors were Henry Neville Reynolds and Mr Thrupp.

The will, which was hand written by the testator, Sir Robert Mitford, recited the provisions made for his ex wife and excluded his brother from all benefit and gave a moiety (one-half) of the family estate he held jointly with his brother to another Robert Mitford – the son of the brother, with an annual cash legacy. After certain other personal bequests such as leaving a sufficient sum to keep his horses (in retirement) without work during the remainder of their lives, Sir Robert gave the residue of his property to the Government of Bengal, to be applied to charitable purposes for the benefit of the city of Dhaka and especially the native inhabitants in such a manner as they and the Government should think best. The executors each received a generous lump sum to ensure that all would be done correctly and properly and he finally declared that whatever alterations in the will that might become necessary, would if practicable, be made by a codicil.

On the 24th March 1836, Sir Robert travelled to Paris and shortly after his arrival took ill and booked into the Hotel Mirabeau, in Rue de la Paix. On 14th April Sir Robert asked Dr Morgan, one of three medical doctors attending to Sir Robert, to summon his nephew Henry Reynolds to come and meet him. A few days later his condition deteriorated and, realising the seriousness of his condition, Sir Robert attempted to write to Mr Thrupp to ask him to bring his will but was unable to finish the letter. Captain Jones, also staying at the hotel, kindly obliged and finished the letter. Henry Reynolds arrived in Paris on the 18th and remained with Sir Robert until his death.

The next day the three doctors, Dr Morgan, Sir Robert Churnside and Sir Augustus West, suggested to Henry that he should attend to the wishes of Sir Robert with delicacy. In the presence of two of the doctors Sir Robert dictated a few statements as a codicil to his will. "I make this a codicil to my will. Ann (referring to his sister) and you (meaning Henry and his wife), must sink everything for your own use". With his last statement he also left some money to his servant, George Chenery.

After hearing all the facts and details the court judge was obliged to give his decision. In summary with the depositions of the principal witnesses being George Chenery, Sir Robert Churnside and Sir Augustus West, the court said that the main problem was that they could not fully understand what was meant by "must sink everything for your own use"? If Sir Robert had expressed himself in a clear and intelligible manner to benefit the people mentioned, the court would have been bound, without hesitation to pronounce the papers valid.

However, throughout this conversation between Henry Reynolds and Sir Robert, Sir Robert was in the greatest agony and no mutual understanding existed as the latter was at the time suffering from biliary fever which had affected his throat and his voice, making it very difficult to make himself clearly understood.

After much deliberation and thought the learned judge said that, under the circumstances of the case, he felt himself bound to pronounce against the validity of the statements made, but with respect to the money bequeathed to his servant and analysis of former papers, he was of perfect mind and granted probate to the latter with the original will.

As such, the funds became available to establish the Mitford Hospital in Dhaka in 1854. Twenty years later Lord Northbrook the Viceroy of India travelling by special train en route for Assam* made an official state visit to Dhaka and his first call was to visit the patients at Mitford Hospital.

Later, in 1930 Mitford Hospital featured in media headlines. The acting Inspector General of Police, Francis Lowman, and Eric Hodson, Chief Superintendent of Police, were shot at and seriously wounded leaving Mitford Hospital. Francis Lowman aged 46 was shot and the bullet lodged in his spine and Eric Hodson aged 36 was wounded in the hip. Both police officers were shot by a Bengali youth who was seized by a hospital contractor, but managed to break away, leaving his revolver and slippers behind.

Today and tomorrow, its history and goodwill continues.

It is with deep gratitude and kind thanks to those who have worked and continue to work in Mitford Hospital over the many years who continue to uphold and acknowledge the goodwill of how and why it was created and the person that made it happen, Judge, Sir Robert Mitford.

Mitford Hospital, Dhaka, Bengal, taken by Fritz Kapp in 1904

(v) Admiral Robert Mitford

(1786-1780)

From Cleopatra's Needle to Howard Carter

Aged 21 years William Tyssen-Amhurst (Lord Amhurst) married his childhood sweetheart - Margaret Susan Mitford, the only daughter of Admiral Robert Mitford of Mitford, Northumberland and Hunmanby, Yorkshire. Not only did William gain a wife but also a father-in-law who had a deep passion for Egypt.

With youthful enthusiasm and energy, combined with the unlimited Tyssen-Amhurst funds William set about building up a large and remarkable collection of Egyptian artefacts. The Tyssen-Amhursts were an extremely wealthy family. The Tyssen family had been Flemish traders and acquired vast wealth which was used to purchase large estates in Hackney (north east London) and Norfolk.

Due to Admiral Mitford's long and celebrated naval career, it is believed he was on excellent terms with Khedive Mahomet Ali of Egypt and this provides the basis of an intriguing family mystery. According to family legend as recorded by one of Admiral Mitford's seven granddaughters Mary Rothes Tyssen-Amhurst - she was born in 1857 and was the eldest of the seven daughters of William Tyssen-Amhurst and Margaret Susan Mitford, they had been given an obelisk as a gift. Mary grew up surrounded by Egyptian artefacts and was known to her family and friends as May. In her memoirs Mary wrote of a visit to Alexandria. The following is taken from an unpublished document, entitled 'A Few Egyptian Memories', family photograph albums and Mary's sketchbook (dated 1873/4).

"Another drive along the sea-shore by a very bad road full of deep ruts and holes, took us to Cleopatra's needles. There were two of them. One obelisk was standing, the other one had fallen down and was partly covered with sand and rubbish. This needle belonged to us, so we looked at it with great interest. It was given by Mahomet Ali to my grandfather, after he had fitted out for him the first Egyptian man-of-war. He also gave him his portrait, a sword, and a rosary and many other things, which are in our museum at home.

We longed to be able to take the needle away, but the trouble and expense were too great – there was no possible apparatus to move it and no ship that would carry it; but after all it has reached England and now stands on the Thames Embankment, where other people besides ourselves may see and admire it". The lithograph by David Roberts 1839 clearly shows the two needles, one lying down the other standing before they were moved.

The remarkable story of the journey of Cleopatra's Needle to its present position on the Embankment, in London, is well documented. However, any part that Admiral Mitford played in the fitting out of Egyptian corvettes after being given the needle as a reward has not apparently been recorded elsewhere. However, the needle given as a reward, does have credence.

During the mid 1800s there was much discussion about bringing the obelisk to London. According to Sir Ernest Alfred Wallis Budge (1857-1934), Keeper of Egyptian Antiquities - British Museum and one of the world's leading Egyptologists, His Highness the Khedive of Egypt (Sa'id Pasha) brought the question of the removal of the obelisk to England before the British Government. As the story goes, the Khedive had let the land on which the monument lay to a certain Greek called Dimitri, who wished to develop the property he had rented, and the obelisk made it impossible for him to carry out his plans for his building project. He therefore applied to the Khedive, either to remove the obelisk or to have it buried. (This story was presented to nudge the British government to have the obelisk removed once and for all).

In turn, the Khedive politely asked the British government to remove the obelisk which Mahomet Ali had given to England more than once! So, Mary's claim is quite possible as Mahomet Ali had given the obelisk to many people with the probable thought that no one would actually remove it, due to its size and weight.

It was only in 1877 that funding and a contract was signed and finally Cleopatra's Needle arrived in London on 20 January 1878 and erected on the Victoria Embankment, between the Waterloo and Charing Cross bridges. The author visited the needle and on the pedestal are four inscriptions, which read –

North Face - Through the patriotic zeal of Erasmus Wilson FRS, this obelisk was brought from Alexandria, encased in an iron cylinder; it was abandoned during a storm in the Bay of Biscay, recovered and erected on this spot by John Dixon CE in the 42nd year of the reign of Queen Victoria 1878.

East Face - This obelisk quarried at Syene was erected at (Heliopolis) by the Pharaoh Thothmes III about 1500 BC. Lateral inscriptions were added nearly two centuries later by Rameses the Great. Removed during the Greek dynasty to Alexandria, the royal city of Cleopatra. It was there erected in the 18th year of Augustus Caesar BC 12.

West Face - This obelisk, prostrate for centuries on the sands of Alexandria was presented to the British nation AD 1819 by Mahomet Ali Viceroy of Egypt. A worthy memorial of our distinguished countrymen Nelson and Abercromby.

South Face - William Askin, Michael Burns, James Gardiner, William Donald, Joseph Benbow & William Patan. Perished in a bold attempt to succour the crew of the obelisk ship "Cleopatra" during the storm 14 October 1877.

Many questions remain unanswered. However, there is little doubt that the Amhursts were always welcomed in Egypt and this was perhaps due to the Admiral.

The Tyssen-Amhurst family home, Didlington Hall became one of the leading private museums of Egyptian artefacts in England. Seven Sekhmet statues stood outside one wing, which housed the museum. There was one statue for each of William's seven daughters. These had been part of Dr John Lee's collection at Hartwell House, acquired by William in 1865. These statues originally stood in the Temple of Mut at Karnac in Egypt, and were probably brought to Europe by Belzoni (a celebrated Egyptologist) or slightly later by one of his assistants. Now they can be seen in the Metropolitan Museum in New York.

It was at Didlington Hall that Howard Carter began his lifelong interest in Egyptology. As a boy he spent a great deal of time in Didlington Hall museum, while his artist father, Samuel Carter, was employed elsewhere in the sprawling mansion. Howard first visited Egypt with Admiral Mitford and the Amhursts on one of their trips to buy Egyptian artefacts, clearly Howard found the trip interesting and enjoyable. When the Amhurst collection, catalogued by Howard Carter, came to be sold by Sotheby's in 1921, it was the third largest private collection in England.

(vi) Squire Osbaldeston

(1786-1866)

"The best sportsman of any age or country"

The importance of the Osbaldeston family to the existence of the Mitford family has been mentioned in previous sections. This chapter is devoted to the memory of the Osbaldestons and their estate of Hunmanby in Yorkshire. Whilst there many interesting Osbaldestons, it is worth exploring an individual who was perhaps the most famous, colourful and publicised family member – the squire and sportsman George Osbaldeston, or Squire Osbaldeston, who famously rode 200 miles in 8 hours 42 minutes. He lived through India's First War of Independence and the American Civil War.

The name is pronounced Osbaldéston with the accent on the third syllable and his family home was known as Hutton Buscel as pronounced Bushell. The squire was not descended in tail male from the ancient Yorkshire family, which traces back to Richard I. His father George, son of the Rev. Dr and Mrs Wickens, assumed the name on succeeding to part of the Osbaldeston property according to the Fountayne Wentworth Will along with the Mitford family.

Robert Mitford of Mitford Castle married Mary, youngest daughter of Sir Richard Osbaldeston Kt., of Hunmanby by his second wife, Elizabeth. Philadelphia, eldest daughter of Robert and Mary Mitford, married the Rev. John Wickens, Rector of Petworth and Tillington in Sussex and they had two children George and Philadelphia. In 1770 George Wickens inherited from his mother's brother, his uncle, Fountayne Wentworth Osbaldeston, a share of the Hutton Buscel property and as required by the will had to change his name to Osbaldeston. This happened often when there was no male heir to be found and inheritance went via a maternal line. Failure to do so within six months of the will being read would have cost him his inheritance.

The other Osbaldeston property Hunmanby was inherited by the Mitford family on the same basis. Sir Richard Osbaldeston Kt., (1655-1728) was succeeded by his fourth son, Fountayne Wentworth (1695-1770). Fountayne Wentworth Osbaldeston left Hunmanby to his grand-nephew (son of his niece) Humphrey Brooke, who was likewise, obliged to change his name to Humphrey Brooke Osbaldeston. Humphrey died in 1835 leaving two daughters. The estate then passed to Bertram Mitford and then to his brother Admiral Mitford, who lived at Hunmanby Hall because the Mitfords had no family seat. This was when Mitford Hall was built. The old Osbaldeston family ended in the female line.

Squire Osbaldeston was described by his contemporaries as "the best sportsman of any age or country". It was a time when men were gentlemen and horses were transportation. His greatest fame was as Master of Hounds. His greatest failure was when he left the chase for the turf and lost more than £200,000 pounds on horse racing. Hunting proved to be his greatest passion. He had his own pack of hounds at the age of 16 and was master of 9 hunts, the most well known being the Atherstone and the Quorn Hunt. I think it was due to his short temper that he kept changing from one hunt to the other. He could also afford it!

With cricket he played for the MCC, Surrey and Sussex and, being both a gifted fast bowler and batsman, enjoyed single wicket competitions that invariably involved large side bets. In 1810 Osbaldeston teamed up with the professional Lambert and played Lord Frederick Beauclerk and Thomas Howard. The Squire fell ill and withdrew from the match but his opponents insisted it must proceed. Lambert deliberately bowled wide and to Beauclerk's fury won by 15 runs. As a direct result the MCC changed the rules of cricket to ban bowling wide.

Osbaldeston, who never could resist an opportunity for a match or wager of any kind, backed himself to the sum of 1,000 guineas to ride 200 miles in less than ten hours. A number of different horses were used, each being ridden four miles. Some were used several times – one of them Tranby, afterward imported to the USA, was ridden four times. The time of the four mile

Each squire of Mitford had his own, individual Coat of Arms, shown here are two examples. Top left John Philip Mitford. 27th Squire and top right, Edward Ledwich Mitford 28th Squire.
Below, left the London 'needle', right obelisk plaque. Bottom, Major Roland Mitford with plane and two friends.

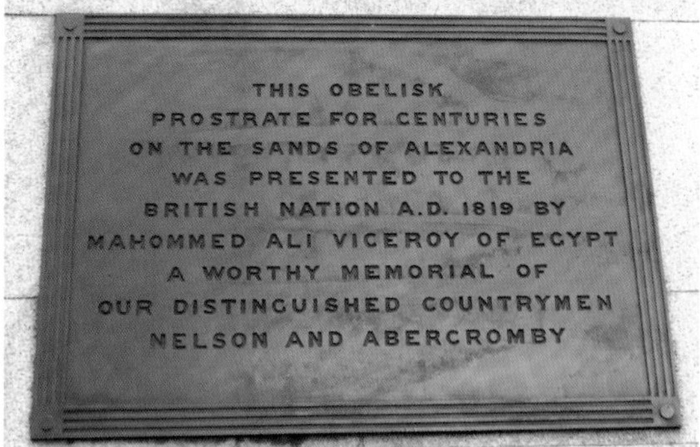

THIS OBELISK
PROSTRATE FOR CENTURIES
ON THE SANDS OF ALEXANDRIA
WAS PRESENTED TO THE
BRITISH NATION A.D. 1819 BY
MAHOMMED ALI VICEROY OF EGYPT
A WORTHY MEMORIAL OF
OUR DISTINGUISHED COUNTRYMEN
NELSON AND ABERCROMBY

Above. Bertram Lane & Brenda (McLeod) Mitford (30th Squire) arriving at Mitford Hall after the wedding and 'being pulled in' by the villagers.

Left, Bertram Mitford with son, Roland.
Above, Edward (Teddy) Mitford & Patricia Mitford in Turkey.

Opposite page top right.
Four generations of Mitford's, seated Rev. Edward holding baby John with grandfather Edward and Robert Mitford at back.
Opposite page bottom.
Squire Osbaldeston depicted in his 200 mile race against time.

Above is Bertram Mitford FRGS with young son Roland and daughter Yseulte.

George Osbaldeston

Bertram Mitford

Edward L. Mitford

SQUIRE OSBALDESTON ON EMMA IN HIS WAGER OF 200 MILES AGAINST TIME

Reproduced from the Print after Alken in the collection of General A. H. Cowie.

Above and top of page. Three plates taken from 'The Adventures of Johnny Newcome in the Navy' written by John (Jack) Mitford and published in 1904 by Methuen and Co.

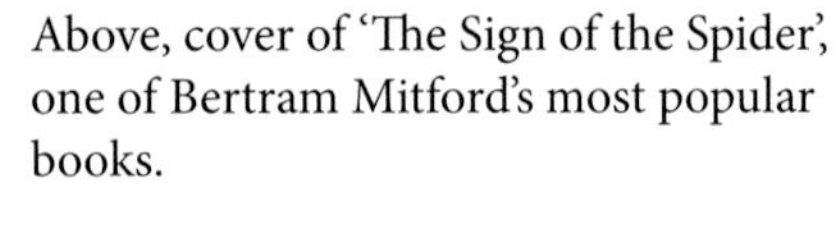

Above, cover of 'The Sign of the Spider', one of Bertram Mitford's most popular books.

Left, bronze leopard created and given to the Hout Bay community in 1963 by Ivan Mitford-Barberton in Cape Town (photograph courtesy of Matt Mercer).

Below, artwork by Admiral Mitford, on left jay and on right a common coot.

Above, Mitford coach house.

Right, An example of some rare Mitford china plate (c. 1881) showing Mitford Bridge and castle.

Below.
The grounds of Mitford Cricket Club showing the original, old red roofed pavilion and clubhouse and the new clubhouse. To the right is a large section of concrete laid down during WW II, used for armoured tank training.

Top, Blackburn Aeroplane Company 1910.

Middle, Robert Blackburn's – Blackburn Mercury plane 1911 on Filey sands – note the hanger in the background on the right. (Pictures courtesy of Filey Bay Museum).

Left, Admiral's Arch, entrance to All Saints Church, Hunmanby, Yorkshire.

Next two pages, two estate documents.

The First Schedule above referred to

First All that the Mitford Estate situate or arising in the Parishes of Mitford Dinnington Mason and Dinnington and Longframlington in the County of Northumberland including the Manor and Barony of of Mitford with its rights members and appurtenances the mansion house at Mitford together with the pleasure grounds gardens and closes enjoyed therewith and the messuages farm lands and other properties and mines and minerals held therewith particulars of which Estate are as follows:—

Name of Place	Tenant	Parishes	Acreage
The Manor and Barony of Mitford with its rights members and appurtenances.			
Mansion House at Mitford together with the pleasure grounds gardens and closes enjoyed therewith	In owners hands	Mitford	60·398
Mitford Steads	George Scott	"	474·022
East Coldside	Excors of J. Smith	"	304·775
Middle Coldside	J. Frazer	"	11·460
West Coldside	Thomas Hunter	"	316·736
Dene House	Charles Frazer	"	56·772
Mill Farm	T. P. Carmichael	"	156·530
West Molesden	Excors T. Potts	"	316·741
East Molesden	M. C. Potts	"	351·680
Land at Molesden (River Green)	S. Relph	"	3·246
Molesden Wood Cottage	J. Dixon	"	·100
West Throphill	James Smith	"	458·671
East Throphill	J. & R. Ogle	"	407·240
Newton Underwood	Wm Frazer	"	163·742
Cottage and land at Newton Underwood	J. G. Walton	"	1·600
Newton Park	Excors A. Hindmarsh	"	298·599
Newton Mill	Edward Gill	"	83·022
Lightwater	Isaac Renton	"	82·705
Cottage at Lightwater	In hand	"	·100
Pigdon	Richard Elliott	"	468·916
Maidens Hall	Misses Potts	"	444·818
Nunriding Hall	W. W. Potts	"	282·762
Cottage at Nunriding Hall	W. H. Thornton	"	·100

Name of Place	Tenant	Parishes	Acreage
Nunriding Moor	Excors R. Gill	Mitford	177·809
House at West Throphill	J. W. Swinhoe	"	·150
Quarry House (Farm, and Quarry at Coalhouses)	G. Young	"	10·635
Prestwick Carr Allotment	W. McCain	Dinnington	12·000
Longframlington Allotment	Excors G. Renwicks	Longframlington	125·000
Pigdon House and land	H. B. Speke	Mitford	11·665
House and land at Mitford	J. Brown	"	
Shop at Mitford	A. Fisher	"	3·500
House and land at Mitford	Mrs Morton	"	
Cottage and Garden at do do do do	J. Brown	"	
Garden at Mitford	J. Brown	"	
Cottage and Garden at Mitford	B. Buddles	"	
House, Garden, byre and land	Mrs Marshall	"	24·000
Post Office (Old School House and Garden)	Miss Brown	"	
House and Garden (View Cottage)	N. Hood	"	
House and Garden		"	
Cottage & Gardens at Dinnington	Various tenants	Dinnington	2·500
The mines and minerals under the allotments of Longframlington Common	Not let	Longframlington	920·119
The mines and minerals under the allotments of Prestwick Carr Common	East Walbottle Coal Company Limited	Mason and Dinnington	1012·119
Woodlands Mitford Township	In Owners hands	Mitford	113·000
" Molesden "	"	"	97·000
" Newton Parks "	"	"	64·500
" Newton Underwood "	"	"	25·000
" Throphill "	"	"	14·000
" Pigdon "	"	"	187·000
" Nunriding "	"	"	94·000
Rivers and Roads Mitford Township	"	"	45·781
Rivers and Roads Newton and Throphill Townships	"	"	27·950
Rivers & Roads Pigdon Township	"	"	9·306

The Advowson and perpetual right of presentation of and to the Vicarage and Parish Church of Mitford in the County of Northumberland and the rights and appurtenances thereto belonging.

turns, ranged between 8 and 12 minutes. Some of the horses used were hacks and hunters owned by George himself, but in order to make better time he hired or borrowed a number of racehorses. This celebrated match took place at Newmarket Racecourse on 5 November 1831.

The Squire, dressed in purple silks and black velvet cap rode through several rain showers, one fall and many stops for brandy and food, achieved the 200 mile in less than 9 hours riding a total of 28 horses. To this day, his autobiography serves as a thoroughly entertaining story of his life & escapades. Here follow some of his words, taken from his autobiography.

George was born a Cockney in Welbeck Street, London in 1787, but was also called a Yorkie because his inherited estate was in Yorkshire. In those days mothers preferred to have their babies in London rather than chance the Yorkshire countryside. Being the only son George was the object of the greatest anxiety and interest to his doting mother, especially being the heir to a large fortune and estate. He had the power to terminate the entail when he reached 21 years, which he did.

In his own words. "My mother was very extravagant, fond of society, gave large parties and led a very fashionable life. Here I may be permitted to make use of a sporting phrase 'great truth in breeding' – I inherited her propensities, extravagance and imprudence. Bred up in luxury and extravagance from the age of six years with the prospect of a large family estate to come my way at twenty-one, I became reckless and thoughtless of the future and trusted to men who proved to be untrustworthy.

A fair calculation will show I have lost nearly £200,000 from betting and horse racing over a period of 45 years and a further £100,000 through the misdeeds of shady people! I blame my own folly and extravagance. I am an example of 'A fool and his money are soon parted'.

When I was thirteen, I was transferred to Eton. Having arrived at a more mature age for mischief, I committed a good many sins and broke many rules, most of them athletic in character. I could beat any boy at single-handed cricket or any boy of my age at boxing. I belonged to the first rowing boat in the school and our crew could beat any other from Windsor Bridge to Surley Hall. Bumping one another's boats was the fashion then, but now it's called fouling.

Being a wild, playful and healthy boy, I was fonder of sport than attending to my lessons and I frequently got flogged for not being perfect in them, along with other transgressions. Dr Goodall, or 'Silvertip' as old Etonians will remember, was headmaster and Dr Keate under master. The former was an excellent master and a fine man, good and kind, the latter was a little crab – very unpopular, severe and overly eccentric".

It was during his time at Eton and his weekends and time out that George took to hunting and shooting.

"I became the laughing stock of my sisters who used to say that if I ever shot anything they would eat it raw, feathers, fur and all. Shortly after that I bought home my first victims, a partridge and a hare and tried to make the girls keep their word. Of course I failed, but they left me alone after that.

Having sown some wild oats I was not so reckless at Oxford. I settled down a little and enjoyed life at Brazenose college. I kept two hunters and hunted three days a week. I went poaching and kept up my rowing as this provided the chance to have a meal and a few pints at the Star and Garter and we generally got drunk and ended up in fights and rows with the villagers when retuning to our colleges. I also took up cricket, tennis and pigeon shooting.

When I turned twenty I left Oxford and went home. It was soon after my return that the present Earl Fitzwilliam, then Lord Milton, contested the county of York (1807), his opponents being William Wilberforce and Lord Harewood, then Lord Lascelles. I believe 20,000 voters polled and of these Lord Milton had 9,000 voters, but he obtained a majority over his opponents of only 150 or 200 votes. He was a Whig. Lord Lascelles was a Tory, as also, I believe, was William Wilberforce.

Had Wilberforce not been standing Lord Milton's majority would have been much larger, for he was supported by most of the Dissenters as well as by a good proportion of the gentry". A dissenter (from the Latin dissentire, "to disagree"), is one who disagrees in matters of opinion, belief, etc, in the social and religious history of England and Wales. "I am not sure whether William Wilberforce was a Dissenter or not; his extraordinary popularity with all sects and classes was chiefly due of course, to his unrelenting energy and the freedom of slaves. He was a little thin man and looked exactly like a primitive Methodist priest and his voice corresponded with his appearance. I believe his election expenses were almost entirely defrayed by subscription (£64,455). It was said that the election cost Lord Milton £100,000.

My mother was a most enthusiastic politician, devoted to supporting Lord Milton. She actually canvassed every voter within 25 miles of Hutton Bushell, and was universally acknowledged as the major reason for his victory. Not many ladies did such a thing in those days. During this election stories flowed showing the pride of some of our aristocrats.

Lord Fitzwilliam, father of the late earl and grandfather of the present peer, was an intimate friend of the then Earl of Carlisle, who had been a school fellow of his. As the Earl had considerable influence locally, owing to his large estates adjoining Malton, for which borough Lord Fitzwilliam returned two members, the latter applied to the Earl to render him all the assistance he could in favour of his son, Lord Milton. The Earl's answer – according to popular report was 'My dear Fitzwilliam, whatever votes I can command you shall have – but cannot stoop to ask a favour of any plebian'."

"I was, as I have said, the only son and had the power to cut off the entail – thus being of intense interest to my mother and far more value to her than all my sisters". The first thing George did was to cut the entail, so securing the future security of his mother and sisters. With the entail the Hutton Buscel estate and its annual income of £10,500 for life would go to the nearest male heir and would completely exclude all George Osbaldeston's four sisters and they would lose their home and income. Hence the reason for the daughters to make a good marriage to ensure their future security. Entail was abolished in 1925.

When George turned 21 a big party was arranged by the family with the usual display of joy and good fun for all, including roasting an ox and inviting everyone from far and wide. The horses were moved to the farm yard and the stables, coach-houses and out buildings were made available for temporary accommodation for the helpless guests to be made as comfortable as possible until they recovered from the merriment, beer and wine.

He eventually exhausted what was left of his considerable fortune but achieved his life ambition of being one of England's greatest sportsmen. Pierce Egan's excellent Book of Sports, consisting of some 400 pages and published in 1832 is dedicated to George Osbaldeston. In his day he was Master of Hounds, best rider, best shot, best boxer and best cricketer in England. Along with all the stories about the Squire's hunting exploits on and off the field that fuelled his reputation his petulance and temper gave cause to his numerous disputes and amazing lifestyle. He sold his estates to cover his debts and with what was left over at 65 married Elizabeth Williams, a wealthy widow and lived in Regents Park until he died in 1866. A life well lived.

(vii) Mary Russell Mitford

(1787-1855)

Her life and the great British mudbath

Mary Mitford wrote only because she had to, to make ends meet. Money was needed to pay for the debts and extravagances of her lovable but spendthrift father, Dr George Mitford. In her school letters home she called her parents "my darlings" and her father was, in her own words, "a cheerful and speculative man – who not only enjoyed life but spent everyone's money and something more – he made every living creature around him love him, lend to him and forgive him". As a result, his daughter's life was sacrificed to writing and literature.

Mary was born at Alresford in Hampshire. Her mother Mary Russell was a wealthy heiress related to the dukes of Bedford her father was from the Mitford family of Northumberland, he graduated from Edinburgh University and assisted with a famous, pioneering London medical practice as a doctor for a short time (this will be covered in more detail later). Mary was a precocious only child and the apple of her parents eyes. Her education was the best that could be had, she was sent to St Quentin's school in Chelsea, London and encouraged in every area to distinguish herself. She did just that. She developed a lifelong interest in French literature and studied Latin.

This Mitford family was wealthy in those days so their daughter participated in society activities and learned everything that was considered right for a young lady to do. Her youthful confidence with her own judgement and wisdom provided her with an early degree of independence and maturity.

At fifteen she could confidently state her preference to various works of the classical writers Pope, Homer and Dryden. "Dryden is so fond of triplets and Alexandrines that it is much heavier reading, although being more harmonious than Pope, some of his lines are so careless that I shall not be sorry when I have finished it .... I am now reading that beautiful opera of Metastasio (Italian poet), Themistocles (Greek politician and general), and when I have finished that, I shall read Tasso's 'Jerusalem Delivered' she adds. How you would dote on Metastasio, my sweet Tod!" (a nickname for her father). "I am much flattered my darlings" (referring to her parents) she writes, "by your praises for my last letter, but don't have the vanity to deserve them. It has never been my ambition to write like my darlings, though I fear I shall never attain their style." This amiable, confident, affectionate, warm-hearted and self assured girl was a born writer.

For over fifty years she continued to present her rash, sudden judgements, opinions some sound, some superficial and her outbursts of exaggerated fondness for her father. He was her "sweet Tod" her "best-beloved darling", and always the object of gushing fondness and if any negatives did exist, they were well concealed. Her letters were charming, amusing and enjoyable. Mary's relationship with her father gave shape and colour to her life.

Considerable misfortune which took hold of her later life was in total contrast to her cheerfulness and good natured spirit. Although she suffered bleak adversity and selfishness from her father, her noble and affectionate character never yielded for a moment to one single unloving thought. His career as a doctor was beyond belief as explained in later paragraphs.

By 1820, her father with his card playing, lavish entertaining, running packs of greyhounds, his house building and horse stables had reduced the family to poverty. He squandered thirty thousand pounds in a few years and twenty thousand more which his daughter won on the Irish lottery. A birthday present from her father she chose the numbers 2224, which added together makes ten, her age at the time. Her father promptly spent the money!

Apparently, having spent all his wife's money he then ran through this glorious windfall, the lottery prize of £20,000 around £1,000.000 today. When the money ran out, he had to depend on his daughter's talent. The nearest disagreeable comment she ever made about him is "I have to provide for expenses over which I have no more control than my dear dog Dash". She loved dogs.

It was Mary who gave the famous spaniel Flush to her friend Elizabeth Barrett Browning. Flush was three times stolen in London, causing his mistress great distress. Virginia Woolf wrote an imaginative biography of Flush.

Mary's father George was a great lover of coursing and Mary was initiated into the running of the family kennels at an early age. Her letters to her friends were full of descriptions of the greyhounds, their breeding, activities and training. Her comments were later criticised in the press as being "unladylike". However, she could write about animals in a style that other writers like Scott or Cowper could not equal. The tenderness, the humour and wonderful sympathy which she always displays upon her favourite topic are possibly unrivalled in English literature. Here follows a quote from a small part of what she wrote about the memories and virtues of Moss-trooper, a beloved greyhound, which was never intended for publication and was found in a sealed envelope with some of the dog's hair. In perfect elegance she writes…

"His coat was of the finest and most glossy black, with no white, except a very little under his feet (pretty white shoe-linings, I used to call them) – one little beautiful white spot, quite small in the very middle of his neck, between his chin and breast – and a white mark on his bosom. His face was singularly beautiful; the finest black eyes, very bright and yet sweet and fond and tender – eyes that seemed to speak; a beautiful complaisant mouth, which used sometimes to show one of the long, white teeth at the side; a jet black nose; a brow which was bent and flexible, like Mr Fox's, and gave great sweetness and expression and a look of thought to his dear face. There was never such a dog!

His temper was beyond comparison, the sweetest ever known. Nobody ever saw him out of temper. Thank God, he went off without suffering. He must have died in a moment. I thought I should have broken my heart when I came home and found what had happened. George and Frank buried him and Granny, Drum and I, Moses, Whim and Molly were mourners. Everybody is so sorry. Everybody loved him – "dear saint," as I used to call him, and as I do not doubt he now is!

No human being was ever so faithful, so gentle, so generous and so fond. I shall never love anything half so well. My own beloved Mossy, Heaven bless you! His delight at seeing me when I had been out in the gig was inexpressible. He knew the sound of the wheels and used to gallop to meet me, talking his own pretty talk. He met me in this way at the white gate on the Thursday before he died on the Saturday. Whilst I had him I was always sure of having one who would love me alike in riches or in poverty – who always looked at me with looks of the fondest love – always faithful and always kind. To think of him was a talisman against vexing thoughts. A thousand times I have said "I want my Mossy," when that dear Mossy was close by, and would put his dear black nose under my hand on hearing his name".

These lines were written in 1819, the turning point of her life with the ruin of her family.

In 1820, their grand and spacious family home Bertram House, built and named after the barons of Mitford, was sold and they moved to a small tumble-down cottage at Three Mile Cross, a little village between Reading and Basingstoke. Here Mary discovered that her literary talent, instead of supplementing the family income must now provide it. She kept up her friendships with many of the leading literary personalities of the time. Sir Walter Scott who wrote the series of Waverley novels, Robert Burns, Percy Bysshe Shelley, William Wordsworth, Samuel Taylor Coleridge, John Mitford and Jane Austen. For nearly twenty years her writing was incessant. Tragedies, essays, tales and her book "Our Village" poured from her pen and kept the wolf from the door. Here is an amusing note penned with an excellent ending, about Jane Austen.

"I have discovered that our great favourite Miss Austen is a fellow country woman and mother knew all the family very intimately. She an old maid (I beg her pardon, I mean a young lady) that Mamma knew before her marriage. Mamma says she was the prettiest, silliest, most affected, husband-hunting butterfly she ever remembers. A friend who visits her now, says she has stiffened into the most perpendicular, precise, taciturn piece of single blessedness that ever existed, and that till "Pride and Prejudice" showed what a precious gem was hidden in that unbending cause. She was no more regarded in society than a poker or a fire screen. The case is very different now; she is still a poker, but a poker of whom everyone is afraid."

In Reading around 1823 the corn market going down from St Lawrence's Church was one of the best shopping areas. On Saturdays it was packed and the largest in Berkshire. Here follows a vivid insight, to quote Mary Mitford

"From the poor farmer with his load of corn, up to the rich meal man and the great proprietor all the landed interest is there, mixed with jobbers and chapmen of every description, cattle-dealers, millers, brewers, maltsters…..carriers, carters, errand-boys, tradesmen, shop-men, apprentices, gentlemen's servants, and gentlemen in their own persons, mixed with all the riff-raff of the town…

Noise is the prime characteristic of the Reading market-day, from the heavy rumbling of so many loaded wagons over the paved marketplace, to the crash of crockery-ware as the stall is knocked down by the impetus of a cart full of turnips…

But the noisiest place is the Piazza, appropriated by long usage to the female vendors of fruit and vegetables, certain old women…..with the genius for vituperation for which ladies of their profession have long been celebrated".

Of the English countryside and cricket she wrote. "I was this afternoon for an hour on Heckfield Heath, a common dotted with cottages and a large piece of water backed by woody hills; the nearer portion of ground a forest of oak and birch, hawthorn, holly and fern, intersected by grassy glades; a road winding through; and behind us the tall trees of Stratfield Saye Park (the family seat of the dukes of Wellington).

On an open space, just large enough for the purpose, a cricket match was going on – the older people sitting by on benches; the younger ones lying about under the trees; and a party of boys just seen glancing backward and forward in a sunny glade, where they were engaged in an equally merry and far more noisy game. Well, there we stood, Ben and I and Dash, watching and enjoying the enjoyment we witnessed. And I thought if I had no pecuniary anxiety, if my dear father were stronger and our dear friend well, I should be the happiest creature in the world, so strong was the influence of that happy scene.

I doubt if there is any scene in the world more animating or delightful than a cricket match and I don't mean a set match at Lord's. The cricket I mean is a real solid old fashioned match between neighbouring parishes, where each attacks the other for honour and supper, glory and half a crown a man. If there be any gentlemen amongst them, it is well – if not, it is so much the better.

Your gentleman cricketer is in general rather an anomalous character. Elderly gentlemen are obviously good for nothing; and young beaux are, for the most part, hampered and trammelled by dress and habit ; the stiff cravat, the pinched-in waist, the dandy walk – oh, they will never do for cricket!

Now, our country lads, accustomed to the flail or the hammer (blacksmiths are capital batsmen), have the free use of their arms; they know how to move their shoulders; and they can move their feet too – they can run; then they are so much better made, so much more athletic, and yet so much more graceful and supple. A village match is the thing – where our highest officer is but a little farmer's second son; where a day worker is our bowler, and a blacksmith our long stop; where the spectators consist of the retired cricketers, the veterans of the green, the careful mothers, the girls, and all the boys of two parishes, together with a few amateurs, little above them in rank, and not at all in pretension; where laughing and shouting and the very ecstasy of merriment and good humour, prevail"

Mary's father's medical career was in total and complete contrast. For a short while he joined the practice of a famous London quack, a Scotsman called Dr James Graham, a pioneer sexologist (as someone has called him), who opened what he called "The Temple of Health" in a house in Adelphi Terrace. The rooms were apparently full of glass globes and bottles, marble statues, figures of dragons, stained glass and other theatrical props, and buzzing electrical equipment while the air was drugged with incense and the ears charmed with the strains of music. All this was well advertised in the only newspapers available in those days. In one of the advertisements or announcements as they were referred to then, he expounded on his transcendent abilities which the world could not match.

He professed to be able to provide the whole art of enjoying health and vigour of body and mind and of preserving and exalting personal beauty and loveliness for at least 100 years. His rooms were well frequented by the rich and aged London population. One of his remedies for ensuring fabulous health and longevity was the frequent use of mud baths. To gain acceptance to this practice he would often host demonstrations assisted by Dr Mitford and was seen in his garden immersed in mud and accompanied by a lady he called Vestina the Goddess of Health. This was no other than the notorious Emma Lyon, also known as Emma Hart, who afterwards became celebrated as the second wife of Sir William Hamilton, the British Ambassador at Naples and the fascinating Cleopatra who infatuated Lord Nelson. While sitting in the mud bath she had her hair elaborately dressed in the current fashion (like an elevated bird's nest I believe) with powder, flowers, feathers and pearls. To round off the experience there was a sumptuously furnished room with an enormous celestial bed as the centrepiece. The bed was filled with fresh oat straw mixed with rose leaves, lavender and horse hair from English stallions.

As lovers lay in the bed, listening to soft music perhaps played on harps and violins, breathing the fragrant scented air they could gaze up and stare into the large mirror suspended from the ceiling. The phrase "Be fruitful, multiply and replenish the earth" was inscribed on the headboard. For the night it cost £50.

The full course consisted of a lifelong supply of the elixir of life (the doctor's secret potion), until they reached a 'century of age' and as many mud baths as they would care to have until 100 years for a payment of £100 in advance. Apparently half the nobility of London flocked to this miracle- working professor and doctor, especially the frustrated nobility that were desperate for a heir. Even the young Sir Walter Scott attended to have his leg cured but more so to watch the spectacle of well-known London personalities immersed naked in the all British mud bath or twitching and jolting about while undergoing electrical and magnetic treatment.

This Temple of Health reminds the author of the charming film starring Hugh Dancy, Maggie Gyllenhaal and Rupert Everett entitled "Hysteria" Based on the true story of Joseph Mortimer Granville's invention of the first electro mechanical vibrator around 1883 called "Granville's Hammer". This was originally designed for muscular disorders and later used by London doctors (quacks) for the treatment of hysteria.

From the Adelphi, Drs Graham and Mitford moved onwards and upwards to Schomberg House in Pall Mall to a new and more dazzling Temple of Health. Dr Graham engaged the services of two enormous porters or doormen and dressed them up in gold lace and huge hats and when off duty their job was to wander about London and distribute flyers from house to house. Apparently these giants were called Gog and Magog associated with Guildhall. The place was crowded day after day by a charmed audience eager to hear Vestina the Goddess of Health present her evening lectures and health services.

As advertised, "Vestina, the rosy goddess of health, presides at the evening lecture, assisting at the display of the celestial meteors and of that sacred vital fire over which she watches and whose application in the cure of diseases she daily has the honour of directing." The descriptive exhibition of her apparatus in the daytime is conducted by the officiating junior priest. This was of course, Dr George Mitford. Naturally this was all too much to continue forever and it soon lost its charm. It eventually closed down after someone was apparently murdered there by having a red hot poker thrust through his body. Dr Graham then decided onto take a grand tour of England and Scotland and off he went. At his is point Dr George Mitford decided to end his medical career. Mary nursed her mother and father through ill health right up to their deaths in 1830 and 1842 respectively. She was able to provide an income that embraced their needs of a pony-chaise, food on the table, a bottle of claret and well fed dogs at heel – in front of the fire place on a cold winter's night. Her father left a debt of over £1,000 which she accepted to pay.

Mary's difficult situation didn't pass unnoticed and it was addressed in the form of a subscription of 37 people headed by the Earl of Radnor, Sir Throckmorton, Philip Pusey, Lord Barrington, Charles Russell, Lord Viscount of Chelsea, Sir Claudius Hunter – Lord Mayor of London and the support of four banks (now part of the London banks today) and friends, £1,500 was raised and the debt was settled. Her health broke down and in 1837 she received a pension from the Crown that kept her comfortable for the last 18 years of her life. She died at Swallowfield, in Berkshire in 1855 at the age of 68 years.

Mary Russell Mitford

(viii) Edward Ledwich Mitford

FRGS (1811-1912)

7000 Miles on horseback through 16 countries

The first person to present a plan to the British Government leading to the Balfour Declaration and the creation of Israel.

Edward Ledwich Mitford lived to be over 100 years of age. Born on the 31st October 1811, and four years old during the Battle of Waterloo, when George III was King – Edward lived through the reigns of six sovereigns.

It is possible to view in Mitford Church, Northumberland, a framed telegram message of goodwill sent by King George V from Sandringham to Edward Mitford, dated and stamped on 31 October 1911 at Mitford Post Office, exactly 100 years to the day.

Edward's reply was as follows. "To Lord Stamfordham – please convey to His Majesty the most loyal expression of my thanks for his very gracious message of congratulation, and pray assure him of my deepest devotion at all times to his throne and person". Two days later Edward was out and about greeting the Morpeth Hunt in Mitford Hall Park.

With a love of life, travel and adventure, combined with a remarkable facility for acquiring languages Edward travelled to many strange and distant lands, where no Englishman had been before.

After completing his education in France (his studies included French and German) Edward started his travels, at the age of 18 in Morocco, and four years later as Consular Agent at Mazagan or El Jadida, as it is known today, a port city on the Atlantic coast of Morocco. In this capacity as British Consul, he soon found himself "up against" the Moorish government who had kept the trade of the country in their own hands. The young consular agent did his utmost to open the port to worldwide trade, a step which brought him into sharp conflict with the ruling powers, who were naturally disinclined to give up their pleasures and profitable privileges. He resigned and left the country in 1835. His five years in residence and travelling about Morocco had been of great advantage to him in many ways, notably in enabling Edward to gain a good knowledge of Arabic, which was of inestimable value to him in his later travels.

Based on tragic facts, he wrote a story entitled "The Arab's Pledge – A Tale of Morocco in 1830", published by Hatchards, 187 Picadilly, London in 1867. This book covers some stirring incidents during his residence there and the state of oppression under which Jews suffered in Morocco. The book illustrates the character of the people of West Barbary. The Barbary Coast is the old term for the coastal regions and cities throughout the middle and western coastal regions of North Africa – what is now known as Morocco, Algeria, Tunisia, and Libya. It is believed that as a result of this book and the demands made by Sir Moses Montefiore (President of the Jewish Board of Deputies) along with the forceful protests from the British Government, there was some measure of relief from repression. Clearly it was this experience that motivated his later appeal to the British Government.

Around 1840, religious and political groups alike favoured the resettlement of Palestine by Jews or even the creation of a Jewish commonwealth.

In Franz Kobler's book "The Vision Was There - A History of the British Movement for the Restoration of the Jews to Palestine", possibly the best reference written on the subject at the time, "Franz Kobler writes of my great-great grandfather Edward Ledwich Mitford". This book shows the trends in British thinking that gave rise to the Restoration Movement and resulted in the British Mandate over Palestine from which emerged the State of Israel.

"In 1845, two high colonial officials Edward Ledwich Mitford and Colonel Gawler, presented two opposite political opinions which were to set the course of history as we know it today. Edward Mitford stood for the establishment of a Jewish State, while Gawler distrusted such "wild schemes" and recommended the colonization of Palestine as part of the Turkish Empire". To this, Edward published his second book "An Appeal in Behalf of the Jewish Nation in connection with British Policy in the Levant" also published by Hatchards, London in 1845. Edward's plan laid out the foundations leading to the Balfour Declaration of 2 November 1917.

In his 1845 book, Edward Mitford, one of Lord Palmerston's colleagues in the Foreign Service (served as both Foreign Secretary and as Prime Minister), highlighted his opinion of the Jewish people possessing the qualities of "fortitude and perseverance" being responsible for the miracle of their continuity. For this remarkable and creative people, Edward Mitford demanded an independent State. Up until this time there had never been a state in Palestine, an Arab State, a Muslim State or a Palestinian State. Britain was not in the business of making nations and countries but rather wanted to ensure continued stability and economic continuity and control for its long term strategic protection of its trade route to India and the opening of the Suez Canal in 1869. Edward was one of the very few British Government officials who had an intimate, detailed and documented knowledge of Palestine and Middle East countries. He was fluent in Arab dialects.

"The plan I would propose is, first, the establishment of the Jewish nation in Palestine, as a protected state, under the guardianship of Great Britain, secondly their final establishment, as an independent State, when the parent institutions shall have acquired sufficient force and vigor to allow this tutelage being withdrawn..."

With various waves of settlers arriving in Palestine (likewise in South Africa and other British colonies) from the early 1820's, Edward Mitford astutely was quick to highlight the dilemma of the indigenous population and their attitude towards Jewish immigrants - his statement was very relevant. "The country, compared with its size, is at present thinly populated, yet the pressure caused by the introduction of so large a body of strangers upon the actual inhabitants might be attended with injurious results. Before attempting to make a settlement it would be desirable that the country should be prepared for their reception. This might be done by inducing the Turkish Government to make the local inhabitants fall back upon the extensive and partially cultivated countries of Asia Minor, where they might be put in possession of tracts and allocations, equally advantageous and far superior in value to those they abandoned". As well appreciated - the early settlers had to carve out their existence and living from barren and rocky land, which later led to the kibbutz programme and creation of employment and agricultural projects, continued to this day.

In the build up to his appeal Edward includes a synopsis from his book "An Arab's Pledge – A Tale of Morocco" published in 1867 which presents factual evidence of the cultural differences between the Muslim and Jewish cultures portrayed through the fatal and brutal killing of an innocent Jewish girl, burnt alive. This book vividly recalls pieces from his manuscript of a third and later book that was published in 1884, in two volumes, covering his overland journey on horseback from London to Colombo in (Ceylon) Ski Lanka, where he experienced the actual circumstances, as related in this book.

In his own words, the introduction to his book starts off as follows. "The purpose of this book is three-fold. Firstly – to expose the injustice and cruelty which the Jewish nation endures, especially at the hands of the Muslims. Secondly, to appeal to the British people and the ministers of the British Empire, in their behalf, and thirdly to point out how England may remedy the evils complained of, and at the same time very considerably... promote the strength of her political position and the prosperity of her colonial dependencies". The direct religious question is avoided as much as possible.

"The time is right for mighty changes and whatever events may happen, will be brought about by the natural course of providence". He leaves the reader to form his own judgement and decision. It was around this time that the popular phrase was used "A country without a people for a people without a country" or "A country without a nation for a nation without a country".

His appeal goes on to state the practicalities and process of achieving an independent state with regards to worldwide opinion, how it is to be achieved and managed - the position of Russia and other European countries and their influence in the Middle East. Edward died five years before the Balfour Declaration of 2 November 1917. Everything detailed in Edward's book and the plan he laid out in 1845 took place and happened, it set the framework for the British mandate that followed in 1920-1948. This important, historical document, out of print and hidden in the family archives, has now been edited and republished in 2015 by Edward's great-great grandson Hugh, under the title "British Policy in the Middle East and the Creation of Israel".

Foreign Secretary, Arthur James Balfour sent the following letter to Baron Rothschild in regard to the establishment of a national home in Palestine for the Jewish people. "His Majesty's Government view with favour the establishment in Palestine of a national home for the Jewish people, and will use their best endeavours to facilitate the achievement of this object, it being clearly understood that nothing shall be done which may prejudice the civil and religious rights of existing non-Jewish communities in Palestine, or the rights and political status enjoyed by Jews in any other country".

Edward was a recognized specialist on the Middle East - actively engaged in British foreign policy and intimate friends with many of the leading Politicians including Sir Moses Montefiore, President of the Jewish Board of Deputies for 28 years. Little did he know that some years later in the 1930's the British Labour Party Politician, Sir Oswald Mosely, (a potential candidate for Prime Minister) would establish a new party called the "British Union of Fascists, which claimed the Jews were leading Britain to war?

Not only that, a relative, Diana Mitford married Bryan Guinness, heir to the Guinness brewery fortune, and several years later, having met at a dinner party, fell in love with Sir Oswald Mosley. They married in secret while staying with Joseph and Magda Goebbels (Hitler's second in command) in Berlin. Based on her older sister Nancy's testimony and Diana's attempt to set up a German radio station across Europe, to broadcast propaganda – with an income from advertising, Diana and Sir Oswald spent three years in Holloway prison. The Mitford girls are detailed in a later chapter.

To cap it all, along with this, Unity Mitford, Diana's sister, having established herself as an intimate friend of Adolf Hitler - openly publicized herself as a "Jew hater", reported throughout the British and international press. Hitler himself, provided Unity with an apartment to live in, in Munich, Germany. As recorded, when Unity went to look over the flat and her new home she was delighted, while the Jewish owners cowered, unable to say anything - they were later removed. In fact most of Lord Redesdale's, or the David Freeman-Mitford family and children, the Mitford Girls... became Nazi, fascist and communist sympathizers. A third sister, Jessica, became a communist and emigrated to America.

According to my parents, the family, uncles and cousins took a long time to get over all this, if at all. No love was lost and the rift was never healed.

Back to Edward. After a brief spell back in England, and once again with the irresistible call of the Middle East, Edward was to find himself, this time with a young companion who would later rise to fame as Sir Austen Henry Layard, to become Under-Secretary of State for Foreign Affairs in the reign of Queen Victoria. Edward was about to undertake the most adventurous and perilous journey of his life. To ride 7,000 miles on horseback through 16 countries.

A journey that would take two years and ten months and covered 10,000 miles overland, with 7,000 miles on horseback. It was completed before telephones existed and photography was invented. The reasons which induced Edward to undertake this amazing journey are best explained by Edward himself, in the opening paragraph of his book, "A Land March from England to Ceylon".

"In the year 1839, after five year's residence and travelling Morocco, I found myself in the unenviable position of being without occupation, when my attention was directed to the probability of employment in the colony of Ceylon, either in the government service or in the newly opened enterprise of coffee planting. To reach Ceylon I must either take the long sea voyage round the Cape or the shorter and inconvenient one by the Mediterranean and the Red Sea, with a caravan across the Isthmus of Suez. But moved by the love of travel, after consulting the map, I resolved to take the journey entirely by land. By taking a south-east line through southern Europe, Central Asia and India, I could reach my destination with no more sea than the Straits of Dover, the ferry of the Bosphorus and the Strait of Adam's Bridge, through most interesting and little known country.

As a matter of fact, due to tiredness and ill health, Edward made an addition to the distance covered by sea, by accepting an invitation to travel a short distance by boat to Bombay. This avoided taking a circuitous land route and allowed him time to rest and recover. Also, the reader may like to reflect and take a perspective view on the enormity of Edward's undertaking especially when compared to circumstances in the 21st century.

As mentioned earlier, Edward, who was then 28 years of age, had Austen Henry Layard, a young man of 22 years as a companion. Apparently, an agreeable companionship for as long as it lasted, as to Edward's regret (or otherwise) when they parted company half way. Austen Layard admits in his autobiography that one of his independent ventures to visit the ruins of Petra was foolhardy. In fact he was lucky to come out of it alive. "The consul and acquaintances considered me guilty of unjustifiable foolhardiness in undertaking so dangerous a journey under such conditions and foretold that all manner of mishaps were certain to befall me, the least of which would be that I should be stripped to the skin and have to find my way back to Jerusalem naked and barefoot.

They were right. I had little experience of Arabs and of travelling the desert. I should have listened. But, I had romantic ideas about Bedouin hospitality and believed in the culture of the Bedouin tribes, trusting to their respect for their guests, that I should incur no danger. I did not know that the Arab tribes who inhabit the country to the south and east of the Dead Sea differ much from the Bedouins of the desert".

Layard and Mitford travelled through the Ottoman lands, visiting Constantinople (where Layard nearly died of malaria, which recurred in following years) and Jerusalem. As stated, his reckless journey alone to see Petra and other ancient sites east of the Dead Sea, where he was robbed and nearly killed by tribesmen was frowned upon. They stayed in Mosul and Baghdad. In August 1840, in Persia, now Iran, the two parted company, as Layard, who had become enamoured with the simplicity and independence of local life, preferred to stay in the region. He read local history, learned Arabic and Persian, and spent time in the Bakhtiari Mountains with a tribe which was resisting the oppression of the Shah.

As it happened, Edward decided that his traveling companion was incorrigible. If Layard was going to join with the Bakhtiari — a tribe regarded as "a race of robbers, treacherous, cruel, and bloodthirsty", then he wanted none of it. By luck, he gained the patronage of a great and powerful Bakhtiari chieftain, Mehemet Taki Khan, a man able to command a force of thousands of men with a dramatic outcome. In the fortress of Kala Tul the Khan's ten-year-old son lay dying of fever. Apparently at the point of death, "the father appealed to me in the most heartrending terms, offering me gifts of horses and anything that I might desire if I would only save the life of his son." Taking a chance Layard gave the boy some quinine. Within hours the boy broke into "a violent perspiration"; and was soon on the way to recovery. After this Layard had not a trouble in the world and was welcomed into the most intimate areas of the Bakhtiari tribe and lived in the residential harem itself.

Of the entire journey of nearly 10,000 miles, Edward accomplished 7,000 miles on horseback – a mode of travel much enjoyed by "Squire Osbaldeston" who famously rode 200 miles in 8 hours and forty two minutes, as you have read.

Throughout Edward Mitford's life story and travels, there is continuous evidence of his great knowledge and love of horses. He even wrote and published a poem dedicated to the horse. As his great-great grandson, luckily as I can say, it was a talent and passion I continued with training and breeding racehorses in Southern Africa and as Pupil Assistant to Major Dick Hern, Queens Trainer at West Illsley, Berkshire.

To continue the story...Edward rode past the Cilician Gates when Ibrahim Pasha was holding them for Mohammed Ali against the Sultan. He mixed and mingled with the Kurds and spoke very highly of that much-abused people. His most unpleasant experiences occurred in Persia, now Iran. He traversed Afghanistan via Herat, Kandahar and Quetta, at a time when General Nott was commanding the valley of Helmand. All on horseback. On reaching Kandahar in Afghanistan, the British Political Agent, Sir Henry Rawlinson exclaimed "Goodness gracious Edward, you're still alive". An understandable statement considering his journey.

Sir Henry and Edward remained lifelong friends, sharing their experiences of the Middle East countries and politics. Many have heard the famous quotation "Dr Livingstone I presume?" made by Henry Morton Stanley in 1871. It was Sir Henry Rawlinson (1810-1895), President of the Royal Geographic Society that was one of David Livingstone's supporters during his last years in Africa. Sir Henry's signature appears on Edward Mitford's certificate of election as Fellow of the Royal Geographic Society in 1883.

It took Edward one year and seven months to reach Karachi, the largest city of Pakistan and its main seaport, and another year and three months to reach his journey's end at Colombo on the west coast of Sri Lanka. A total of two years and ten months in all – free of harm, which in those days, and even now, including Baghdad and Afghanistan, is a most remarkable achievement.

How many hardships he endured on that long and often tedious pilgrimage through practically unknown countries – how, at the risk of health and even life, he had to sleep in sodden clothes under the star-lit sky – how he was delayed by sickness and hunger, and weather bound by rain – how he had to encounter the suspicions of responsible governments and the cut-throat irresponsibility of thieves and robbers – all this Edward graphically relates so the reader can easily imagine his real life journey.

Edward observed closely, took careful notes from day to day of the countries and people he saw. He got to know all the unmapped, hidden routes and passages through all the Middle East countries he travelled. Another talent was drawing and painting and his book is exquisitely illustrated with original hand drawn sketches throughout. The result is an impressive and thoroughly interesting book. His writing is truly impressive. I choose a small extract which refers to the cypress trees found in Turkish cemeteries.

"Taken individually the almost black unfading cypress is a sublime object – standing rich in unearthly grandeur, it presents an emblem of a Christian dweller in a world of trial unshackled by its thrall – it faints not in the summer's heat, nor shrinks under the winter's cold; it laughs not in the sunbeams, nor wantons with the passing zephyrs; the clouds may lower, but cannot further darken it; and even when the tempest raging bows the sapling to the dust, or rives the gnarled oak, trusting its sure foundation in the tomb, the towering cypress, unsubdued, defies the blast; sculptured stillness, and its summit still points heavenward".

Questions often received at the time included, how many horses did he use, what money did he carry and what languages were spoken? Apart from walking and spring less carts, he was able to use hired horses in-between intervals of buying a total of six horses to complete the journey. For money, there was a bank at Constantinople (now Istanbul) and after that he cashed notes with the various consuls along the way. The small eastern coins of gold and silver were convenient to carry and conceal and traveling with one horse with no baggage, his wants and needs were few.

Edward writes with characteristic modesty. Throughout the journey Edward wore English clothes, never attempting any disguise, which would have been both impolite and useless. "Impolite because the open profession of an Englishman, accompanied by ordinary prudence will always be found the greatest safeguard in all eastern countries – useless because in no case have I ever known an Oriental deceived by it".

His knowledge of Arabic was invaluable to him up to a certain point. But it was the Arabic of Morocco that he knew and could speak fluently. Although he found it different from the dialects spoken in Syria and Mesopotamia, (from the ancient Greek, the land between the Tigris–Euphrates river system, corresponding to modern-day Iraq, Kuwait, the north eastern section of Syria and to a much lesser extent south eastern Turkey and smaller parts of south western Iran), the roots of the language being the same, he found it most useful for ordinary purposes. In Persia, now Iran however, Arabic was of no use, but a stay of six to eight weeks at Baghdad enabled him to master Persian sufficiently to continue his journey.

Edward arrived in Colombo, on 2 May 1842 and was greeted by the Governor, Sir Colin Campbell. He settled and lived in Ceylon for 25 years, working for the Ceylon civil service. He gained rapid promotion and was Government Agent – Consul when he retired in 1866, aged 55 years. Government Agents or GA's as they were known received a salary of between £1,200 and £1,500 per annum. It was in 1866 that the civil servants petitioned Parliament for an increase in salary of 25%, due to the heavy rise in the cost of living, supported by the Governor of Ceylon. A 20% salary increase was approved in 1877.

In 1844 Edward married Janet Bailey, daughter of the Archdeacon of Ceylon, Benjamin Bailey, my great-great grandmother. They produced nine children, five boys and four girls. The first born, Cuthbert (died of an infection at the age of ten), then followed Robert, Frances, Edith, Edward, Bertram, William, Margaret (my great grandmother) and Sybil. All raised and educated in the temperate and idyllic climate of the British colony.

Of his time in Colombo there is a charming and amusing story to relate. One thing Edward totally disagreed with and made every effort to have stopped was what he regarded as "a scandalous misuse of public money". It was the practice of the British Government to pay for the hire of a number of dancing girls in the temples. At the time, as Assistant Commissioner it was his duty to certify that they had been so employed! Apparently this was simply too much for him as his conscience would not allow him to witness "this degrading performance". His superiors and the clergy of the island, all – excepting Archdeacon Benjamin Bailey, whose daughter Edward married, urged him to certify to no avail. The matter (out of sheer frustration I think) was eventually referred to the British Home Office in London and it was recorded that, "with shame", they had to abandon the practice of employing dancing girls in temples!

Not only did Edward write books about his overland adventures and times in Morocco, he also, in complete contrast... mentally climbed mount Parnassus (in ancient Greece, Parnassus is the home of poetry, music and learning – also there is a Montparnasse area in Paris, where he spent time as a student) by publishing in 1869 "Poems, Dramatic and Lyrical". Of two dramas, in verse, one entitled "Prince Edward", deals with the conflict between King Henry III and Simon de Monfort, Earl of Leicester. This subject specially appealed to the author from the fact that Baron Mitford sided with the Earl, and consequently forfeited his castle and his barony to the King. This actually happened and is detailed in this book.

"Gaston de Foix" is the title of the other drama, the scene of which is set in France, one of the characters being Edward the Black Prince. Edward of Woodstock, Prince of Wales, Duke of Cornwall, Prince of Aquitaine, (1330-1376) was the eldest son of King Edward III of England as well as father to King Richard II of England, known as the Black Prince. He was an exceptional military leader, and his victories over the French at the Battles of Crécy and Poitiers made him very popular during his lifetime. In 1348 he became the first Knight of the Garter, of whose Order he was one of the founders. I can only imagine that Edward chose to feature the Black Prince due to some link from his student days in France along with that, as you have read, David de Strathbolgie (1332-1375) the 13th and last Earl of Athol was once owner of Mitford castle and also participated in the wars of France with the Black Prince.

Edward Mitford was the third son of Robert Mitford (1780-1818) of the Government Audit Office in London and his mother was the daughter of the Rev. Dr Edward Ledwich of Dublin, Ireland, a well known antiquary and author. Dr Ledwich was the editor of The Antiquities of Ireland in 2 volumes, the first in 1794 and the second in 1796. He survived both his elder brothers who died without children and on the death of Lt Col. John Philip Mitford in 1895, the eldest of the three brothers; he succeeded to the family estates in Northumberland and Yorkshire at the grand age of 85 . As such, due to mention in a will, he was obliged to use the additional name of Osbaldeston.

Two of his sons, two grandsons and one great grandson went on to become squires and owners of Mitford Castle and estates. His youngest son Bertram Mitford FRGS, became a well known author, writing 43 bestselling novels about South Africa. Edward Ledwich Mitford FRGS also served on the bench of Newcastle Magistrates' Court for many years.

Entranced, enthralled and befriended by the Persian nightingale on his long and lonely rides through eastern lands during his 10,000 mile journey, with 7,000 miles on horseback from London to Ceylon… Edward wrote this enchanting poem. From his book "Poems Dramatic and Lyrical" by E L Mitford, published in 1869. Now reprinted 140 years later by his great-great grandson Hugh Mitford Raymond, in The Mitford Family.

The Nightingale By Edward L Mitford

Hail, fairy bird! If bird thou art,
And not a spirit sent on earth
From realms of woe, with burning heart,
Or fields of bliss, where joy has birth
Hail, fairy thing! wafted on angel wing,
Pouring thy joys and woes in liquid song.
Whether at night upon the moonlit trees,
Or midday warm, warbling the shades among.
Hark! How it rises – up and up –
Thrilling clear;
Then sinks in startling plaintive fall,
Low and near;
Now droning dreamily a dulcet symphony:
Then rolling recklessly in rippling harmony,
Or bubbling o'er in daring melody;
As torrent strong
Rushing along,
An anguished scream, telling of fears;
Then a low wail, melting to tears:
A deep, deep roll,
As though its soul
Went gushing out from its bursting threat
In mellifluous waves of sound:
Then sweeping round
Once more it sours,
Wreathing eddies bright
Of coruscated light;
Leaping, flashing in a flame of song;
While joy on joy, and woe on woe,
The glorious tones prolong,
Upwelling from its heart, from off its silver tongue;
Sudden it stops With uplifted hand
Under the moon I see Silence stand,
Listening attent in suspensive pain,
Until once more outpours the soul-absorbing strain.

As mentioned earlier, Edward was also a talented artist, his exquisite painting of a dove can be found on the ceiling of the Mitford Church bell tower. The author chose this picture for the cover of Edward's book, republished in 2015 under the title "British Policy in the Middle East and the Creation of Israel". The original title was "An Appeal in behalf of the Jewish Nation", published by Hatchard & Son in 1845.

He led a remarkable and adventurous life. To quote the words inscribed on his gravestone in Mitford Churchyard – "There the tears of earth are dried - there the hidden things are clear".
Books published by Edward Ledwich Mitford. Title - publisher and year of publication.

An Appeal in behalf of the Jewish Nation	Hatchard	1845
The Arab's Pledge – A Tale of Morocco	Hatchard	1867
Poems, Dramatic & Lyrical	Provost	1869
A Land March from England to Ceylon	Allen & Co	1884

Elected FRGS

At the end of the book there is a list of people that bought Edward's books.

(ix) Algernon Mitford

(1837-1916)

Old Japan, legends and culture

The ancient culture of Japan is both fascinating and brutal. The Meiji Restoration in 1868 (it could also be described as a revolution) marked the end of the Shogunate. Japan went through many political and social changes, restoring the Emperor of Japan and paving the way towards Japan becoming the modernized nation that it is today, Algernon decided to record an insight to the old Japanese customs and culture, a civilisation that he observed first hand, in an excellent book. The first volume contains the legends of the Rônins or knights-errant (medieval knights at large) of old Japan, and a selection of fairy tales and the second book is devoted to ancient superstitions, sermons, rites and ceremonies.

Algernon was the great-grandson of William Mitford who wrote the History of Greece, as mentioned earlier in this book. He became First Baron Redesdale (1837-1916) known as Lord Redesdale, and was grandfather to the Mitford Girls. As Secretary in the London Office of Works he was involved with the restoration of the Tower of London and landscaping Hyde Park. He served in the Diplomatic Corps and was Second Secretary to the British Legation in Japan during the time of the Meiji Restoration.

Algernon Mitford in the story of the "Forty-seven Rônins" tells us how readily the old knights of Japan engaged in some bloody enterprise, committed wholesale murder in revenge of a petty indifference upon themselves or their lords, and then, to satisfy the requirements of Japanese justice, killed themselves by hari-kiri. The 47 knights who lie buried in the groves and graves of the Sengakiyi cemetery are the famous Japanese heroes of history. Incense is still burned upon their graves and every sixty years a commemorative festival is held for two months, attended by people from all over the country to do honour to those brave men, who with their swords, avenged the death of their lord and then committed suicide.

To the Samurai or a man of the military class, his sword is the most prized treasure which he possesses. These fabulously costly swords are crafted by master sword smiths and become heirlooms passed from father to son and are almost part of the wearer's identity. Iyéyasu, the founder of the last dynasty of Shoguns, wrote "The girded sword is the living soul of the Samurai". The occupation of a sword smith is regarded as an honourable profession reserved for gentlemen, the traditions of the craft are many and curious. The forging of the sword is conducted in secret; the doors of the workshop are closed and the finishing strokes are added in darkness and gloom.

As recorded in a rare Japanese manuscript. Seppuku or hari-kiri is the mode of suicide adopted amongst Samurai when they have no alternative but to die. Some commit suicide of their own free will; others who have committed some crime which does not put them outside the pale of the privileges of the Samurai, are ordered by their superiors to put an end to their own lives. In 1869 a motion was brought forward in the Japanese Parliament by Ono Seigorô, a clerk of the house, advocating the abolition of the practice of hari-kiri. Two hundred members out of a house of 209 voted against the motion, which was supported by only three speakers, with six members not voting on either side. In this debate the seppuku or hari-kiri, was called "the very shrine of the Japanese national spirit, and the embodiment in practice of devotion to principle. A great ornament to the empire; a pillar of the constitution; a valuable institution tending to the honour of the nobles, and based on a compassionate feeling towards the official caste; a pillar of religion and a spur to virtue". The entire debate shows the affection with which the Japanese cling to the traditions of a medieval and chivalrous past. Of note, is that the proposer, Ono Seigorô, who by introducing motions based upon the admiration of the Western way of civilisation, was murdered not long after this debate took place. This was 140 years ago.

From the doom and gloom of murder and bloodshed it is refreshing to turn to the fairy tales that Algernon has selected.

Apart from the amusing but regular mother and child fables he has included several which have a good moral story to them and tell us of the evils resulting from cruelty and covertness and the potential blessings to be gained from charity and kindness. Many of these stories contain the delightful adventures of cats, foxes and badgers which are regarded by the Japanese with superstitious awe and are supposed to possess the power of assuming the human shape in order to bewitch men and women.

Some of the stories selected bear a strong resemblance to the "Arabian Nights" and some to the medieval myths of Western Europe. The fox in Japan does not seem to possess the same ingenuity, cunning and tact of the European version. The Japanese badger presents a better example of mind over matter and love appears to be generally the motive power used by the cat, fox, and the badger as the general cause and effect of the ruin of man.

One story relates how Rônin, who killed a priest for his money, was tormented by his ghost and lost his reason. The ghost in the form of the priest comes to visit him in his sickness and tells him how he was miraculously saved from death, gives the Rônin his blessing and forgives him. He tells the unhappy murderer that the heart of man, "pure by nature, is corrupted by circumstances"; that "poverty drives a man to crimes which he repeats in his wealth", and that "a guilty man shudders at the rustling of the wind and the chattering of a stork's beak; a murderer's conscience preys upon his mind till he sees what is not".

Of the sermons translated is the text of the Chinese philosopher, Mêng Tse "Benevolence is the heart of man; righteousness is the path of man. How lamentable a thing is to leave the path and go astray, to cast away the heart and not know where to seek for it". In the course of this sermon the preacher has something to say about the education of young, Japanese ladies. He enlarges on the folly of teaching them only to make tea, arrange flowers, play the harp and sing songs while they are quiet ignorant of such useful accomplishments as shampooing the shoulders and loins and other household duties. What use would such a girl be as a wife? "If her honoured father-in-law or mother-in-law fall ill, her being able to plait flowers and paint pictures and make tea will be of no use in a sick room. To shampoo her parents-in-law and nurse them affectionately, without employing either shampooer or servant-maid, is the right path of a daughter-in-law".

(x) Godolphin Mitford

(1844-1884)

Converting to Islam and the 'Elixir of Life'

"The mind is its own place, and in itself can make a Heaven of Hell, a Hell of Heaven."
John Milton (1608-74) Satan, in Paradise Lost.

Synonymous with the name Mitford is the word eccentricity. Godolphin it would appear took eccentricity to another level. In fact we perhaps move to another planet and level of thinking? Apart from his nervous and excitable manner he not only converted to Islam, he also adopted Indian dress and changed his name to Moorad Ali Beg. He then became an atheist then joined the Roman Catholic Church. He wrote his mind, as is detailed across the pages that follow.

Godolphin was born and grew up in Madras in 1844 during the time his father was employed by the East India Company. As a young man he later worked for the Maharajah of Bhavnagar as chief cavalry officer. He was not strong minded or confident, in fact completely the opposite and drifted away from social norms into the horrors of black magic and the workings of sorcerers. For all he went through he is acknowledged for a famous article he wrote entitled "The Elixir of Life", published in The Theosophist in 1882. This article is mentioned several times in Theosophical literature and included in this chapter.

In 1881, he apparently went to the Headquarters of the Theosophical Society, then located in Bombay, and met the Founders and Masters. Colonel Henry Olcott was an American military officer, journalist and first President of the Theosophical Society. He was the first person of western descent to make a formal conversion to Buddhism. From an old diary Henry Olcott wrote a little about this extraordinary character. Henry Olcott describes him as a strange looking creature with a fair complexion and light blue eyes who, with his long, light brown hair tied up in a Grecian knot behind his head looked more like an actor made up for the part than anything else. "The writing of the "Elixir of Life" occurred sometime later but when I first met him he seemed to be engaged in a strong mental and moral conflict with himself. He complained of being dragged hither and thither, first by good, then by bad influences. He explained all the sufferings he had passed through the previous years were due to his teachings from a Muslim guru.

Godolphin had a fine mind and had done a great deal of reading and he wanted to join our Theosophical Society but, as I had no confidence in his moral stamina, I refused him. My colleague Helena Blavatsky relented and offered to become responsible for him. Some months later, he went mad by running about with a sword while shouting that all the Mahatmas were devils. Mahatmas in theosophical literature are teachers, elder brothers, masters, sages, and seers and generally, a person who is respected for being good, wise, and holy".

The Elixir Of Life
By Godolphin Mitford

The article that follows merits a few words of introduction. The details given in it on the subject of what has always been considered as one of the darkest and most strictly guarded of the mysteries of the initiation into occultism — from the days of the Rishis until those of the Theosophical Society — came to the knowledge of the author in a way that would seem to the ordinary run of Europeans strange and supernatural.

He himself, however, we may assure the reader, is a most thorough disbeliever in the Supernatural, though he has learned too much to limit the capabilities of the natural as some do. Further, he has to make the following confession of his own belief. It will be apparent, from a careful perusal of the facts, that if the matter be really as stated therein, the author cannot himself be an adept of high grade, as the article in such a case would never have been written. Nor does he pretend to be one. He is, or rather was, for a few years a humble Chela (a Chela is the pupil and disciple of an initiated Guru or Master).

Hence, the converse must consequently be also true, that as regards the higher stages of the mystery he can have no personal experience, but speaks of it only as a close observer left to his own surmises — and no more. He may, therefore, boldly state that during, and notwithstanding, his unfortunately rather too short stay with some adepts (a person who understands) he has by actual experiment and observation verified some of the less transcendental or incipient parts of the course. And, though it will be impossible for him to give positive testimony as to what lies beyond, he may yet mention that all his own course of study, training and experience, long, severe and dangerous as it has often been, leads him to the conviction that everything is really as stated, save some details purposely veiled. For causes which cannot be explained to the public, he himself may be unable or unwilling to use the secret he has gained access to.

Still he is permitted by one to whom all his reverential affection and gratitude are due - his last guru — to divulge for the benefit of Science and Man, and specially for the good of those who are courageous enough to personally make the experiment, the following astounding particulars of the occult methods for prolonging life to a period far beyond the common.

Godolphin Mitford.

"If you are anxious to drink the "Elixir of Life," and live a thousand years or so, you must take our word for the matter at present, and proceed on the assumption. For esoteric science does not give the faintest possible hope that the desired end will ever be attained by any other way; while modern, or so-called exact science - laughs at it".

Godolphin Mitford continues.

"Probably one of the first considerations which move the worldly-minded at present to solicit initiation into Theosophy is the belief, or hope, that, immediately on joining, some extraordinary advantage over the rest of mankind will be conferred upon the candidate. Some even think that the ultimate result of their initiation will perhaps be ex-emption from that dissolution which is called the common lot of mankind. The traditions of the "Elixir of Life," said to be in the possession of Kabalists and Alchemists, are still cherished by students of Mediaeval Occultism — in Europe. The allegory of the Abé Hyat or Water of Life, is still credited as a fact by the degraded remnants of the Asiatic esoteric sects ignorant of the real great secret. The "pungent and fiery Essence," by which Zanoni renewed his existence, still fires the imagination of modern visionaries as a possible scientific discovery of the future.

Theosophically, though the fact is distinctly declared to be true, the above-named conceptions of the mode of procedure leading to the realization of the fact, are known to be false. The reader may or may not believe it; but as a matter of fact, Theosophical Occultists claim to have communication with (living) Intelligences possessing an infinitely wider range of observation than is contemplated even by the loftiest aspirations of modern science, all the present "Adepts" of Europe and America — dabblers in the Kabala — notwithstanding. But far even as those superior Intelligences have investigated (or, if preferred, are alleged to have investigated), and remotely as they may have searched by the help of inference and analogy, even they have failed to discover in the Infinity anything permanent but — Space.

All is subject to change. Reflection, therefore, will easily suggest to the reader the further logical inference that in a Universe which is essentially impermanent in its conditions, nothing can confer permanency. Therefore, no possible substance, even if drawn from the depths of Infinity; no imaginable combination of drugs, whether of our earth or any other, though compounded by even the Highest Intelligence; no system of life or discipline though directed by the sternest determination and skill, could possibly produce Immutability. For in the universe of solar systems, wherever and however investigated, Immutability necessitates "Non-Being" in the physical sense given it by the Theists — Non-Being which is nothing in the narrow conceptions of Western Religionists — a reductio ad absurdum. This is a gratuitous insult even when applied to the pseudo-Christian or ecclesiastical Jehovite idea of God.

Consequently, it will be seen that the common ideal conception of "Immortality" is not only essentially wrong, but a physical and metaphysical impossibility. The idea, whether cherished by Theosophists or non-Theosophists, by Christians or Spiritualists, by Materialists or Idealists, is a chimerical illusion. But the actual prolongation of human life is possible for a time so long as to appear miraculous and incredible to those who regard our span of existence as necessarily limited to at most a couple of hundred years.

We may break, as it were, the shock of death and instead of dying, change a sudden plunge into darkness to a transition into a brighter light. And this may be made so gradual that the passage from one state of existence to another shall have its friction minimized, so as to be practically imperceptible. This is a very different matter, and quite within the reach of Occult Science. In this, as in all other cases, means properly directed will gain their ends, and causes produce effects. Of course, the only question is what are these causes, and how, in their turn, are they to be produced. To lift, as far as may be allowed, the veil from this aspect of Occultism, is the object of the present power.

We must premise by reminding the reader of two Theosophic doctrines, constantly inculcated in "Isis" and in other mystic works — namely,

(a) that ultimately the Cosmos is One — one under infinite variations and manifestations, and

(b) that the so-called man is a "compound being" — composite not only in the exoteric scientific sense of being a congeries of living so-called material Units, but also in the esoteric sense of being a succession of seven forms or parts of itself, interblended with each other.

To put it more clearly we might say that the more ethereal forms are but duplicates of the same aspect, — each finer one lying within the inter-atomic spaces of the next grosser. We would have the reader understand that these are no subtleties, no "spiritualities" at all in the Christo-Spiritualistic sense. In the actual man reflected in your mirror are really several men, or several parts of one composite man; each the exact counterpart of the other, but the "atomic conditions" (for want of a better word) of each of which are so arranged that its atoms interpenetrate those of the next "grosser" form. It does not, for our present purpose, matter how the Theosophists, Spiritualists, Buddhists, Kabalists, or Vedantists, count, separate, classify, arrange or name these, as that war of terms may be postponed to another occasion.

Neither does it matter what relation each of these men has to the various "elements" of the Cosmos of which he forms a part. This knowledge, though of vital importance in other respects, need not be explained or discussed now. Nor does it much more concern us that the Scientists deny the existence of such an arrangement, because their instruments are inadequate to make their senses perceive it. We will simply reply — "get better instruments and keener senses, and eventually you will."

All we have to say is that if you are anxious to drink of the "Elixir of Life," and live a thousand years or so, you must take our word for the matter at present, and proceed on the assumption. For esoteric science does not give the faintest possible hope that the desired end will ever be attained by any other way; while modern, or so-called exact science, laughs at it.

So, then, we have arrived at the point where we have determined — literally, not metaphorically — to crack the outer shell known as the mortal coil or body, and hatch out of it, clothed in our next. This "next" is not spiritual, but only a more ethereal form. Having by a long training and preparation adapted it for a life in this atmosphere, during which time we have gradually made the outward shell to die off through a certain process (hints of which will be found further on) we have to prepare for this physiological transformation.

How are we to do it? In the first place we have the actual, visible, material body — Man, so called; though in fact, it's his outer shell — to deal with. Let us bear in mind that science teaches us that in about every seven years we change skin as effectually as any serpent; and this so gradually and imperceptibly that, had not science after years of unremitting study and observation assured us of it, no one would have had the slightest suspicion of the fact.

We see, moreover, that in process of time any cut or lesion upon the body, however deep, has a tendency to repair the loss and reunite; a piece of lost skin is very soon replaced by another. Hence, if a man, partially flayed alive, may sometimes survive and be covered with a new skin, so our astral, vital body — the fourth of the seven (having attracted and assimilated to itself the second) and which is so much more ethereal than the physical one — may be made to harden its particles to the atmospheric changes.

The whole secret is to succeed in evolving it out, and separating it from the visible; and while its generally invisible atoms proceed to concrete themselves into a compact mass, to gradually get rid of the old particles of our visible frame so as to make them die and disappear before the new set has had time to evolve and replace them . . . . We can say no more. The Magdalene is not the only one who could be accused of having "seven spirits" in her, though men who have a lesser number of spirits (what a misnomer that word!) in them, are not few or exceptional; they are the frequent failures of nature — the incomplete men and women.

Each of these has in turn to survive the preceding and more dense one, and then die. The exception is the sixth when absorbed into and blended with the seventh. The "Dhatu" of the old Hindu physiologist had a dual meaning, the esoteric side of which corresponds with the Tibetan "Zang" (seven principles of the body). (Dhatu — the seven principal substances of the human body — chyle, flesh, blood, fat, bones, marrow, semen).

We Asiatics, have a proverb, probably handed down to us, and by the Hindus repeated ignorantly as to its esoteric meaning. It has been known ever since the old Rishis mingled familiarly with the simple and noble people they taught and led on. The Devas had whispered into every man's ear thou only, if thou wilt, art "immortal." Combine with this the saying of a Western author that if any man could just realize for an instant, that he had to die some day, he would die that instant. The illuminated will perceive that between these two sayings, rightly understood, stands revealed the whole secret of Longevity. We only die when our will ceases to be strong enough to make us live. In the majority of cases, death comes when the torture and vital exhaustion accompanying a rapid change in our physical conditions becomes so intense as to weaken, for one single instant, our "clutch on life," or the tenacity of the will to exist. Till then, however severe may be the disease, however sharp the pang, we are only sick or wounded, as the case may be. This explains the cases of sudden deaths from joy, fright, pain, grief, or such other causes. The sense of a life-task consummated, of the worthlessness of one's existence, if strongly realized, produces death as surely as poison or a rifle-bullet. On the other hand, a stern determination to continue to live has, in fact, carried many through the crises of the most severe diseases, in perfect safety.

First, then, must be the determination — the Will — the conviction of certainty, to survive and continue. Without that, all else is useless. And to be efficient for the purpose, it must be, not only a passing resolution of the moment, a single fierce desire of short duration, but a settled and continued strain, as nearly as can be continued and concentrated without one single moment's relaxation. In a word, the would-be "Immortal" must be on his watch night and day, guarding self against — himself. To live, to live, to live — must be his unswerving resolve. He must as little as possible allow himself to be turned aside from it.

It may be said that this is the most concentrated form of selfishness, that it is utterly opposed to our Theosophical professions of benevolence, and disinterestedness, and regard for the good of humanity. Well, viewed in a short-sighted way, it is so. But to do good, as in everything else, a man must have time and materials to work with, and this is a necessary means to the acquirement of powers by which infinitely more good can be done than without them.

When these are once mastered, the opportunities to use them will arrive, for there comes a moment when further watch and exertion are no longer needed: — the moment when the turning-point is safely passed. For the present as we deal with aspirants and not with advanced chelas, in the first stage a determined, dogged resolution, and an enlightened concentration of self on self, are all that is absolutely necessary. It must not, however, be considered that the candidate is required to be inhuman or brutal in his negligence of others. Such a recklessly selfish course would be as injurious to him as the contrary one of expending his vital energy on the gratification of his physical desires. All that is required from him is a purely negative attitude. Until the turning-point is reached, he must not "lay out" his energy in lavish or fiery devotion to any cause, however noble, however "good," however elevated.

Such, we can solemnly assure the reader, would bring its reward in many ways — perhaps in another life, perhaps in this world, but it would tend to shorten the existence it is desired to pre-serve, as surely as self-indulgence and profligacy. That is why very few of the truly great men of the world (of course, the un-principled adventurers who have applied great powers to bad uses are out of the question) — the martyrs, the heroes, the founders of religions, the liberators of nations, the leaders of reforms — ever became members of the long-lived "Brotherhood of Adepts" who were by some and for long years accused of selfishness. (And that is also why the Yogis, and the Fakirs of modern India — most of whom are acting now but on the dead-letter tradition, are required if they would be considered living up to the principles of their profession — to appear entirely dead to every inward feeling or emotion.)

Notwithstanding the purity of their hearts, the greatness of their aspirations, the disinterestedness of their self-sacrifice, they could not live for they had missed the hour. They may at times have exercised powers which the world called miraculous; they may have electrified man and subdued Nature by fiery and self devoted Will; they may have been possessed of so-called superhuman intelligence; they may have even had knowledge of, and communion with members of our own occult Brotherhood; but having deliberately resolved to devote their vital energy to the welfare of others, rather than themselves, they have surrendered life; and, when perishing on the cross or the scaffold, or falling sword in hand, upon the battle-field, or sinking exhausted after a successful consummation of the life-object, on death-beds in their chambers, they have all alike had to cry out at last: "Eli, Eli, lama sabachthani!" ("My God, My God, why have You forsaken Me?").

So far so good. But, given the will to live however powerful, we have seen that, in the ordinary course of mundane life, the throes of dissolution cannot be checked. The desperate, and again and again renewed struggle of the Cosmic elements to proceed with a career of change despite the will that is checking them, like a pair of runaway horses struggling against the determined driver holding them in, are so cumulatively powerful, that the utmost efforts of the un-trained human will acting within an unprepared body become ultimately useless.

The highest intrepidity of the bravest soldier; the intensest desire of the yearning lover; the hungry greed of the unsatisfied miser; the most undoubting faith of the sternest fanatic; the practised insensibility to pain of the hardiest red Indian brave or half-trained Hindu Yogi; the most deliberate philosophy of the calmest thinker — all alike fail at last.

Indeed, sceptics will allege in opposition to the verities of this article that, as a matter of experience, it is often observed that the mildest and most irresolute of minds and weakest of physical frames are often seen to resist "Death" longer than the powerful will of the high-spirited and obstinately egotistic man, and the iron frame of the labourer, the warrior and the athlete.

In reality, however, the key to the secret of these apparently contradictory phenomena is the true conception of the very thing we have already said. If the physical development of the gross "outer shell" proceeds on parallel lines and at an equal rate with that of the will, it stands to reason that no advantage for the purpose of overcoming it is attained by the latter.

The acquisition of improved breechloaders by one modern army confers no absolute superiority if the enemy also becomes possessed of them. Consequently it will be at once apparent, to those who think on the subject, that much of the training by which what is known as "a powerful and determined nature," perfects itself for its own purpose on the stage of the visible world, necessitating and being useless without a parallel development of the "gross" and so-called animal frame, is, in short, neutralized, for the purpose at present treated of, by the fact that its own action has armed the enemy with weapons equal to its own. The force of the impulse to dissolution is rendered equal to the will to oppose it; and being cumulative, sub-dues the will-power and triumphs at last. On the other hand, it may happen that an apparently weak and vacillating will-power residing in a weak and undeveloped physical frame, may be so reinforced by some unsatisfied desire, the lchcha (wish), it is called by the Indian Occultists (for instance a mother's heart-yearning to remain and support her fatherless children), as to keep down and vanquish, for a short time, the physical throes of a body to which it has become temporarily superior.

The whole rationale then, of the first condition of continued existence in this world, is:

(a) the development of a Will so powerful as to overcome the hereditary (in a Darwinian sense) tendencies of the atoms composing the "gross" and palpable animal frame, to hurry on at a particular period in a certain course of Cosmic change; and

(b) to weaken the concrete action of that animal frame as to make it more amenable to the power of the Will. To defeat an army, you must demoralize and throw it into disorder.

To do this then, is the real object of all the rites, ceremonies, fasts, "prayers," meditations, initiations and procedures of self-discipline enjoined by various esoteric Eastern sects, from that course of pure and elevated aspiration which leads to the higher phases of Adeptism Real, down to the fearful and disgusting ordeals which the adherent of the "Left-hand-Road" has to pass through, all the time maintaining his equilibrium. The procedures have their merits and their demerits their separate uses and abuses, their essential and non-essential parts, their various veils, mummeries and labyrinths.

But in all, the result aimed at is reached, if by different processes. The Will is strengthened, encouraged and directed, and the elements opposing its action are demoralized. Now, to anyone who has thought out and connected the various evolution theories, as taken, not from any occult source, but from the ordinary scientific manual accessible to all, from the hypothesis of the latest variation in the habits of species, say, the acquisition of carnivorous habits by the New Zealand parrot, for instance, to the farthest glimpses backwards into Space and Eternity afforded by the "Fire Mist" doc-trine, it will be apparent that they all rest on one basis. That basis is, that the impulse once given to a hypothetical Unit has a tendency to continue; and consequently, that anything "done" by something at a certain time and certain place tends to repeat itself at other times and places.

Such is the admitted rationale of heredity and atavism. That the same things apply to our ordinary conduct is apparent from the notorious ease with which "habits," — bad or good, as the case may be — are acquired, and it will not be questioned that this applies, as a rule, as much to the moral and intellectual, as to the physical world.

Furthermore, History and Science teach us plainly that certain physical habits conduce to certain moral and intellectual results. There never yet was a conquering nation of vegetarians. Even in the old Aryan times, we do not learn that the very Rishis, from whose lore and practice we gain the knowledge of Occultism, ever interdicted the Kshatriya (military) caste from hunting or a carnivorous diet. Filling, as they did, a certain place in the body politic in the actual condition of the world, the Rishis as little thought of interfering with them, as of restraining the tigers of the jungle from their habits. That did not affect what the Rishis did themselves.

The aspirant to longevity then must be on his guard against two dangers. He must beware especially of impure and animal thoughts. For Science shows that thought is dynamic, and thought-force evolved by nervous action expanding outwardly, must affect the molecular relations of the physical man. The inner men, however sublimated their organism may be, are still composed of actual, not hypothetical, particles, and are still subject to the law that an "action" has a tendency to repeat itself; a tendency to set analogous action in the grosser "shell" they are in contact with, and concealed within.

And, on the other hand, certain actions have a tendency to produce actual physical conditions unfavourable to pure thoughts, hence to the state required for developing the supremacy of the inner man.

To return to the practical process. A normally healthy mind, in a normally healthy body, is a good starting-point. Though exceptionally powerful and self-devoted natures may sometimes recover the ground lost by mental degradation or physical misuse, by employing proper means, under the direction of unswerving resolution, yet often things may have gone so far that there is no longer stamina enough to sustain the conflict sufficiently long to perpetuate this life; though what in Eastern parlance is called the "merit" of the effort help to ameliorate conditions and improve matters in another.

However this may be, the prescribed course of discipline commences here. It may be stated briefly that its essence is a course of moral, mental, and physical development, carried on in parallel lines — one being useless without the other. The physical man must be rendered more ethereal and sensitive; the mental man more penetrating and profound; the moral man more self-denying and philosophical. And it may be mentioned that all sense of restraint, even if self-imposed, is useless.

Not only is all "goodness" that results from the compulsion of physical force, threats, or bribes (whether of a physical or so-called "spiritual" nature) absolutely useless to the person who exhibits it, its hypocrisy tending to poison the moral atmosphere of the world, but the desire to be "good" or "pure," to be efficacious must be spontaneous. It must be a self-impulse from within, a real preference for something higher, not an abstention from vice because of fear of the law: not a chastity enforced by the dread of Public Opinion; not a benevolence exercised through love of praise or dread of consequences in a hypothetical Future Life.

It will be seen now in connection with the doctrine of the tendency to the renewal of action, before discussed, that the course of self-discipline recommended as the only road to Longevity by Occultism is not a "visionary" theory dealing with vague "ideas," but actually a scientifically devised system of drill. It is a system by which each particle of the several men composing the septenary individual receives an impulse and a habit of doing what is necessary for certain purposes of its own free-will and with "pleasure." Everyone must be practised and perfect in a thing to do it with pleasure. This rule especially applies to the case of the development of Man.

"Virtue" may be very good in its way — it may lead to the grand results. But to become efficacious it has to be practised cheerfully not with reluctance or pain. As a consequence of the above consideration the candidate for Longevity at the commencement of his career must begin to eschew his physical desires, not from any sentimental theory of right or wrong but for the following good reason. As, according to a well-known and now established scientific theory, his visible material frame is always renewing its particles; he will, while abstaining from the gratification of his desires, reach the end of a certain period during which those particles which composed the man of vice, and which were given a bad predisposition, will have departed.

At the same time, the disuse of such functions will tend to obstruct the entry, in place of the old particles, of new particles having a tendency to repeat the said acts. And while this is the particular result regards certain "vices," the general result of abstention from "gross" acts will be (by a modification of the well-known Darwinian law of atrophy by non-usage) to diminish what we may call the "relative" density and coherence of the outer shell (a result of its less-used molecules); while the diminution in the quantity of its actual constituents will be "made up" (if tried by scales and weights) by the increased admission of more ethereal particles.

What physical desires are to be abandoned and in what order? First and fore-most, he must give up alcohol in all forms; for while it supplies no nourishment, nor any direct pleasure (beyond such sweetness or fragrance as may be gained in the taste of wine, to which alcohol, in itself, is non-essential) to even the grossest elements of the "physical" frame, it induces a state of well being and in extreme, a violence of action, a rush so to speak, of life, the stress of which can only be sustained by very dull, gross, and dense elements, and which, by the operation of the well known law of Reaction (in commercial phrase, "supply and demand") tends to summon them from the surrounding universe, and therefore directly counteracts the object we have in view.

Next comes meat-eating, and for the very same reason, in a minor degree. It increases the rapidity of life, the energy of action, the violence of passions. It may be good for a hero who has to fight and die, but not for a would-be sage who has to exist.

Next in order come the sexual desires; for these, in addition to the great diversion of energy (vital force) into other channels, in many different ways, beyond the primary one (as, for instance, the waste of energy in expectation, jealousy etc), are direct attractions to a certain gross quality of the original matter of the Universe, simply because the most pleasurable physical sensations are only possible at that stage of density. Alongside with and extending beyond all these and other gratifications of the senses (which include not only those things usually known as "vicious," but all those which, though ordinarily regarded as "innocent," have yet the disqualification of ministering to the pleasures of the body, the most harmless to others and the least "gross" being the criterion for those to be last abandoned in each case) must be carried on the moral purification.

Nor must it be imagined that "austerities" as commonly understood can, in the majority of cases, avail much to hasten the "etherealizing" process. That is the rock on which many of the Eastern esoteric sects have foundered, and the reason why they have degenerated into degrading superstitions. The Western monks and the Eastern Yogees, who think they will reach the apex of powers by concentrating their thought on their navel, or by standing on one leg, are practising exercises which serve no other purpose than to strengthen the will-power, which is sometimes applied to the basest purposes. These are examples of this one-sided and dwarfed development. It is no use to fast as long as you require food. The ceasing of desire for food without impairment of health is the sign which indicates that it should be taken in lesser and ever decreasing quantities until the extreme limit compatible with life is reached. A stage will be finally attained where only water will be required.

Nor is it of any use for this particular purpose of longevity to abstain from immorality so long as you are craving for it in your heart; and so on with all other unsatisfied inward cravings. To get rid of the inward desire is the essential thing, and to mimic the real thing without it is barefaced hypocrisy and useless slavery.

So it must be with the moral purification of the heart. The "basest" inclinations must go first — then the others. First avarice, then fear, then envy, worldly pride, uncharitableness, hatred; last of all ambition and curiosity must be abandoned successively. The strengthening of the more ethereal and so-called "spiritual" parts of the man must go on at the same time.

Reasoning from the known to the unknown, meditation must be practised and encouraged. Meditation is the inexpressible yearning of the inner Man to "go out to-wards the infinite," which in the olden time was the real meaning of adoration, but which has now no synonym in the European languages, because the thing no longer exists in the West, and its name has been vulgarized to the make-believe shams known as prayer, glorification, and repentance. Through all stages of training the equilibrium of the consciousness, the assurance that all must be right in the Cosmos, and therefore with you a portion of it, must be retained. The process of life must not be hurried but retarded, if possible; to do otherwise may do good to others, perhaps even to yourself in other spheres, but it will hasten your dissolution in this.

Nor must the externals be neglected in this first stage. Remember that an adept, though "existing" so as to convey to ordinary minds the idea of his being immortal, is not also invulnerable to agencies from without. The training to prolong life does not, in itself, secure one from accidents. As for as any physical preparation goes, the sword may cut, the disease enters, the poisons disarrange. The adept may be more secure from ordinary dangers than the common mortal, but he is so by virtue of the superior knowledge, calmness, coolness and penetration which his lengthened existence and its necessary concomitants have enabled him to acquire; not by virtue of any preservative power in the process itself. He is secure as a man armed with a rifle is more secure than a naked baboon; not secure in the sense in which the deva (god) was supposed to be secured than a man.

If this is so in the case of the high adept, how much more necessary is it that the neophyte should be not only protected but that he himself should use all possible means to ensure for himself the necessary duration of life to complete the process of mastering the phenomena we call death! It may be said, why do not the higher adepts protect him? Perhaps they do to some extent, but the child must learn to walk alone; to make him independent of his own efforts in respect to safety, would be destroying one element necessary to his development — the sense of responsibility.

What courage or conduct would be called for in a man sent to fight when armed with irresistible weapons and clothed in impenetrable armour? Hence the neophyte should endeavour, as far as possible, to fulfil every true canon of sanitary law as laid down by modern scientists. Pure air, pure water, pure food, gentle exercise, regular hours, pleasant occupations and surroundings are all, if not indispensable, at least serviceable to his progress. It is to secure these, at least as much as silence and solitude, that the Gods, Sages, Occultists of all ages have retired as much as possible to the quiet of the country, the cool cave, the depths of the forest, the expanse of the desert, or the heights of the mountains. Is it not suggestive that the Gods have always loved the high places; and that in the present day the highest section of the Occult Brotherhood on earth inhabits the highest mountain plateaux of the earth.

Nor must the beginner disdain the assistance of medicine and good medical regimen. He is still an ordinary mortal, and he requires the aid of an ordinary mortal.

"Suppose, however, all the conditions required, or which will be understood as required (for the details and varieties of treatment requisite, are too numerous to be detailed here), are fulfilled, what is the next step?" the reader will ask. Well if there have been no backslidings or remissness in the procedure indicated, the following physical results will follow:–

First the neophyte will take more pleasure in things spiritual and pure. Gradually gross and material occupations will become not only uncraved for or forbidden, but simply and literally repulsive to him. He will take more pleasure in the simple sensations of Nature — the sort of feeling one can remember to have experienced as a child. He will feel more light-hearted, confident, and happy. Let him take care the sensation of renewed youth does not mislead, or he will risk a fall into his old baser life and even lower depths. "Action and Re-action are equal."

Now the desire for food will begin to cease. Let it be left off gradually — no fasting is required. Take what you feel you require. The food craved for will be the most innocent and simple. Fruit and milk will usually be the best. Then as till now, you have been simplifying the quality of your food, gradually — very gradually — as you feel capable of it diminish the quantity. No, but before you mock, consider the character of the process alluded to. It is a notorious fact that many of the lowest and simplest organisms have no excretions.

The common guinea-worm is a very good instance. It has rather a complicated organism, but it has no ejaculatory duct. All it consumes, the poorest essences of the human body, is applied to its growth and propagation. Living as it does in human tissue; it passes no digested food away. The human neophyte, at a certain stage of his development, is in a somewhat analogous condition, with this difference or differences, that he does excrete, but it is through the pores of his skin, and by those too enter other etherealized particles of matter to contribute towards his support.

Otherwise, all the food and drink is sufficient only to keep in equilibrium those "gross" parts of his physical body which still remain to repair their cuticle-waste through the medium of the blood. Later on, the process of cell-development in his frame will undergo a change; a change for the better, the opposite of that in disease for the worse, he will become all living and sensitive, and will derive nourishment from the Ether. But that epoch for our neophyte is yet far distant.

Probably, long before that period has arrived, other results, no less surprising than incredible to the uninitiated will have ensued to give our neophyte courage and consolation in his difficult task. It would be but a truism to repeat what has been alleged (in ignorance of its real rationale) by hundreds and hundreds of writers as to the happiness and content conferred by a life of innocence and purity. But often at the very commencement of the process some real physical result, unexpected and unthought-of of by the neophyte occurs.

Some lingering disease, hitherto deemed hopeless, may take a favourable turn; or he may develop healing mesmeric powers himself; or some hitherto unknown sharpening of his senses may delight him. The rationale of these things is, as we have said, neither miraculous nor difficult of comprehension. In the first place, the sudden change in the direction of the vital energy (which, whatever view we take of it and its origin, is acknowledged by all schools of philosophy as most recondite, and as the motive power) must produce results of some kind. In the second, Theosophy shows, as we said before, that a man consists of several men pervading each other, and on this view (although it is very difficult to express the idea in language) it is but natural that the progressive etherealization of the densest and most gross of all should leave the others literally more at liberty.

A troop of horses may be blocked by a mob and have much difficulty in fighting its way through; but if every one of the mob could be changed suddenly into a ghost, there would be little to retard it. And as each interior entity is more rare, active, and volatile than the outer and as each has relation with different elements, spaces, and properties of the Cosmos which are treated in other articles on Occultism, the mind of the reader may conceive — though the pen of the writer could not express it in a dozen volumes — the magnificent possibilities gradually unfolded to the neophyte.

Many of the opportunities thus suggested may be taken advantage of by the neophyte for his own safety, amusement, and the good of those around him; but the way in which he does this is one adapted to his fitness — a part of the ordeal he has to pass through, and misuse of these powers will certainly entail the loss of them as a natural result. The Itchcha (or desire) evoked anew by the vistas they open up will retard or throw back his progress.

But there is another portion of the Great Secret to which we must allude, and which is now, for the first, in a long series of ages, allowed to be given out to the world, as the hour for it is come.

The educated reader need not be reminded again that one of the great discoveries which has immortalized the name of Darwin is the law that an organism has always a tendency to repeat, at an analogous period in its life, the action of its progenitors, the more surely and completely in proportion to their proximity in the scale of life. One result of this is, that, in general, organized beings usually die at a period (on an average) the same as; that of their progenitors. It is true that there is a great difference between the actual ages at which individuals of any species die.

Disease, accidents and famine are the main agents in causing this. But there is, in each species, a well-known limit within which the Race-life lies and none are known to survive beyond it. This applies to the human species as well as any other. Now, supposing that every possible sanitary condition had been complied with, and every accident and disease avoided by a man of ordinary frame, in some particular case there would still, as is known to medical men, come a time when the particles of the body would feel the hereditary tendency to do that which leads inevitably to dissolution, and would obey it.

It must be obvious to any reflecting man that, if by any procedure this critical climacteric could be once thoroughly passed over, the subsequent danger of "Death" would be proportionally less as the years progressed. Now this, which no ordinary and unprepared mind and body can do, is possible sometimes for the will and the frame of one who has been specially prepared. There are fewer of the grosser particles present to feel the hereditary bias, there is the assistance of the reinforced "interior men" (whose normal duration is always greater even in natural death) to the visible outer shell, and there is the drilled and indomitable Will to direct and wield the whole.

From that time forward the course of aspirant is clearer. He has conquered "the Dweller of the Threshold" — the hereditary enemy of his race, and, though still exposed to ever-new dangers in his progress towards Nirvana, he is flushed with victory, and with new confidence and new powers to second it, can press onwards to perfection.

For, it must be remembered, that nature everywhere acts by Law, and that the process of purification we have been describing in the visible material body, also takes place in those which are interior, and not visible to the scientist by modifications of the same process. All is on the change, and the metamorphoses of the more ethereal bodies imitate, though in successively multiplied duration, the career of the grosser, gaining an increasing wider range of relations with the surrounding cosmos, till in Nirvana the most rarefied Individuality is merged at last into the infinite totality.

From the above description of the process, it will be inferred why it is that "Adepts" are so seldom seen in ordinary life; for, pari passu, with the etherealization of their bodies and the development of their power, grows an increasing distaste, and a so-to-speak, "contempt" for the things of our ordinary mundane existence. Like the fugitive who successively casts away in his flight those articles which incommode his progress, beginning with the heaviest, so the aspirant eluding "Death" abandons all on which the latter can take hold. In the progress of Negation everything got rid of is a help. As we said before, the adept does not become "immortal" as the word is ordinarily understood. By or about the time when the Death-limit of his race is passed he is actually dead, in the ordinary sense, that is to say, he has relieved himself of all or nearly all such material particles as would have necessitated in disruption the agony of dying. He has been dying gradually during the whole period of his Initiation.

The catastrophe cannot happen twice over. He has only spread over a number of years the mild process of dissolution which others endure from a brief moment to a few hours. The highest Adept is, in fact, dead to, and absolutely unconscious of, the world; he is oblivious of its pleasures, careless of its miseries, in so far as sentimentalism goes, for the stern sense of duty never leaves him blind to its very existence. For the new ethereal senses opening to wider spheres are to ours much in the relation of ours to the Infinitely Little. New desires and enjoyments, new dangers and new hindrances arise, with new sensations and new perceptions; and far away down in the mist — both literally and metaphorically — is our dirty little earth left below by those who have virtually "gone to join the gods."

And from this account too, it will be perceptible how foolish it is for people to ask the Theosophists to "procure for them communication with the highest Adepts." It is with the utmost difficulty that one or two can be induced, even by the throes of a world, to injure their own progress by meddling with mundane affairs. The ordinary reader will say: "This is not god-like. This is the acme of selfishness." . . . . But let him realize that a very high Adept, undertaking to reform the world, would necessarily have to once more submit to Incarnation. And is the result of all that have gone before in that line sufficiently encouraging to prompt a renewal of the attempt?

A deep consideration of all that we have written, will also give the Theosophists an idea of what they demand when they ask to be put in the way of gaining practically "higher powers." Well, there, as plainly as words can put it, is the path. . . . Can they tread it?

Nor must it be disguised that what to the ordinary mortal are unexpected dangers, temptations and enemies also beset the way of the neophyte. And that for no fanciful cause, but the simple reason that he is, in fact, acquiring new senses, has yet no practice in their use, and has never before seen the things he sees. A man born blind suddenly endowed with vision would not at once master the meaning of perspective, but would, like a baby, imagine in one case, the moon to be within his reach, and, in the other, grasp a live coal with the most reckless confidence.

And what, it may be asked, is to recompense this abnegation of all the pleasures of life, this cold surrender of all mundane interests, this stretching forward to an unknown goal which seems ever more unattainable? For, unlike some of the anthropomorphic creeds, Occultism offers to its votaries no eternally permanent heaven of material pleasure, to be gained at once by one quick dash through the grave. As has, in fact, often been the case many would be prepared willingly to die now for the sake of the paradise hereafter. But Occultism gives no such prospect of cheaply and immediately gained infinitude of pleasure, wisdom and existence. It only promises extensions of these, stretching in successive arches obscured by successive veils, in an unbroken series up the long vista which leads to Nirvana. And this too, qualified by the necessity that powers entail new responsibilities, and that the capacity of increased pleasure entails the capacity of increased sensibility to pain. To this, the only "answer" that can be given is two-fold:

First the consciousness of Power is itself the most exquisite of pleasures, and is unceasingly gratified in progress onwards with new means for its exercise and secondly as has been already said — this is the only road by which there is the faintest scientific likelihood that "Death" can be avoided, perpetual memory secured, infinite wisdom attained, hence an immense helping of mankind made possible, once that the adept has safely crossed turning-point.

Physical as well as metaphysical logic requires and endorses the fact that only by gradual absorption into infinity can the Part become acquainted with the Whole, and that, that which is now something can only feel, know, and enjoy Everything when lost in Absolute Totality in the vortex of that Unalterable Circle wherein our Knowledge becomes Ignorance, and the Everything itself is identified with the nothing.

(xi) Bertram Mitford FRGS

(1855-1914)

South African Novelist and a founder of South African literature

Often when asked about apartheid and Nelson Mandela, and life in my home country - South Africa - I feel it's always best to speak as an English – South African, after enjoying over 40 years of living in what I consider to be one of the best countries in the world. Firstly, to understand any country one needs to know its history and culture.

Bertram Mitford, my great uncle, is considered to be one of the founders of South African literature, is perhaps best known for the classic statement which he coined – 'two bulls and a fence', and one of his best selling books 'The Sign of the Spider'. [Book cover illustrated in plate section.]

In one of the books he wrote, "The Induna's Wife" (Induna means chief or headman in Zulu), he describes a conference between the Amabuna (Afrikaners or Boers) and Dingane, King of the Zulus. The Afrikaners argued they could live on good terms with the Zulus with only the waters of the mighty Tugela River dividing them. Bertram writes. "I know not" answered King Dingane. "When two great bulls stand looking at each other over one fence, are they friends for long?"

The Boers replied that the land on each side of the proposed boundary was large enough for both. "The kraal (African name for enclosure or paddock) in which stands each of those bulls is large enough for both" said Dingane, "yet it will not be long before one of them is through the fence to drive out the other. Then he rules over both kraals". Dingane knew exactly what he was saying (a rather crafty fellow, as the Boers were to discover) as he had no intention of giving any lands to the Boers or the British. The book 'The Indunas Wife' deals with death and destruction, fighting with witch-doctors, impis (singular, is a group of armed men) and naked warriors – a classic Zulu story. All this, was exciting stuff during the Victorian era. Today it is still exciting.

Born in Bath, England, Bertram was the third son of nine children, five boys and four girls. His father was Edward Ledwich Mitford FRGS, a "GA" or Government Agent / Consul for 25 years in the British colony of Colombo, Ceylon (now Sri Lanka). He married Janet Bailey, daughter of the Archdeacon of Ceylon, Benjamin Bailey, my great-great grandparents. His father, Edward (previously covered) became the 27th Squire of Mitford at the grand age of 85 years, followed by his two sons Robert and Edward.

Bertram grew up in the temperate climate of Ceylon and later attended Hurstpierpoint College in England from 1870 to 1874, where he excelled in English writing. His father, having led an adventurous and exciting life himself, was a great influence on his career encouraging him to follow his passion and explore South Africa, which at the time was the new colony. Bertram Mitford did just that and first arrived in South Africa aged 20 in 1875 to try his hand at farming then became fascinated with the country – its space, beauty and engaging tribal culture.

Bertram was a government official in the Cape Civil Service during the times of the Zulu wars in 1877/8 and gained varied experience travelling about the African bushveldt hunting and shooting, in the new and developing South African gold and diamond mines where he first met and became a friend of British mining baron, Cecil John Rhodes (1853-1902 famous for his Rhodes Scholarships and more recently debate over his statue). Bertram's youthful and adventurous spirit took him further afield to visit northern India, Afghanistan and America, before settling down in South Africa and writing 44 books over a period of 32 years from 1881 to 1913.

In 1886 Bertram married Helen Zima and they produced two children, daughter Yseulte Helen in 1887 and son Roland Bertram in 1891. Both daughter and son married but did not produce any grandchildren. Bertram died in Cowfold, England of liver disease in October 1914 and his wife died five months later in 1915.

Through The Zulu Country

Bertram Mitford was the first person to visit the battlefields of Zululand, to gather the opinions of the survivors of the Zulu war at Isandlwana where the British experienced their worst defeat during the Victorian era in 1879. Just one year later in 1880, starting from Rorke's Drift, he visited Isandlwana and the scene of the Prince Imperial of France's death in the Ityotyozi Valley. In his book, Bertram gives a detailed account of the site, a report of the Prince Imperial's death and people involved.

The Prince Imperial of France – was born Eugene Louis Napoleon on 16th March 1856. He was the only child of Emperor Napoleon 3rd of France and his consort, Empress Eugene. He was the nephew of Napoleon Bonaparte 1 - his paternal grandfather was Louis Bonaparte, King of Spain, and his maternal grandfather, Count de Montijo, Grandee of Spain, and heir to the most powerful court in Europe. He was killed aged 23 in Zululand.

Bertram writes "I was at some pains to get at the facts of the whole affair, which, according to the story of Sabuza and his followers, were these. The Zulus who surprised the Prince numbered sixty men belonging to the Ngobamakosi, Umbonambi, and Nokenke regiments — a scouting party, in fact. The presence of white men was reported by one of the number, who, from a peak overlooking the valley, directly opposite the scene of the catastrophe, had seen the Prince's party off saddle at the kraal. Thereupon the whole body moved stealthily down a deep donga opening into the Ityotyozi ; gaining the river they crept along beneath its high banks and advanced upon the unsuspecting group under cover of the standing corn.

Those fatal ten minutes! But for that disastrous delay the Prince would have been alive now. The savages were scarcely in position when the word was given to mount, but fearing lest their prey should escape them after all, they made the attack. A hurried volley; a wild shout ; and the rout was complete. One of the troopers was unable to mount his horse, that of the other was shot; but the Prince still had hold of his — a large grey — which plunged and reared, becoming quite unmanageable. 'We fired again,' said my informant, ' and charged forward, shouting "Usutu." The big horse broke away, and ran after the other white men who were riding out as fast as they could, round the slope.

He fought hard when we came up to him; the scuffle with the horse had brought him here (about 150 yards from where the attack was made). The first man to stab him was Xamanga, he belonged to the Umbonambi regiment, and was afterwards killed in the battle of Nodwengu. We did not know at the time who the Prince really was, but thought he was an English induna. His sword was taken to Cetywayo." His body was recovered with numerous assegai wounds down his chest. There ended the last hope to continue the Napoleon dynasty. He was finally buried in St Michael's Abbey, Farnborough.

"The Prince Imperial's monument where he died seems to be kept in good order. There is about a quarter of an acre of ground walled in, and within that a small inner enclosure where the Queen's cross stands. The original wreath placed round it is still intact, though much faded. The monument was handed over by Major Stabb, to a chief called Sabaza and his tribe, who promised to take care of it and they have kept their word well. When we entered the enclosure the Zulus stood a moment, one after another, and, raising the right hand above the head, gave the salute of honour, 'Inkos' which ceremony they told me was always gone through whenever they had occasion to visit the place. The bones of the trooper's horse were still lying near where that of the Prince broke away, but other traces of the sad affair were there none"

As a memento of this visit Bertram kept the hoof bone of the fallen horse and later back in England had it mounted with a silver replica of the Queens cross. This was once kept at Mitford Hall, but sadly is now lost.

Bertram's tour of all the battle sites ended up with a visit to Cetewayo, the Zulu King under house arrest in the Cape. There is a great deal that is valuable in Bertram's observation. He met and became acquainted with nearly all the Zulu chiefs. Bertram never grew tired of praising the Zulus. He maintains that instead of thinking of them as fierce, untameable barbarians whose every thought is war, we ought to know that they, unless provoked, are really a quiet, kindly, light hearted race, sober, clean and honest.

"It would be idle, of course, not to expect occasional turbulence and disquiet, among a brave, warlike people with great military traditions. I maintain that the Zulu is by nature of a quiet and kindly disposition, not wanting in generosity, and good humoured to a degree; in short, far from being a brutal savage. He has his faults indeed; and if merciless and cruel in the madness and exultation of victory, at any rate it is the blind ferocity of the wild beast, whose rage is satiated with the death of an enemy – not the refined barbarity of the Red Indian, or of the Oriental delighting in the prolonged torments of the victim".

Bertram formed a high opinion of John Dunn, a well known settler and hunter of Scottish descent who married 48 African wives and fathered 117 children. A remarkable accomplishment of energy and fortitude. He also dabbled in the liquor trade. His network or territory which was studded with African liquor canteens (or shebeens as we call them today), enjoyed an almost unrestricted right of sale. Bertram and John, with their good friendship were no doubt part of the many – gathered around some of these canteens in various stages of intoxication.

Hangovers or no hangovers, Bertram interviewed a great many men who had fought in the various battles, and managed to get accounts from men who had actually taken part in the battles. The local natives in Pietermaritzburg were mesmerised with the cannon and Gatling guns used at the time. The cannon gun they called "Ubain-bai" and Bertram records the following tale.

"At Pietermaritzburg, every morning a gun was fired at 8 am, signalling the hour when all the servants and labourers were expected to be at work. Later it was changed to 9 am. Jack who had some idea of time but none of punctuality still persisted in sticking to the old time and from sheer force of habit would go to his master for his daily task. The "baas" however, would put him off – 'don't bother me now, come by-and-by when the gun fires!' So Jack reports back to his friends and relates what he has been told "Come by-and-by". Directly after the expected detonation at 9 am was heard – nearly every native throughout the city of

Pietermaritzburg would exclaim 'Haow, Ubain bai!' and go to work, and so the name of the gun became Ubain bai".

"Through the Zulu Country – its Battlefields and its People" was his first book published in 1883 when he was 28. In recognition he was elected Fellow of the Royal Geographic Society on 5 April 1890. The certificate was signed by Arthur Montefiore FRGS and two others whose signatures are quite undecipherable to myself.

Another book he wrote entitled "The Gun Runner" is the story of Zululand. To quote Vanity Fair – 'As a story of Zululand, this book takes high rank in historical fiction.' Bertram writes. "I have refrained from terming this work a 'historical' novel; yet many of the incidents recorded are history". The bulk of the Zulu chiefs and indunas who feature in it are real characters, and, including the king, were personally known to Bertram. The same holds good of the localities used. The narrative deals with history and the remarkable military power and ultimate downfall of the finest and most intelligent race of savages in the world – now, thanks to the 'beneficent' policy of England, crushed and 'civilized' out of all recognition." A graphic tale of Zululand – not the mythical Zululand of Rider Haggard, but the real thing written in contemporary language of the time.

Exactly 86 years later, in 1969, at the age of 16 Bertram's great nephew, myself, also got to meet one of the chiefs of Zululand. I remember my father saying to my mother, "Absolutely ridiculous. In fact crazy, driving into the heart of Zululand to discuss horses in a deal with a Zulu chief, is totally absurd". My father declared he would have nothing to do with the expedition, except he did end up paying for it. My mother didn't falter and carried on. At that young age I thought this was all rather exciting. What adventure!

In a nutshell, the "deal" we were about to do concerned an exchange of horses. The Zulu chief had bought a stallion that was the brother to one of the horses I rode and my mother wanted to rescue it from the wilderness. The only way the chief would part with the horse was by replacing it with another stallion. So my mother bought another young stallion and we transported the animal several hundred miles to Zululand by Land Rover and horse-box then exchanged the stallion with the horse she wanted to rescue. My mother didn't bat an eyelid and it was all done as she did this sort of deal every day, much to the amazement of my father and friends. I didn't get to spend much time with the Zulu chief as I was running around the African bush veldt trying to catch and then load up a wild stallion.

All Bertram's books have gripping tales of adventure, desperate fights and hair breadth escapes set with a background of African wars, tribal life and stories of the early pioneering and colony settlements of southern Africa. Bertram has often been compared with the novelist Rider Haggard. Indeed they became good friends and often lunched together when in London. Their roots are much the same – both have links to English country gentlemen.

Whilst Rider Haggard wrote popular romance, Bertram ventured into areas to challenge Britain's role in Africa and to reveal the truth behind the scenes, presenting a more rustic, true life account than other writers on South Africa. At the heart of many of his books lie the politics and relations between the Boers, British and African tribes. His heroes include settlers, slave traders, renegade whites and savage tribesmen. His heroines court physical danger and rescue endangered men folk. He shows a liberal, progressive and humane attitude through his work and stories.

An example of one of the statements can be found in his book entitled "The Curse of Clement Waynflete", when news of the British defeat at Isandlwana is reported at a family dinner table, when a heated dialogue follows one of the ladies present simply asks – "Surely even the Zulus can't be blamed for defending their country?" Her father replies "What's the girl talking about, defending their fiddlesticks? They've no business fighting against the British flag." "But I was always under the impression that we invaded their country" she persisted. Her father then turns to another person at the dinner table "Royston, do you know anything about this affair – why are we at war with the Zulus?" His reply follows "I'll be hanged if I do know exactly – I suppose the long and the short of it is that we want their country…."

Interestingly, in several books, Bertram presents the world from a black perspective to explore Zulu and Matabele society and their response to the encroaching white domination. One of his most successful books, "Sign of the Spider" 1896, written while staying at Westbourne Park Road, W2 in London, highlights the relations between the Boers, British, Uitlanders, and the Transvaal government during the discovery of gold and diamonds. To quote from a description of the book, "The story bristles with incident. The terrific episode of the spider is narrated with extraordinary force. A thrilling adventure and absorbing romance".

Above all, Bertram possessed an intimate knowledge and understanding of black African tribes. On the following pages are some examples. On one occasion, he even took Rider Haggard to task in a public letter. Bertram wrote to the Editor of the Pall Mall Gazette.

Dear Sir, I should like to ask Mr Rider Haggard whence he draws his authority for stating that Charka, King of the Zulus ever "commanded an army of about a hundred thousand soldiers," or anything like that number. If the statement is inaccurate, what has become of the odd 70,000? But so far from there being any suggestion – at the time of the Anglo-Zulu invasion – of such enormous diminution of the Zulu army, the "formidable man-slaying machine" of Sir Bartle Frere was estimated to be as formidable and as man-slaying as ever. Yet the largest impi which King Cetewayo was able to put into the field for a decisive battle numbered about 25,000 shields.

This was at Isandhlwana and, adding the 4,000 or so who attacked Col Pearson at the Inyezane river on the same day, and a few fighting men who would be sure to have remained at home near the king, would total about 30,000 Zulus under arms and no more. Again I ask, how are we to account for that missing 70,000? – for it is a large order, mind. The migration of the present Matabele and Gaza would account for less than half – the Boer battles for a mere fraction, and any wars waged by the Zulus against neighbouring tribes since have been mere police expeditions, so far as meeting with any serious resistance was concerned.

What, again, does Mr Haggard mean when he writes about "Umzilikaze or Mosilikatze, the Lion"? So far as I know there are only two words in Zulu which mean lion – viz "Ingonyama" and "Ibubéshe." But "The Lion" is one of the titles of the Zulu kings, and for a sub-chief to usurp it would mean death – especially under the rule of Charka. It could not, therefore, be used by Umzilikaze as a title. Where then, does it come in?

With all due respect to worthy Pieter Bezuidenhout and Mr Haggard, I take leave to doubt that from four to five hundred Boers, armed with muzzle-loading guns, killed 3,500 Zulus in any one battle. Still more that when "the Zulus in thousands were no further than ten paces" the Boers would have had any time – let alone "scarcely any"… "to throw a handful of powder into the gun etc."

The fact is that in narratives of this kind a wider margin of discount must be allowed for the exaggeration natural to the winning side in totting up the enemy's losses and in duly setting forth its own prowess, and something of an experience of Boers and natives (including Zulus) has not as yet convinced me that the former are prone to err on the side of ungarnished veracity, or that the latter are ingenuously open in holding up their losses to the gaze of their present or wily foe. So we still have about thirty to forty of those disappearing thousands unaccounted for. Have they gone on a search after the Lost Ten Tribes? Signed - Bertram Mitford 23 October 1893.

In 1899 he again wrote to the editor of the Pall Mall Gazette.

Sir, - The writer of "The Attitude of the Zulus" in your last night's issue sums up the situation concisely and accurately enough – but he enunciates one statement which is calculated to convey an erroneous impression. This is it. "The memory of Boer brutality, the days of ancestral slavery…" The fact is the Zulus have no such memory. When the Boers under Pieter Retief, swarmed over the Drakensberg, with their families and possessions, into Natal, Dingane, the then Zulu King recognized that they had come to stay and adopted towards them the short and simple method in favour with barbarian potentates under the impression that their sway is menaced. He massacred as many as he could lay his hands on. Nor did the Boers even conquer the Zulus, as the popular error is. With the help of half the nation under Dingane's revolted brother Umpande, they drove back the other half into the forest country beyond the Black Umfolosi. There Dingane was collecting his forces with the object of trying conclusions again, when his murder at the hands of a Swazi conspiracy settled the matter in favour of the Dutch. Cetywayo, too (the name should be spelled as I have written it, not with "e" twice), had no notion of submitting to Boer encroachment – an important raison d'être of his splendid and disciplined standing army. But neither the Zulus nor the erstwhile powerful and warlike Amaxosa tribes in the Transkei and Cape Colony have ever had occasion to cherish the memory of "ancestral slavery" at the hands of the Boers. I am, Sir, yours faithfully, Bertram Mitford; Junior Athenaeum Club.

P.S. It may be of interest at the present juncture to note that during the late hotly-contested Cape elections, when racial feeling had probably touched the highest point it has ever yet attained, the native vote in the Cape Colony preponderated in favour of the Bond. This may only prove the superior astuteness of Bond electioneering methods. Or, – it may be a straw.

In 1896, Bertram wrote an article for a London newspaper entitled "The Boer as I know him", as follows. "The term "Boer" means simply and solely a farmer. Although the Dutch language, Dutch tradition, Dutch religion and Dutch sympathies preponderate, yet by no means is the Boer by origin a Dutchman pure and simple. You see the large massive Scandinavian or Teutonic type – blond, blue eyed, slow moving, side by side with the dark, vivacious, dapper Latin element. You find such characteristically Dutch names as Bezuidenhout, Oosthuisen, Wessels, Hattingh, and of course, all the innumerable family of the "Vans" – Van Aardt, Van Niekerk, Van Wyk, Van de Merve, and so forth. But alongside of and all intermingled with them, there are such unmistakably Gallic sounding patronymics as Labuschagne, Roux, Lombard, De Villiers, and Joubert, and that not uncommon, Hispano sounding one, Ferreira. Refugee French Huguenots have had far more to do with building up the Boer factor in South Africa than we are accustomed to think –

probably, too, there is an admixture of Iberian blood, as a relic of Spanish occupation of the Netherlands.

The Boer is, as a rule, essentially domestic and stay-at-home. He delights to sit down under his own vine, and, when they become too destructive, shoot spreuws (starlings) in his own fig trees. He hates English rule – less as a matter of feeling than of tradition. Practically, however, he rubs along exceedingly well with his English neighbour. He will drop in as a matter of course and shake hands all round, and drink his *sopje* of Congo or a cup of coffee, and light his pipe and discuss the latest news; take what there is going, and get on his horse and wend his way – the last no sooner than he likes. And his English neighbour will look in upon him in like unceremonious fashion. "Help yourself and your friends will love you", is a Boer saying; and taking it as it is meant, wholly without satire, it throws a telling sidelight upon the Boer character. In a word, the instinct of hospitality and neighbourliness of the Boer is innate, ingrained. Even his horse will stop of its own accord on the road when meeting another, to have a chat, exchange the news and a "fill" of tobacco from each other's skin pouch. If you spend the night at his house, whether belated or of set purpose, you get what is going, or if too late for the family meal, the first thought on the part of the huis-vrou (housewife) is to start culinary operations on your behalf.

As far as the external aspect goes, there can hardly be said to exist such a thing as a typical Boer. I have seen individuals whom, until they opened their mouths, I would have thought of being French, others again, to all outward appearances, colonial English. There are of all sorts and sizes – from men of fine and towering stature to small and wizened. One characteristic the Boer has is that he does not touch a razor. Shaving is a refinement he regards as effeminate and luxurious, hence the shaggy and unkempt type of countenance so frequently met with.

Of the Boer woman, it cannot be said to err on the side of beauty. The girls, when they have any pretensions to good looks, are comely rather than handsome – bright eyed, rosy cheeked and not altogether wanting in vivacity. But early marriage and lack of healthy outdoor exercise and interest soon ages them and they become shapeless and unwieldy and too often mentally vacuous and listless. Their courting is no more romantic a process than it is among our own rustic population, in that it is done in a few words spread over as many hours at a time. But Piet or Stoffel or Martinus, together with his relatives, is every bit as great a stickler for the dol as Jacques, Alphonse or Polyte of the French bourgeoisie; and the Boer parent seldom fails to set apart from the increase of his flocks and herds to meet such eventual requirement on the part of his own redundant progeny. For the Boer is the most matrimonial mortal on the face of the earth. With dawning manhood his first ambition is to get married. Bachelorhood is a state not well favoured, along with his sisters, cousins and aunts. A middle aged Boer bachelor is a phenomenon. It is no uncommon thing to meet with Boers only just touching middle age, yet wedded to their third wives; and when we remember that this is a race pre-eminately mindful of the divine command concerning multiplication, it will readily be understood that the population of the paternal farm is soon in excess of what that patriarchal estate can support. Hence the ever present tendency to trek.

The Boer's religion is like himself – hard, unpolished, thorough; but such as it is, he believes in it, and outwardly practises it thoroughly. The predikant (minister) and ouderlingen (elders), the latter to be seen on Sundays in all the dignity of stovepipe hat and full evening dress, are powers in his midst; and Nachtmaal (Lord's Supper) is a quarterly recurring solemnity whose importance he is not disposed to underrate. Even in the naming of his children the Boer is nothing if not scriptural – Abraham, Izaak and Jacob are as popular with him as with the tribesmen who extracted so much gold from out his midst. He is fond of piling up Christian names too, and is frequently to be found groaning under such an accumulation as "Petrus Jacobus Johannjes Elias". So too as to his female counterpart, and "Rachael Petronella Johanna Aletta" will get through life comfortably under the load.

The Boer is essentially clannish. He is full of fight in his own grim deliberate way. He wants it soon, because the sooner it is over the sooner he can return to the farm. I well remember when the news of the Gaika rising in Christmas week 1877, arrived in the small frontier township where at that time I held a Government post. The place was without telephone communication in those days, so the news, startling though not unexpected, was somewhat delayed. Word was sent round to the field-coronets of the district – almost exclusively a Dutch one, and in an astonishing few hours nearly a thousand Boers had mustered at the court house, mounted, armed and ready. We "commandeered" between three and four hundred of them, and these then set to work in the most businesslike way; and the commando, having first marched to the church to listen to an address from the predikant, rode off there and then, and with a clear conscience, to "knock spots of John Kaffir" – returning in a few weeks grim and war torn, but having materially decreased the number of Sandili's fighting men (Mgolombane Sandile 1820-1875, was a Xhosa, Paramount Chief).

If there is one thing more upon which the Boer sets store, it is his rifle. His marksmanship enjoys worldwide celebrity. I remember a Boer who used to sometimes join our buck hunting parties, and who at any distance up to 300 yards would pick off any given one of a line of springbok going at a very fair rate of speed. We only had to name our buck – first, third, middle, tail of the line – and that buck fell. He rather enjoyed banter about being born with a gun in his hand, saying that it was little short of actual fact, for almost before he had ceased to crawl his father would send him out into the veldt with a muzzle-loading gun containing a bullet and a single charge of powder. With this he was going to bring home a buck and the penalty for missing consisted in going supper less to bed with the application of the "strap" frequently thrown in. It followed that his misses were few. Sometimes in a moment of paternal indulgence, he would be allowed one extra charge. And that, he declared, was the way to teach boys to shoot. For the shotgun, the Boer, as a rule, entertains profound contempt. He looks upon birds as poor eating. If he wants meat he shoots a buck. If it is poultry, well, his vrouw is sure to keep a lot of chickens around the homestead. But bird-shooting he regards as poor sport and only fit for Englishmen".

Further, in October 1899, the New York Times quoted Bertram's comments regarding the political situation in South Africa. Bertram said "The Boers will fight like devils. The Jameson raid roused them and ever since they have been preparing for war and practicing shooting and they will resist to the bitter end. I do not believe the Boers will incite the natives against England, but it is impossible to say what the natives will do. The Basutos are loyal to the Queen, but hate the Free State. Though it would be a bad thing for white supremacy if the Basutos were to rise and conquer the Free State, yet it would be hardly possible to stop them. The Swazis are equally bitter against the Transvaal, and it would need little encouragement to lead them to attack the republic. I do not think there is any danger from the Zulus, but the Matabele and the Mashonas might try to repeat the horrors of 1896. All the published estimates of the fighting strength of the boers are exaggerated. It does not exceed 15,000 at the outside".

In June 1900, Bertram and Rider Haggard were still chuckling about his letter to the editor, at a South African Writers' Club luncheon hosted at the Grand Hotel in Charing Cross with Rider Haggard as chairman. In his opening speech, he said much had happened over the past years and the war was now behind them. The settlement would be a long and ugly struggle. The guest speaker was the Hon Hedworth Lambton (later Admiral of the Fleet the Hon Sir Hedworth Meux GCB KCVO), who came to the rescue of the British at Ladysmith during the second Boer war.

Other well known personalities attending included Sir Frederick Mirrielees, head of the Union Castle Shipping Line, Namaqua Copper Mines and Chairman of the Mount Nelson Hotel in Cape Town. It was through Sir Frederick that Bertram become acquainted with Rudyard Kipling. William Garland Soper, lawyer and chairman of the Sheba Gold Mining company. Howard Spensley, lawyer for and during the aftermath of the famous Jameson Raid in South Africa. Henry Bryden, who played rugby for England and wrote many books on South Africa and James Huddart, shipbuilder.

Bertram certainly mixed in the right circles and was fortunate to have the backdrop of the family estates in Mitford,

Northumberland and Yorkshire which no doubt helped. Over his lifetime he amassed a collection of African art treasures. He was a member of the Junior Athenaeum Club and the South African Writers Club in London. As mentioned, he is also considered to be one of the founders of South African literature. His long friendship with Cecil John Rhodes, mining baron, imperialist, statesman, founder of Rhodesia (now Zimbabwe) and the Oxford University Rhodes Scholarship was remembered in his last will and testament.

Apart from his gravestone Rhodes also commissioned a monument to be erected alongside called the Shangani Memorial. It is an oblong, flat-topped structure, about 10m tall, made from local granite and designed by Herbert Baker. Each of the memorial's four sides bears a bronze panel by John Tweed, depicting members of the patrol in relief. The main inscription reads, "To Brave Men erected to the enduring memory of Allan Wilson and his Men who fell in fighting against the Matabele on the Shangani River 4 December 1893. There were no survivors". Originally written in July 1899, the following are passages made public and edited as follows.

"I wish to be buried in the Matopos on the hill which I used to visit and which I called the "View of the World" in a square to be cut in the rock on the top of the hill covered with a plain brass plate with these words thereon " Here lie the remains of Cecil John Rhodes."

Accordingly I direct my Trustees on the hill aforesaid to erect or complete the monument to the men who fell in the first Matabele War at Shangani in Rhodesia the bas-reliefs for which are being made by Mr. John Tweed and I desire the said Mr. Bertram Mitford says.

"For grim, gloomy savagery of solitude it is probable that the stupendous rock wilderness known as the Matopos Hills is unsurpassed throughout earth's surface. Strictly speaking, the term 'hills' scarcely applies to this marvellous range, which is rather an expanse of granite rocks extending some seventy or eighty miles by forty or fifty, piled in titanic proportions and bizarre confusion, over what would otherwise be a gently undulating surface, forming a kind of island as it were, surrounded by beautiful rolling country, green, smiling, and in parts thickly bushed.

High on the outside ridge of this remarkable range, about twenty miles distant from Bulawayo, towards which it faces, there rises a pile of granite boulders, huge, solid, compact. It is a natural structure – an imposing and dominating one withal, and appropriately so, for this is the sepulchre of the warrior King Umzilikazi, founder and first monarch of the Matabele nation."

From old Rhodesia to Zimbabwe, once the bread basket of southern Africa along with the African colonies belonging to Germany, Spain, Portugal and Belgium, much has happened in southern Africa since those early days.

South Africa! The land where the rainbow ends and where an enormous pot of gold was found – and Mother Nature added more. The pots of diamonds, uranium, chrome ore, manganese, asbestos and much other fabulous mineral wealth. In the midst of all this wealth, charm, and breathtaking scenic beauty are found some of the world's trickiest racial problems described by General Jan Smuts (statesman and prime minister, and a founder of the United Nations we have today) in his words. "South Africa is the social and economic melting pot which contains not only its own singular problems but also the social, economic, educational, political, language, racial and other problems of all other countries as well".

Over past years, perhaps because other countries did not have similar problems they complacently took their distant stand of idealism and hollow theories and told South Africa what it ought to do? World opinion is free to criticise, but remember, it does not have the responsibility of governing. That's South Africa's job.

The country was first run by the British and then by Dutch/ Afrikaners, until Nelson Mandela and the ANC (African National Congress) took over in 1994. He gave hope to ALL South Africans, of all colours (gaining its nick name of the rainbow nation), for a new beginning, a new life, new opportunities and a fair deal. That was and is his legacy. This is dramatised in Clint Eastwood's film "Invictus", where Nelson Mandela took the sport of rugby to unite all South Africans under one flag as one nation, joining together - UMOJA, the African word for the spirit of togetherness.

Books published by Bertram from 1881 to 1913, with title, publisher and year of publication.

1. Our arms in Zululand	Poems	1881
2. Through the Zulu Country	(nonfiction)	1883
3. The Fire Trumpet	Blackett	1889
4. The Weird of Deadly Hollow	Sutton	1891
5. Golden Face	Trischler	1892
6. Tween Snow and Fire	Heinemann Cassell	1892
7. The Curses of Clement	Waynflete Ward	1894
8. The King's Assegai	Chatto	1894
9. The Luck of Gerard Ridgeley	Chatto	1894
10. Renshaw Fanning's Quest	Chatto	1894
11. The White Shield	Cassell	1895
12. A Veldt Official	Ward	1895
13. The Sign of the Spider	Methuen	1896
14. The Expiation of Wynne	Palliser Ward	1896
15. Fordham's Feud	Ward	1897
16. The Induna's Wife	White	1898
17. The Ruby Sword	White	1899
18. The Gun-Runner	Chatto	1899
19. Aletta	White	1900
20. War and Arcadia	White	1900
21. John Ames, Native Commissioner	White	1900
22. The Triumph of Hilary Blachland	Chatto	1901
23. The Word of the Sorceress	Hutchinson	1902
24. A Veldt Vendetta	Ward	1903
25. Dorrien of Cranston	Hurst	1903
26. Forging the Blades	Nash	1903
27. Haviland's Chum	Chatto	1903
28. In the Whirl of the Rising	Methuen	1904
29. The Red Derelict	Methuen	1904
30. The Sirdar's Oath	White	1904
31. A Frontier Mystery	White	1905
32. A Secret of the Lebombo	Hurst	1905
33. Harley Greenoak's Charge	Chatto	1906
34. The White Hand and the Black	Long	1907
35. A Legacy of the Granite Hills	Long	1909
36. A Border Scourge	Long	1910
37. A Duel Resurrection	Ward	1910
38. Ravenshaw of Rietholme	Ward	1910
39. The Heath Hover Mystery	Ward	1911
40. The River of Unrest	Ward	1912
41. Seaford's Snake	Ward	1912
42. Selmin of Selmingfold	Ward	1912
43. Averno	Ward	1913
44. An Island of Eden	Ward	1913

(xii) The Mitford Girls
(1904-2014)

The eccentricities of six sisters

Nancy was the first born in 1904, followed by Pamela, Thomas, the only son, then Diana, Unity, Jessica and Deborah in 1920. Deborah passed away on the 24th September 2014. Their parents were David and Sydney Freeman Mitford, 2nd Baron Redesdale (1878-1958), known as Lord and Lady Redesdale. The name Freeman was added earlier due to an inheritance requirement.

What can be said or added to what has already been reported? They created and strutted scandal as a way of life becoming their *raison d'être*. So much has been written about them. Countless pages, long playing records, films and DVD's have been made. As a youngster I was always asked, are you related to the Mitford girls and I'd look at the person with a blank glaze and ask who are they? In South Africa it was only the "grown-ups" that knew of the Mitford sisters. No one talked much about them because it brought back horrible memories of the war and Hitler. My family of course met them and writer, traveller and journalist Lesley Blanch who was great friends with Nancy. Lesley would have been at the top of Nancy's A-list as she was Features Editor of Vogue Magazine in London and friends with Diana Vreeland (a cousin of Pauline Rothschild). Nancy, in one of her rare, overly generous moods paid for a stained glass window in Lesley's bedroom. The only sister I met and knew was the youngest sister Deborah, the dowager Duchess of Devonshire. Lesley of course was also great friends with Deborah as well. In a letter I received from Deborah while staying with Lesley she wrote "my goodness, is Lesley still alive"? Lesley actually lived to the grand old age of over 102! My insight to the life of the 'Mitford sisters' developed through women who knew them.

I knew Lesley for over 15 years (she was great friends with everyone) and I actually lived with her and her happy cats for two months while moving house from Italy to France. I got porridge in the mornings and whisky in the evenings. The main meal was usually served at lunch time by Alice (a rather charming Scots woman, with red hair who was a great help to Lesley) but I was never at home as I was running around looking for somewhere to live. Until one evening that is impossible to forget. Lesley invited some guests for dinner and I arrived back early to be well prepared and be at hand for whatever, like a dutiful butler. "May I take your coat, this way please" Lesley lived in a much organised jungle. What got my attention was that there was one place missing at the dinner table! Lesley I remember did a very quick move and created another place. Had I not said that Alice would have had her dinner in the kitchen and served at table! This memory perhaps reflects the world that Lesley and the Mitford sisters lived in, Alice always called Lesley "Madam".

Lesley often used to ramble on about Nancy and their times together. They were all born at the same time Nancy in 1904, Lesley in 1904 and Diana Vreeland in 1903. All became wildly successful. They all had something in common and something to trade. Lesley and Diana craved the aristocratic eccentricities of England and Nancy and sisters craved publicity - scandal, a common denominator. Socialising was an art and par for the course. Nancy had started her writing career with her first book published in 1931 and her success followed in 1945 with "Pursuit of Love" (apparently it made around £7,000 in the first six months of publication) and then "Love in a Cold Climate" in 1949. She wrote articles for Vogue and Harper's.

In one of her books, Nancy wrote "My father was quite uneducated – like a clever peasant. He had nothing much to do and when he filled in forms, he wrote next to occupation – honourable". Nancy never had children but she wrote "I love children, especially when they cry, for then someone takes them away". Nancy even has a bedroom named after her which is mentioned in the book entitled "The British Ambassador's Residence in Paris", kindly presented to me after giving a talk on the Mitford family to members of the British Association of Monaco. The one bedroom is called "Wincham", named after the fictitious ambassador in Nancy's book "Don't Tell Alfred" (1960).

This book was inspired by Lady Diana Cooper's extravagant personality, wife of Sir Alfred Duff Cooper the new ambassador after the liberation of Paris.

Lesley studied at the Slade for two years and later became Features Editor for Vogue in London from 1937 to 1944 then worked for the ministry of information with Lee Miller as photographer. In 1945 she married the French diplomat, novelist and icon Romain Gary, and later both became best selling novelists. With Romain's diplomatic career, they travelled everywhere and eventually got posted to Los Angeles and Hollywood. Romain won the Prix Goncourt for his book "Roots of Heaven" while Lesley wrote her bestselling book "The Sabres of Paradise". "Roots of Heaven" was made into a film with Errol Flynn, Trevor Howard, Orson Welles and the screen play was by Patrick Leigh-Fermor, great friend of Deborah Mitford, Duchess of Devonshire.

Diana Vreeland wife of American banker and New York socialite arrived in London in 1929 and took up residence at Hanover Square, Regents Park. Diana knew everyone and hosted grand dinner parties - Cecil Beaton, Wallis Simpson (the Windsors), Coco Chanel, and they were presented to King George V and Queen Mary at Buckingham Palace in 1933. Their publishing careers started around the same time and their lives became interwoven with other Mitford sisters. Diana with Harper's, Lesley with Vogue and Nancy writing articles for both.

A few years later the youngest Mitford sister Deborah fell in love and married Andrew Cavendish in 1941. Three years later in 1944 in Chelsea, London, her brother in law William (Billy) Cavendish married American socialite Kathleen Kennedy, sister to Ted, Robert and John, the future President of the United States of America. Four months after this wedding Billy Cavendish, future Duke of Devonshire was killed in the war and Deborah's husband, his younger brother became Duke and Deborah Duchess of Devonshire and Chatsworth.

When John Kennedy became president it was Diana Vreeland who became special advisor to the First Lady, Jackie Kennedy. Diana resigned from Harper's and her time with William

Randolph Hearst and the mighty Hearst Empire ended. She became editor in chief of Vogue from 1963 to 1971. It was Diana and then Lesley who had a lasting link between the Mitford girls up to the time I was introduced to the youngest, Deborah, the Dowager Duchess. A warm and relaxed person with twinkling blue eyes. No airs and graces, just simple down to earth, engaging practicality, with her quiet serenity and inner strength. She had had in part a tough, hard and eventful life and she coped so very well. It's all there. A lovely person. I also met the Duke many years ago while working as pupil trainer to Dick Hern, the Queen's racehorse trainer.

As mentioned earlier the link between Lesley Blanch's husband Romain Gary (before he married Jean Seberg in secret in Corsica), on the film set of Romain's book, "Roots of Heaven" where Patrick Leigh Fermor assisted Lesley's husband with the screenplay. Deborah Mitford's book "In Tearing Haste" gives the letters written between Deborah and Patrick and their long friendship. Interesting to note are the other films produced from the books by Romain Gary, all made in Nice, at the famous Victorine Film Studios on the French Riviera. In 1957 "Bonjour Tristesse" starred Jean Seberg (Romain Gary's second wife) and David Niven and in 1964 "Lady L", directed by Peter Ustinov, starring Sophia Loren, Paul Newman and David Niven (adapted by Lesley Blanch). The title of the book, "Lady L" refers to the L in Lesley Blanch and there is also a haunting song written about Lesley, called "Lady L". Lesley was a Fellow of the Royal Society of Literature, appointed MBE in 2001 and received the medal of Officier de l'Ordre des Arts et des Lettres from the French government. I was much involved with Lesley's last 15 years, a fascinating life. Lesley was friends with Elvis Presley, Gary Cooper, Sophia Loren and Laurence Olivier to name a few.

The other Diana was of course Diana Mitford, considered the most beautiful of all the Mitford girls. She became engaged to Bryan Guinness within several months of them knowing each other. Their marriage lasted long enough to produce an heir and a spare to the huge Guinness Brewery fortune before Diana fell in love with Sir Oswald Mosley, leader of the British Union of

Fascists, three years after her marriage to Bryan Guinness. Diana successfully and amazingly created several scandals. Her divorce created the first scandal and then the second scandal was her secret marriage to Sir Oswald while staying with Joseph and Magda Goebbels (Hitler's second in command) in Berlin and then the third scandal was when (based on her sister Nancy's testimony) Diana and Sir Oswald spent three years in Holloway prison. Lady Mosley was detained under the Defence Regulations by plain clothes officers at her home, Sanehay Farm, Denham, Buckinghamshire on Saturday 29th June 1940. My parents said it was due to her planned business agreement with Hitler to set up a radio broadcasting station across Europe to broadcast propaganda. Apparently they did have their own little house or apartment and a vegetable garden within the prison walls to entertain guests, so it was perhaps… reasonably agreeable? They could also order things from Harrods I believe. Diana was also an intimate friend with the Duke and Duchess of Windsor and they became neighbours when Diana took up residence at her new home Temple de la Gloire, Orsay, Paris.

Diana's two children were taken care of by the one and only sister who kept out of the public eye due to her passion for farming and animals. Pamela Mitford was perhaps like her mother who subsidized the family brood with cooking, chicken farming and other animals. Pam married Derek Jackson and much enjoyed a quiet country life remaining great friends with Bryan Guinness her one time brother in law.

Apparently, Jessica Mitford was the most organized of the girls as from a very early age she started a "running away account". All her pocket money was saved for the big day. As we have read before, Jessica did eventually run away and joined Winston Churchill's nephew Esmond Romilly, who had also run away and joined the Republicans in the Spanish Civil War. They married in Spain and continued their devotion to communism. The notice in the Evening Telegraph dated 18 May 1937 stated. "In March, after the Foreign Office had asked its consular officials to assist in tracing the couple, Esmond Romilly and Jessica Mitford were found in Spain, both working as journalists. Lord Redesdale objected to his daughter marrying Romilly, and she was made a ward of court, but eventually the couple obtained consent and duly got married".

However, I believe someone said that Churchill got rather upset and sent a warship of some kind to recover his nephew? Much later and sadly, Esmond was killed in the war and Jessica emigrated to the United States and later married Robert Treuhaft, a lawyer. She never saw her father again.

Both communists at heart they worked on a book entitled The American Way of Death, which became a best seller. Jessica gives an excellent presentation which may be seen on youtube.com. I personally was intrigued by this book, because it stirred a link with some memories of life and growing up in South Africa. As a youngster during my teenage years I briefly became friends with the children of a family that ran a funeral parlour company in South Africa. As kids, I was amazed at the enormous and palatial home they had built and lived in, along with all the cars and their statement that went with it. They were more posh than posh! My parents said they were nouveau riche, the new money. Old or new, I was more intrigued by the fact that how on earth can they live in this fabulous and dazzling home, because they are burying people?

Obviously, burying the dead made lots of money, but at the time it was difficult for a youngster to understand! However, Jessica's book hits home with the realities and truth of her investigation into the American funeral industry. The American Federal Trade Commission made a ruling on funerals such as itemizing costs, choice and display of coffins, obtaining permission from the next of kin for embalming and quoting prices via telephone if requested. Even David Bowie considered The American Way of Death to be a great read. Likewise, J K Rowling, author of the Harry Potter books was impressed with Jessica's earlier book Hons and Rebels, of sticking to her beliefs and her running away from home that she named her daughter Jessica.

Moving on to Unity, we find perhaps the best example of the Mitford single mindedness with her infatuation of Hitler. She had a plan and as a result of her dedication and total focus on what she wanted, she got. She needed to make a statement perhaps related to sibling rivalry from her younger childhood years when she had shared a room with Jessica. The room was divided into two, one side being communist and the other fascist – the continuation of her childhood ideology?

Unity's strength of character and her youthful, aristocratic presence and arrogance captivated Hitler and they became solid friends until war was declared between Germany and England. With shock and disbelief Unity attempted to commit suicide by shooting herself, unsuccessful she lingered on and became an invalid for the rest of her life. It has been said that Unity worked with MI6? It makes sense. How did she pay her bills incurred running around Germany, her car and staying at various hotels? It has also been said that Unity was shot by one of Hitler's inner circle because she presented a security risk? There are a number of unanswered questions that we will never know for sure? Her unique friendship with Hitler gave her direct access to the Nazi leadership which was frowned upon by many. Her dedication was demonstrated by stating publicly and internationally that she was a "Jew Hater". It's not difficult to imagine the exchange of guarded information between England and Germany? When the war ended Hitler, Eva Braun and the entire Goebbels family with their children, all committed suicide.

A remarkable family in many ways. The girls and their parents must have known (as the 1st Lord Redesdale, their grandfather, was on my great-great grandfather's mailing list) that the head of the Mitford family (Mitford, Northumberland) had in part, dedicated his life to establishing a homeland for the Jewish nation when J. Hatchard & Son, of 187 Piccadilly, London, Booksellers to H.R.H. the Princess of Wales, published An Appeal in Behalf of the Jewish Nation in Connection with British Policy in the Levant 1845 (republished by the author as British Policy in the Middle East & the Creation of Israel 2015). Covered in detail in a previous chapter, this book was addressed to the ministers of the British Government and provided the framework leading to the creation of the country of Israel. It would have been freely available within the Batsford Park family library, Asthall Manor, Swinbrook and 26 Rutland Gate, the homes the girls grew up in.

Had my great-great grandfather Edward Ledwich Mitford 27th Squire of Mitford, been alive to witness the later antics of the Mitford girls he would have gone ballistic and straight through the roof! As it was, this mental state of being was left to his sons, my great uncles and cousins.

There was also an only son and brother to the Mitford girls. Major, the Honorable Thomas Freeman-Mitford of The Queens Westminsters, he studied law and followed his sisters Diana and Unity's passion for Germany and also met Hitler but remained conservative. He studied German and music in Vienna. He fought for England in World War II and died in Burma on Good Friday on 30th March 1945 from wounds received in action on the previous Saturday while attached as 2nd in Command to the Devonshire regiment aged 36 years. The only son of Lord and Lady Redesdale - David and Sydney Freeman-Mitford. This ended the succession of the Exbury branch of the Mitford family.

However, there is first cousin once removed from the Mitford sisters, Rupert Mitford, 6th Baron Redesdale who is a British Liberal Democratic politician. The Duchess of Devonshire, Deborah Mitford who with her late husband the Duke, was active in the Social Democratic Party. The later merged with the Liberal party to become the Liberal Democrats, for whom the current Lord Redesdale sits in the House of Lords. He is well known for the protection and survival of the native British red squirrel population against grey squirrels. Long live red squirrels.

To discover more of these amazing sisters I would recommend, the finest and foremost books written about the Mitford girls are by Mary Lovell. Excellent books, along with all the books Mary Lovell has written. Further, The Swan Inn and restaurant in Swinbrook, close to the birthplace of the Mitford girls, owned by the late Deborah Mitford continues to accommodate and serve excellent food at reasonable prices.

Apart from the Mitford girls, if by chance you are in the opposite end of England, why not visit the village of Mitford and The Plough Inn? Situated two and a half miles from Morpeth and 16 miles from Newcastle in Northumberland. You may be assured of a warm welcome and excellent food. I raise a glass!

Chapter 9
Mitford's Estate Act (1854)

Epilogue – Perfect Indifference

You have read – the history of an extraordinary family. But what remains of this long and amazing journey that has taken us all over the world? It is possible to find plaques on walls in England - a private family chapel that someone thought to transform into a storage room – a number of books that have been continuously re-edited for the benefit and memory of a branch of the family that has maintained international interest for a century due to scandals and love affairs, and certainly the rights owners? A hospital in one of the poorest parts of the world that wanted to change its name because the Mitford family has lost interest?

How did this incredible story conclude at 19 Ennismore Gardens, Knightsbridge, a small apartment near Hyde Park in London (the home of the last squire) with nothing remaining from the family fortunes, lands, family jewels and prized family heirlooms and possessions dating back nearly 1,000 years? How come what's left is like the remains of a large and long banquet with just the crumbs, bones and empty plates scattered around in the most perfect indifference?

But how and why did the last squire decide to write the last words and put the final full stop in the story of this once great family, dispersing the remains of the Mitford fortune, instead of establishing a trust to pass on the baton and stewardship as has been done for the previous 960 years? Having sold assets held by generations, the last chance to revive the Mitford family into the 21st century was lost? With the millions available…was he unable to find or create a solution or was he careless during his last few years of ill health and simply signed away the left-overs of a dynasty? Did he appreciate the significance our great-great grandfathers' motivation and deeds towards the creation of

Israel and our great uncle to record the early history of South Africa and our ancestors to force King John to sign the Magna Carta? Of course he did, but he did nothing. Was he correctly or incorrectly advised, unable to adapt and change with forethought and creativity towards future generations?

As the last on the original mainline I felt obliged to consolidate the family history inside one cover. This book is a small token to all the Mitfords around the world. Here follows proof positive of what was originally intended. As I discovered, the Mitford estate was offered to several people who all turned it down and no trust was set up. The original trust that does exist with a term of 900 years and sets out the succession guidelines via my great-great grandfather was not acknowledged. At the time the estate was being sold I was working in the Middle East and totally unaware of what the last squire and his counsel was planning. My parents simply said to me "you will always have a home in England" and "as long as you hold a British passport you will be contacted when the time is right". I duly contacted the trustees, had dinner with some and talked to others over the telephone.

Mitford's Estate Act 1854 - By Royal Assent

With several Mitford fortunes, one to sustain an other, with nothing left after 964 years it would appear that the complete opposite of what was intended has happened. All trace of the Mitford family's estate and stewardship of Mitford has disappeared. With several million pounds from the sale of the Mitford estate the capital asset should have been invested in a family trust to sustain the consolidation of Mitford history and continuation through a heritage foundation (as originally intended) for generations ahead.

The Mitford's Estate Act was passed in the Houses of Parliament, Westminster, London on 31st July 1854 by Royal Assent. This is shown on the first page of the act as the formula used for personal acts. Through an age old process the act is presented by summarised title (as above) and "Soit fait comme il est désiré" – "Let it be done as it is desired" is read out in Norman French. When all the bills have been presented – the Clerks of Parliament and the Crown bow to the Lords Commissioners and return to their places at the Table. The Commons and the Lords Commissioners then retire. This then becomes a law within the British Parliament.

As you have read, this Act and trust with a term of 900 years was created as a result of the sale of part of the Hunmanby Estate in East Riding, Yorkshire, inherited and owned by the Mitford family via the marriage of Mary Osbaldeston to Robert Mitford in 1716. This sixteen page document includes an estate schedule of 26 farms consisting of 5,000 acres with an annual rental income of £4,800.

The proceeds from the sale via Bank of England, Court of Chancery – as abolished in 1875, and now High Court of Justice, were for the purchase & increase of estates in Mitford, Northumberland with rents and profits to surviving descendants. Taking a total of 5,000 acres one can work out a rough high and low estimation of the land values at the time. In 1870, before the property slump, farm lands were on average £53 an acre, therefore 5,000 X £50 = £250,000 and at worst £25 an acre = £125,000, a sizeable fortune in those days. I imagine this did not come in one lump sum but was realised over a period of time.

As stated previously, these funds were for increasing the Mitford estate, Mitford Hall and Mitford Park.

The registered beneficiaries of the Mitford's Estate Act and trust, as stated on page 6 paragraph 10 of the original document, are Edward Ledwich Mitford (my great-great grandfather) with two of his sons Robert and Edward (my great uncles). Therefore, the Mitford main line continued from Edward Ledwich Mitford FRGS as he outlived his older brother. To quote "On behalf of himself and of his said infant sons, and of their respective issue male, and of any other issue male, which he, the said Edward Ledwich Mitford may hereafter have".

In 1925, the Administration of Estates Act came into being, changing the rule of inheritance from primogeniture (the right of succession belonging to the firstborn child, under feudal conventions it required succession to be the first born son), to that of modern day norms.

When it was realized by the families that the last squire of Mitford, Brigadier Edward Cecil Mitford would not produce a heir after his second marriage in 1949 to Patricia Kirrage in Turkey, when I was born four years later in 1953 in South Africa, I was naturally christened Mitford. As such, becoming a natural descendant on the direct main bloodline – and as evidenced by the Mitford's Estate Act, a descendant & heir.

With regards to continuation and succession, with all male lines dying out, succession can go via the eldest female with a surviving male line.

To recap from earlier chapters, the timeline & my relationship to the last 7 squires of Mitford is as follows.

1 John Philip Mitford 27th Squire
  (my great, great uncle) his brother
2 Edward Ledwich Mitford 28th Squire
  (my great-great grandfather), his daughter, Mary Margaret Mitford (my great grandmother and matriarch of the family),
3 his son, Robert Cuthbert William Mitford 29th Squire
  (my great uncle)
4 his son, Bertram-Lane Mitford 30th Squire
  (my 1st cousin 2 x removed) with no children succession reverted back to Edward Ledwich Mitford's 3rd son,
5 Rev. Edward L Mitford 31st Squire
  (my great uncle)
6 his son, John Philip Mitford 32nd Squire
  (my 1st cousin 2 x removed) and
7 his son, Edward Cecil Mitford 33rd Squire
  (my 2nd cousin 1 x removed) no children.

With this Act of Parliament and according to legal counsel this places myself "beyond any reasonable doubt as a legal blood heir". I am the closest living blood relative to the last squire and next of kin. Through the legal minefield with quotes ranging from £20,000 to £30,000 plus hourly research fees of £900 to simply identify what should be done without legal advice on how to proceed, which would then incur further lump sums of cash on the table, I was simply and quite naturally unable to continue with this largesse of thought. And to what purpose - the estate was sold and the money spent?

With various letters I wrote to everyone enquiring of the situation, simply to put everything in perspective and in order to gauge where I stood it took months and years to receive a reply. I was advised that the entirety of the Mitford Estate was held by the last squire personally as at the date of his death and none of it was held in trust.

By this, does it mean that the Mitford's Estate Act of 1854 with a term of 900 years has no relevance to this or anything for that matter? The next question follows why, according to the Parliamentary Archives and Law Commission – the Chronological Table of Private & Personal Acts from 1539 to 2006, has nothing been put forward to repeal, change or cancel the act, nor has any amendment been made to the Mitford's Estate Act up to 2006?

As the estate was held personally and not in trust, the next question that follows is when was the Mitford's Estate Act changed or cancelled? From my last enquiry nothing had changed since it was made law? Or alternatively has it perhaps become null and void, extinct, outdated or simply totally irrelevant due to lack of interest or application? If so, why was it made a law with a term of 900 years in the first place?

Obviously, this Act was drawn up with a term of 900 years for a reason and it takes us to the year 2754. Also in those days, permission needed to be obtained to sell manorial property. (The reader may recall that the Hunmanby estate was consolidated into separate independent areas prior to the Mitfords taking over). The prime objective at the time was to make funds available to increase the Mitford estate and to pay for the building, furbishment and appointment of Mitford Hall. As you may remember it took 18 years to build.

And thereafter with what funds remained, along with rents and profits was to be invested in trust to provide descendants and beneficiaries, being the future squires with an income to manage the estate towards providing financial stability and continuity.

Much has happened since then including two world wars. Perhaps the money ran out, no one bothered and the Act became extinct as it had done its job and could no longer continue due to lack of funds, bad investments and so forth?

Alas, as you have read, Bertram died before he could invest and consolidate the trust and the money was spent by the following successive squires and the opportunity was lost. Two generations later when it came to my great-great grandfather's turn to inherit, I only think of the dismay he must have encountered with the continuing family crisis and financial woes.

As mentioned, he inherited at the grand old age of 85 with not a penny in the bank, except his civil service pension, but he managed to cope and passed it on to his son. Up to this point his life was full, productive and successful and suddenly to have to cope with all the family problems and holding both the Hunmanby and Mitford estates together required all his energy and fortitude. I can begin to appreciate why Edward wrote those words on his gravestone in Mitford churchyard. From the first time I read them, they intrigued me. I wanted to know why he wrote them?

The one thing that was never ever contemplated by anyone in the family was that the estate would actually be sold. One would think heritage is inalienable, apparently not for the Mitfords. With the current trends and taxes in England not many individuals wanted to take on the management, complications and costly upkeep of a neglected country estate. Patricia Mitford, the squire's wife said at the time, if we don't sell it now it will just go to the Government anyway, best to sell while the time is good. It was simply, of no interest to Patricia. Naturally everyone concerned stood to gain from the sale of the estate.

Once the decision to sell the estate had been made the squire was advised to transfer the administration of the estate from Northumberland to London. In 1993 the 5,000 acre estate with 45 houses and 7 farms bringing in an annual rental income of approximately £48,000 was sold for a reported £2,850,000 and the contents of Mitford Hall auctioned off. The Manorship of Mitford, Pigdon, Maidenhall, Molesden, Benridge and Newton

Park and the advowson and perpetual right of presentation of and to the Vicarage and Parish Church of Mitford and the old buildings adjoining the old Manor house were to be kept. The signing ceremony took place at Mitford Hall and with the last squire's signature on the deed of sale, he not only sold the family estate after 951 years he also lost his wife.

The very next day the squire's wife took ill at the age of 76 and died in York on their journey back to London. Edward then returned to Mitford to bury his wife in the Mitford churchyard a few days later after selling the estate. The very last time he set foot on the family estate.

The last properties to go was the Longframlington property of 126 acres at Lambs Hill, bringing in an annual rental of £300 together with all mineral rights, along with and including the Manorship of Longframlington, a small piece of land at Prestwick Carr, land at Dinnington and the disused railway line at Molesden. With no estate the last squire had no need to visit Mitford ever again. Thereafter he spent his last remaining years in the Middle East and London.

Seven years later and two years after signing a new will, drawn up and prepared by a friend he met in a London club, Edward Cecil Mitford aged 93, died in London in 2002. The net value of the Mitford estate was £2,739,299. This marked the end of the Mitford dynasty. Prior to his death in September 1993, Edward made a donation to Mitford church, to be managed by William Elliot MBE of £60,000 which went to establish a trust to support Mitford Church (solely for the purpose of repair, maintenance and care of the fabric of Mitford Church) continued to this day.

It was only in 2006 that the Mitford Manor Tower was finally sold. Having been specially renovated and funded by family funds and as indicated in the will (previously mentioned) it was to be kept within the Mitford family as a symbol of the family presence in Mitford. However, sadly, the trustees chose to sell the Mitford tower and adjoining piece of land in 2006, totally severing all family ties with Mitford after nearly 1,000 years.

It's common knowledge in England and other countries you can leave your estate to your favourite dog or cat if you so wish.

Beryl Reid left her £1m home to her rescued stray cats Hamish, Coco, Boon and Eileen! Miles Blakewell left £10m to his pet hen, Gigoo, and Alexander McQueen left £50,000 to his dogs.

But when it comes to a family estate that has the amazing longevity of continuous family ownership and a centuries old history, one would expect that no stone would be left unturned in finding a suitable heir and or setting up a trust or heritage project to consolidate this remarkable family history. As a steward of the estate the onus was surely on Edward to ensure the continuation of the family presence in some form or other? He had a lifetime and over 20 years of retirement to establish a suitable trust or heritage project. He did neither.

I unfortunately started my research a few years too late. The sum total of what I knew was as long as I hold a British passport I will be contacted when the time is right and I will always have a home in England. I'm wondering if anyone has actually seen the Loch Ness Monster?

With my research and contacting all the individuals concerned it took one year to receive a reply from Edward Mitford (Teddy's) London lawyer as follows.

"I should have acknowledged your letter before now. Teddy was a client and we were members of the same club, so I got to know him quite well. I have never been to Mitford although I know where it is. It's sad in a way that Teddy and his wife had no children. He was very family minded and I think I remember we had to get his will just right".

No one will know what he meant by "family minded and just right"?

The net value of the Mitford estate being £2,739,299 was granted to three executors and trustees – One, the advising lawyer as above (not a relative), two, Edward's next door neighbour who assisted through his years of ill health (not a relative) and three, a distant, elderly cousin, five times removed from the Mitford mainline, who was left holding the squires ashes at the squire's funeral.

"There the tears of earth are dried – there the hidden things are clear"

Soit fait comme il est désiré

ANNO DECIMO SEPTIMO & DECIMO OCTAVO

VICTORIÆ REGINÆ.

****

Cap. 18.

An Act to authorize the Sale of certain Messuages, Lands, and Hereditaments in the East Riding of the County of *York*, Part of the Estates devised and settled by the Will of *Bertram Osbaldeston Mitford* Esquire, deceased, and for laying out the Money produced by such Sale in the Purchase of other Estates. [31st July 1854]

WHEREAS *Bertram Osbaldeston Mitford*, late of *Mitford Castle* in the County of *Northumberland*, and of *Hunmanby* in the County of *York*, Esquire, deceased, made and duly executed his last Will and Testament in Writing, bearing Date the Ninth Day of *February* One thousand eight hundred and thirty-eight, whereby he devised to his Wife *Frances Osbaldeston Mitford* for her Life, she continuing his Widow, an Annuity of One thousand three hundred Pounds, and to his Cousin *Bertram Mitford* for his Life an Annuity of Fifty Pounds, and he charged the said Annuities respectively on his Real Estates in the County of *York*, and after bequeathing certain Chattels unto his Wife he devised unto her during her Life, she continuing his Widow, his Mansion House at *Mitford*, together

Will of Bertram Osbaldeston Mitford, dated 9th February 1838.

[*Private.*] 5 *d*

First page of Mitford Act of Parliament above, extracts from the act on the opposite page.

Issue of Edward Ledwich Mitford.

And whereas the said Edward Ledwich Mitford, the second cousin of the said testator, is married, and has had issue, Cuthbert Philip Mitford, his eldest son, who was born on the twenty-second of January, one thousand 10 eight hundred and forty-five, Robert Mitford, who was born on the twenty-fifth of November, one thousand eight hundred and forty-six, and Edward Mitford, who was born in the month of October, one thousand eight hundred and fifty-three, and no other male issue :

Wherefore your Majesty's most dutiful and loyal subjects, the said Frances Osbaldeston Mitford and Bertram Mitford, the said Robert Mitford and John Philip Mitford, on behalf of themselves and their respective issue male, if any, who shall hereafter be born, the said Edward Ledwich 25 Mitford, on behalf of himself and of his said infant sons, and of their respective issue male, and of any other issue male, which he the said Edward Ledwich Mitford may hereafter have, and the said John Thomas Lord Redesdale, on behalf of himself and his issue male, if any, who shall hereafter be born :

authorised to be sold as aforesaid, and every or any part thereof respectively, as they and every or any of them had before the passing of this Act, or could or might have had held or enjoyed if this Act had not been passed.

Act printed by Queen's printers to be evidence.

XVII. That this Act shall not be a Public Act, but shall be printed by 5 the several printers to the QUEEN'S Most Excellent MAJESTY, duly authorised to print the Statutes of the United Kingdom, and a copy thereof so printed by any of them shall be admitted as evidence thereof by all judges, justices and others.

Bibliography

2. Where It All Began

History of England by David Hume & Tobias Smollett 1688
History, Directory & Gazette of Durham & Northumberland 1828
History of Northumberland by John Hodgson 1832
The Saturday Magazine 1837
North Country Lore & Legend 1887
Mitford 2000 History of the Village for the last 2000 years by Peter Else
Morpeth Herald
Newcastle Courant
National Sheep Association
Mitford Historical Society
Mitford Raymond Archives

3. The Feudal Barons Of Mitford

History of Northumberland by John Hodgson 1832
Dictionary of National Biography Vol. IV 1885
A Historical View of the County of Northumberland by E Mackenzie 1825
General History of the Counties of Durham & Northumberland 1828
Burke's Peerage 1883

4. Kidnapping The Bishop

North Country Lore and legend 1887
A History of Northumberland by John Hodgson 1832
Mitford 2000 A History of the Village for the last 2000 years by Peter Else 1999
The Mitford Historical Society
Mitford Literary Society

6. Mitford Church

Mitford Church by J.R. Boyle FSA, 1890.
History of Mitford Church by James Fergusson 1884
Mitford 2000 History of the Village for the last 2000 years by Peter Else 1999
History of Northumberland by John Dobson 1832
The Morpeth Herald 1889
The Newcastle Courant 1877
North Country Lore and Legend 1887
Mitford Historical Society
Mitford Literary Society

7. The Squires Of Mitford

History of England by David Hume & Tobias Smollett 1688

History, Directory & Gazette of Durham & Northumberland 1828
History of Northumberland by John Hodgson 1832
The History of Parliament: The House of Commons 1386-1421, C. Rawcliffe, 1993
*History of the World by J M Roberts 1976
History of Mitford Church by James Fergusson 1884
The Monthly Chronicle of North Country Lore and Legend 1887
Woodhorn Archives, Northumberland
British Newspaper Archives
Squire Osbaldeston-His Autobiography 1926
*The Decline and Fall of the British Aristocracy by David Cannadine 1990
The Evening Chronicle
Gloucester Citizen
The Morpeth Herald
*Kings and Queens by Neil Grant 2004
*A History of Central Banking by Stephen Mitford Goodson 2014
*Off With Their Heads by Martin Oliver 2009
Mitford 2000 History of the Village for the last 2000 years by Peter Else 1993
The Mitford Historical Society Archives
Anderson & Garland Auctioneers Catalogue 2010
Mitford Raymond family archives
Mitford Literary Society

8. Extraordinary Characters & Notable People

1. William Mitford (1744-1827)

History of Greece, William Mitford 1838
History of Greece, George Grote 1851
Sheffield and Rotherham Independent 1852

2. Rev John Mitford (1781-1859)

Nichols's Illustrations of Literature, J B Nichols 1848
Dictionary of National Biography Vol 38 William Prideaux Courtney 1885-1900
Gentleman's Magazine – Obituary Anonymous July 1859
The Ipswich Journal 1859
Manchester Evening News 1901

3. John (Jack) Mitford (1782-1881)

Trial of John Mitford on the Prosecution of Lady Viscountess Perceval 1814
Crimes and Horrors of Warburton's Madhouse at Hoxton, by John Mitford 1825
Leicester Chronicle 1832
Monthly Chronicle of North Country Lore and Legend, 1887
National Library of Australia – Kalgoorlie Western Argus 1899

4. Sir Robert Mitford – Mitford Hospital (1783-1836)
   Prerogative Court Papers Sir H Jenner 1837
   Court of Chancery Papers Mitford versus Reynolds 1841
   Morning Post 1874
   Evening Telegraph 1930
   Mitford Raymond Archives
5. Admiral Robert Mitford (1786-1870)
   With kind thanks. Edited from www.amhersts-of-didlington.com - a website designed and written by Angela Cecil Reid, a great-great-great granddaughter of Admiral Robert Mitford.
   Cleopatra's Needles and Other Egyptian Obelisks 1926 by E A Wallis Budge.
6. Squire Osbaldeston (1786-1866) 4 pages
   Squire Osbaldeston His Autobiography 1926
   Thurgarton History, Ellis Morgan 2010
7. Mary Russell Mitford (1787-1855) 5 pages
   Our Village - Mary Russell Mitford 1824-32
   Hampshire Telegraph 1843
   Newcastle Guardian 1855
   Pall Mall Gazette 1870
   Ipswich Journal 1870
   Monthly Chronicle North Country Lore and Legend 1887
   Dictionary of National Biography 1894
   Aberdeen Journal 1925
   National Library of Australia, Kalgoorlie Miner 1920
   Nottingham Post 1932
   Mitford 2000 by Peter Else 1999
   Mitford Historical Society
   Mitford Literary Society
8. Edward Mitford FRGS (1811-1912)
   *Zionism & the British Empire - Stephen P Meyer 2009
   An Appeal in behalf of the Jewish Nation by Edward Ledwich Mitford.1845
   The Vision Was There. A History of the British Movement for the Restoration of the Jews to Palestine by Franz Kobler, originally published by the World Jewish Congress. 1956
   Tranquillisation of Syria and the East: Observations and Practical Suggestions, George Gawler 1845
   Volumes I & II of Austen Henry Lanyard's Autobiography and Letters 1903
   A Land March from England to Ceylon by Edward Ledwich Mitford 1884.
   Poems, Dramatic and Lyrical – Edward Ledwich Mitford 1869
   The Arab's Pledge –A tale of Morocco in 1830 – Edward Ledwich Mitford 1867

Squire Osbaldeston – His Autobiography 1926
Illustrated London News 1870
The Observer 1870
Weekly Dispatch 1870
The Graphic 1884
The Spectator 1869
The Yorkshire Post 1912
Hull Daily Mail 1912
Mitford Historical Society
Mitford 2000 – A History of the Village for the last 2000 years by Peter Else 1999
Mitford Raymond archives
Mitford Literary Society

9. Algernon Bertram Mitford (1837-1916)
   Tales of Old Japan Algernon Bertram Mitford 1871
10. Godolphin Mitford (1844-1884)
   The Theosophist Magazine 1882 & 1885
   Old Diary Leaves Henry Olcot 1974
11. Bertram Mitford FRGS (1855-1914)
   Through the Zulu Country – Its Battlefields and its People by Bertram Mitford 1883
   The Curse of Clement Waynflete by Bertram Mitford 1894
   The Induna's Wife by Bertram Mitford 1898
   The Gun Runner by Bertram Mitford 1894
   Last Will & Testament of Cecil John Rhodes edited by W T Stead 1902
   The New York Times 1899
   The Royal Geographic Society 1890
   Pall Mall Gazette 1893 & 1899
   The Morning Post 1900
   The Morpeth Herald
   The Mitford Historical Society Archives
   Mitford Raymond family archives
   Mitford Literary Society
   All photographs owned by HMR
12. The Mitford Girls (1904-2014)
   The British Ambassador's Residence in Paris by Tim Knox 2011

9. Mitford's Estate Act (1854)

Parliamentary Archives, Houses of Parliament London – Mitford Estate Act 1854
Last Will & Testament – Edward Cecil Mitford 2002
Mitford Raymond Archives

Edward Ledwich Mitford FRGS (1811–1912 Mailing list of subscribers for his books 1870.

G-G grandfathers Mailing list 1870
EDWARD L MITFORD (1811-1912)

MRS ROY ADAMS TUNBRIDGE WELLS

Mr. Tyssen Amhurst, Didlington. 6 copies.
Mrs. Tyssen Amhurst,,, 6 copies.
Mr. Anderson, Little Harle Tower.
Mr. John Anderson, Newcastle-on-Tyne.
Mr. Atkinson, Angerton.
Mrs. Atkinson,,,
Mr. "Wilson-Atkinson, Acton House.
Mrs. Wilson-Atkinson,,,
Mr. Atkinson, Wylam Hall.
Sir Edward Blackett, Bart., Matfen.
Mrs. W. C. Boodle, 33, Connaught Square. 3 copies.
Mrs. T. Salkeld Bramwell, Jesmond Dene House. 2 copies.
Mrs. Brooke, Taney Hill House, Dundrum, Co. Dublin.
The Rev. Dixon Brown, Unthank Hall.
Mrs. Dixon Brown,,,
Mrs. Brown, Houghton.
Mr. Ralph Brown, Whickhain.
Mrs. Ralph Brown,,,
Mrs. T. Brown, Mitford.
Miss M. Brown,,,
Mr. Brumell, Morpeth.
Mrs. Brumell,,,
Mr. M. Brumell,,,
Mr. Burrell, Broome Park.
The Rev. H. B. Carr, Whickham Rectory.
Dr. Charlton, Newcastle-on-Tyne.
Mr. Collingwood, Lilburn Tower.
Mr. Cookson, Meldon Park.
Miss Cookson,,,
Mr. William Cookson, Eslington Park.
Mrs. William Cookson,,,
Mr. Norman Cookson,,,
Mrs. Arthur Coulson, Carham Vicarage.
Mr. Dickson, Alnwick.
Miss Eisdell, The Cottage, Cedars, Epsom.
The Rev. J. Elphinstone-Elliot, Whalton Rectory.
The Rev. T. Finch, Morpeth.
Dr. Fitzgerald, Folkestone.
Mrs. Foster, Selsey Rectory, Chichester. 2 copies.
Mr. W. Sidney Gibson, Tynemouth.
Mrs. Gore, 4, Cheriton Villas, Folkestone.
The Countess Grey, Howick. 2 copies.
The Rev. The Honourable F. R. Grey, Morpeth Rectory.
The Lady Elizabeth Grey,,,

59

Colonel Somerset Grove, Mitford. 3 copies.
Mrs. Somerset Grove,,, 3 copies.
The Rev. H. Teush-Hecker, Misterton Rectory, Lutterworth.
Colonel Teush-Hecker, Folkestone. 3 copies.
Mrs. Teush-Hecker, 3 copies.
Miss F. Hepple, Mitford.
Mr. Hodgson-Hinde, Stella Hall.
The Rev. B. P. Hodgson, Hartburn Vicarage.
Mrs. Hodgson,,,
Mr. Robert Hodgson, Whitburn. 2 copies.
Mr. J. G. Hodgson, North Dene, Gateshead.
The Rev. Thomas Ilderton, Ilderton.
Lady James, Betshanger. 2 copies.
Mr. Edward James, Swarland Park.
Lt.-Colonel Johnson, The Deanery, Chester-le-Street.
The Lord Kenyon, 12, Portman Square.
The Lady Kenyon,,,
Miss Dawson Lambton, Swinburne Castle.
Mr. J. Langdale, Mitford.
Mr. Edward Lawson, Redesdale Cottage.
Mr. Thomas Marshall, Mitford.
Admiral Mitford, Mitford and Hunmanby. 3 copies.
Mrs. Mitford,,, 3 copies.
Mr. Townley Mitford, M. P., Pitshill. 2 copies.
The Honourable Mrs. Townley Mitford, Pitshill.
Major Mitford. 6 copies.
Mrs. J. P. Mitford. 6 copies.
Miss Emma Mitford. 2 copies.
Mr. B. E. Mitford, Royal Regiment.
Sir Arthur Monck, Bart., Belsay Castle.
The Duke of Northumberland, Alnwick Castle. 10 copies.
The Duchess of Northumberland,,, 10 copies.
The Rev. E. C. Ogle, Kirkley. 3 copies.
Mrs. Ogle,,, 3 copies.
Miss Ogle,,, 3 copies.
The Rev. L. S. Orde, Shorestone Hall.
Mrs. L. S. Orde,,,
Mr. Orde, Nunnykirk.
Mrs. Orde,,,
Miss Pack, 32, Devonshire Place. 2 copies.
Mrs. Parker, Darrington Hall, Pontefract.
Mrs. Pidcock, 34, Imperial Square, Cheltenham.
Miss Potts, Mitford.
Mr. Pye, 4, Lancaster Gate, Hyde Park. 6 copies.

100

The Lord Ravensworth, Ravensworth Castle. 2 copies.
The Lord Redesdale, Batsford Park. 1ST LORD (1837-1916) (1878-1958) 2nd LORD
Sir M. W. Ridley, Bart., Blagdon.
Mr. Ridley, M. P.,
Miss Ridley,,,
Mrs. W. R. Sandbach, 10, Prince's Gate.
Mr. T. Eustace Smith, M. P., Gosforth House.
Mrs. Smith, Gosforth House.
The Rev. C. C. Snowden, Mitford Vicarage. 6 copies.
Mr. Harconrt Snowden, Thorpe Mandeville.
Mr. Shum-Storey, Arcot Hall.
Miss Shum-Storey,,, 2 copies.
Miss Nina Shum-Storey,,,
Mr. Honywood Surtees, Benridge.
Mr. Swinburne, Whickam.
Mr. Goldie-Taubman, The Nunnery, Isle of Man.
The Rev. Charles Townley, Little Ahington Vicarage, 3 copies.
Mrs. Gale Townley, Beaulieu, Newbridge, Bath.
Miss Walcott, 1, Victoria Grove, Folkestone.
The Rev. Canou Whitley, Bedlington Vicarage.
Mr. M. C. Woods, Holeyn Hall.
Miss Woods, Newcastle-on-Tyne. 2 copies.
Miss Yea, Monymusk, Aberdeen.
E. Barrett&Sons, Printers, 13, Mark Lane, London.

34

Total 193